Reflective Teacher Development in Primary Science

Peter Ovens

London and New York

First published 2000
by Falmer Press
11 New Fetter Lane, London EC4P 4EE

Simultaneously published in the USA and Canada
by Garland Inc.,
19 Union Square West, New York, NY 10000

Falmer Press is an imprint of the Taylor & Francis Group

© 2000 Peter Ovens

Typeset in Times by Taylor & Francis Books Ltd
Printed and bound in Great Britain by Biddles Ltd,
Guildford and King's Lynn

British Library Cataloguing in Publication Data
A catalogue record for this book is available from the British Library

Library of Congress Cataloging-in-Publication Data
Ovens, Peter
  Reflective teacher development in primary science / Peter Ovens.
        p.   cm.
  Includes bibliographical references and index.
  1. Science – Study and teaching (Elementary) – Great Britain.
  2. Science teachers – In-service training – Great Britain.
  I. Title.
  LB1585.5.G7084 1999   99-36839
  372.3'5044'0941 – dc21   CIP

ISBN 0–750–70863–8 (hbk)
ISBN 0–750–70862–X (pbk)

Contents

Contents

Illustrations

Figures

Illustrations

Tables

Preface

There is currently a great deal of talk about the idea of 'evidence-based practice' as a model for the professional development of teachers. Much of the discussion and debate surrounds how the major components of such a model are to be described, and hinges on two central questions – first: 'What is to count as relevant research evidence?'; and second: 'Does engaging teachers with research evidence involve engaging them in research?'

The dominant model of evidence-based practice answers these questions as follows: *relevant* evidence consists of evidence about the effectiveness of particular pedagogical interventions in improving desired learning outcomes for students. Such evidence is invariably viewed to take the form of objective measures of the effectiveness of interventions conceived in terms of 'treatments'; a medical metaphor. There is little room here for the view that the 'relevance' of evidence is for teachers to judge in the light of the practical problems they subjectively experience in developing their practice. Engaging teachers *with* research evidence need not imply engaging them *in* research. It is a matter of getting them to apply research findings by demonstrating their *technical rationality* as a means of improving their teaching.

In this book, Peter Ovens develops in meticulous and clearly argued detail, which is well-grounded in case study evidence of how teachers improve their teaching of science, an alternative action research model of evidence-based practice as a process of teacher professional development. In doing so, he demonstrates how and why the personal and subjective dimensions of teaching need to be accommodated in any discussion of what constitutes relevant evidence for its improvement. He also demonstrates how and why engaging teachers in research is a necessary condition of engaging them with research.

This book provides us with an empirically grounded, well-articulated and comprehensive theory of teachers' personal professional development. In doing so, it impressively draws on conceptual resources from the fields of curriculum studies, educational theory, philosophy of education and the social psychology of learning. These intellectual resources are in danger of becoming 'lost literatures'. This is because they are witnessing the re-emergence of neo-behaviourist models of teaching and learning in a policy context where highly centralized 'prescriptions' (to use another medical metaphor) are presumed to be the only solution to the problem of raising educational standards in our schools.

Peter Ovens's book shows how the real complexities of teacher professional development can be handled to reap rich rewards for both the teaching profession and the children in our schools who need equal access to learning as a creative and meaningful engagement with the subject matter.

John Elliott
Centre for Applied Research in Education
University of East Anglia
March 1999

Author's acknowledgements

My critical friends during the development of the work described in this book have given vital assistance, both intellectual and emotional, particularly during the dips of this roller-coaster ride experience. Thanks are due to them all, particularly Margaret, Frank and Marion.

The teachers who have been the course members depicted here have taught me so much, and in such a tolerant and good-hearted way.

And many thanks are due to John Elliott, whose clarity of grasp and steadfastness of support for what I was trying to do have been vital.

But without doubt, this book would never have been achieved without Anna.

Peter Ovens
October, 1998

Reflective Teacher Development in Primary Science

Primary school teachers and student teachers who wish to improve their teaching of science will find a distinctive approach offered in this book. The idea that learning is like carrying out a personal inquiry is applied to all three participating groups in the study:

primary school children
achieve significant science learning by *being scientific*, taking an inquiry approach to science with the support and guidance of other children and their teacher

the children's teacher
achieves significant professional learning by *being an action researcher* in taking an inquiry approach to their own teaching of science, with the support of other teachers and an enabler – their CPD course tutor

the teachers' tutor (the author)
achieved significant professional learning by *being an action researcher* in an inquiry approach to his own tutoring, with the support and guidance both of the teachers and of other tutors.

The author describes how a group of teachers took a reflective approach to their own and each others' professional development in relation to problematic aspects of teaching and learning science. Individually and collaboratively, they evaluated their own teaching in the light of their observations and assessments of the children's learning, then carried out action research for improvement. Detailed stories of six of the teachers show that inquiry and reflection can be central parts of the professional development process. Looking across the six studies, the book offers a way of understanding professional development which emphasises the importance of personal qualities, professional contexts and the need for teachers to control their own development. It offers insights into ways in which the complexities of classroom life can be transcended by teachers, showing how they could play a pivotal role in the improvement of school education.

Peter Ovens is Principal Lecturer in Professional and Curriculum Development in the Faculty of Education at Nottingham Trent University, where he teaches science education and action research and supervises research students.

1   Introduction

This book is about the personal professional development of teachers and tutors or others who support teacher development. It is based upon the study of a one year, part-time, day/evening course for primary teachers who developed their teaching of science. The ultimate aim of these developments, of the teachers' teaching, of the course and of the tutor's role has been the improvement of children's learning of science.

The general approach to the improvement of education in the United Kingdom over recent years has been to focus on what is considered to be wrong and to give attention to what teachers cannot do. The government's main methods of prompting for change have been printed words contained in policy documents, prescriptions of curricular aims and methods and other forms of centralized control that amount to a power-coercive approach. It is as if teachers need to be directed by knowledge 'out there', not only about how to teach science better, but also about how to develop themselves professionally. It is expected that this knowledge should be applied by teachers to their practice.

The approach to the improvement of education taken here is of a radically different kind, one that could be said to be educational improvement, that is, improvements which are intended to be educational to those involved rather than managerial or coercive. The focus is upon starting with what are considered to be strengths in teachers' practice and giving attention to what teachers can do (a preferable meaning of the *can do* profession). The main ways of prompting change are: first, harnessing teachers' abilities to deepen their awareness of their own professional needs; second, stimulating close observation of the teachers' own classroom experiences; third, promoting their individual and collaborative reflection about shared learning from their experiences; and fourth, the critical use of others' published ideas to create improvements. The teachers referred to here largely directed themselves not only to improve the science learning of their children, but also to improve their own capacities to develop themselves professionally. Such improvements continued after the main source of support, the course, had ended, and improvements extended beyond the inevitably limited range which was possible within the relatively short time that support could be given. The knowledge involved in these developments is mainly personal in character. It is part of the teachers as people, bound up in their professional thinking and practice. The knowledge is not fully communicable by written accounts, for, as teachers know, the best way for one professional person to understand another's professional practice is to witness it and discuss it with them. Also, the knowledge is generated as it is used, and the effects are immediately tested in the context of the teacher's own classroom.

The claim made by this book, from the experience of evolving this approach with the development of the science teaching of primary teachers, is that the best way of achieving improvements in children's learning and in teachers' teaching more generally is through encouraging teachers to start where they are and to establish a positive framework of support for collaborative action research.

The teachers on this course were encouraged to be teacher researchers and to carry out action research as the main part of their development. The book is about both the teachers' action research and also the tutor's action research into the role of enabling and assessing professional development. It includes six course members' case studies, which consider a series of issues concerning their practice of, and their understanding of, the teaching, learning and assessment of science in the primary school. The book explores the nature of their personal professional development and its assessment. During the course, the teachers developed their use of an investigative pedagogy of teaching science which elicited encouraging examples of pupils' scientific learning. Also, they developed their understandings, abilities, skills and confidence to derive professional growth from reflection about their classroom experiences and their participation in critical friendship discussion with peers and the tutor. Examples are provided of the individual teachers' development of their professional thought and action interdependently within their inquiry work. These examples support and develop a belief in the value of action research for the integration of theory with practice in meeting the practical professional problems of improving teaching for improved learning.

However, there are no infallible recipes for getting teachers to turn their experience into desired professional knowledge or to apply new knowledge to practice. There are no prescriptions for creating the 'right kind of primary science teacher'. There are no formulaic solutions to be imposed dogmatically and hierarchically on the task of teacher development and no predetermined specifications of outcome or product. Instead, the characteristics of professional development processes are explored in the context of an open and dynamic situation in which deeper insights and better qualities of action are encouraged to emerge from reflection on practice and theory, that is to say, action research. All this provides a standpoint from which to question and develop some aspects of action research, its methods, kinds of support and its assessment. It also provides a basis for questioning current ideas about teachers' professional knowledge and how it can be enhanced as part of the desire for educational improvement.

As a profession, it is to be expected that teaching should be the focus of continuing efforts to renew professional knowledge and improve practices, not least because society itself is a dynamic entity. However, curriculum reform initiatives have become increasingly centralized. They were led mainly by educationalists during the 1960s and 1970s, and by politicians during the 1980s and 1990s. Almost all initiatives have assumed that the way of overcoming problems at the periphery of the system, where there is the complexity and unpredictability of classroom teaching, is by the application of centrally designed, technical–rational solutions. Innovators have commonly assumed that teachers construe teaching in the same way as they do – that teaching is about theories and mechanisms rather than about relationships – since mechanisms can be studied 'objectively' and made into 'teacher-proof' packages. (Jerome Bruner is reputed to have mocked 'teacher-proof' packages as 'like trying to make love people-proof'.) The lack of success (unless 'results' are manipulatable) is blamed on the lack of knowledge and, increasingly, the lack of compliance of the teachers. The limitations of the centre-to-periphery model of change were long ago pointed out by Donald Schön (1971), who also described alternative models of change such as the proliferation-of-centres. Only once in the last four decades has a central body devolved power and responsibility rather than sought more for itself. In its last years, the Schools Council set up programmes that harnessed teachers' creativity in the development of personal knowledge and contextualized solutions to professional problems rather than universal, mechanistic ones. For example, the Teacher-pupil Interaction and the Quality of Learning project (Ebbutt and Elliott, 1985) took teachers' perspectives on the problems of teaching for understanding as the starting point for finding solutions. This approach overcomes the deficiencies of a technical–rational approach, including the detachment of questions of technique from questions of value and the isolation of concerns about purpose and theory from concerns about practice. But, apart from these short-lived projects, there has been no serious and sustained attempt to share control over education and responsibility for its quality with teachers in ways which assume that they are professional people. As politicians have taken greater control over education to themselves, they have distorted the character of educational developments. Political time horizons are much shorter than educational ones. It now seems that a politician's need is to be seen to be improving things for their voters' children during the lifetime of one parliament. This creates a predilection for the policy of a 'quick fix' (Sockett, 1989: 130). Until a more intelligent and democratic balance of power can be struck, professional people in education need to find ways to 'cultivate the arts of creative compliance' (Macdonald, B., 1987) with the illusory improvements that some politicians see as vote-winning policy, whilst protecting the long-term improvement, or at least some preservation of real education. In the face of a centrally imposed technicist and managerialist culture, this book is about the maintenance of an educational and professional counter-culture in which it is the teachers' capacities for critical and creative inquiry that enable creative compliance with policy and prescription, whilst seeking genuine improvement.

Parts of the book aim to be of value to primary school teachers both during their initial education and as part of their continuing professional development. It is hoped that they will feel that there is an unfolding, inquiring quality to the stories of teacher development, and that there is an invitation for them to follow a similar approach to their own professional development in some appropriate way. However, the book is mainly intended to be a stimulus to those responsible for the professional develop-ment of teachers, to reaffirm the significance of the personal nature of professional learning and to reassert the necessity of the learner's possession of a good measure of control over their own development.

The Professional Context

The course described in this book is a Certificate in Science Teaching (Primary), validated by the Association for Science Education and run at a large university. The impetus to develop it in this form came not from the world of primary science education, but from the inspiration of the curriculum development initiatives of Lawrence Stenhouse and John Elliott. For example, the Humanities Curriculum Project (HCP) was:

> a very different sort of curriculum from the traditional courses on offer to teachers. It focused on the curriculum problems and issues which arise in particular educational settings, rather than on general theories about educational practice. Its methods aimed not to transmit informa-tion, but to establish conditions which enabled teachers reflectively to develop solutions to the curriculum problems they identified.
>
> (Elliott, 1983: 112)

Both the methodological and substantive features of the Ford Teaching Project (Elliott, 1975) provided insight into the kind of continuing profes-sional development work that I aspired to in primary science. It suggested innovative ways in which the tutor can enable teachers to use an action research approach to develop their pedagogy rather than fulfil conventional course requirements, such as writing essays. The Ford Teaching Project's analysis of inquiry/discovery teaching and learning was a valuable resource for reflection on the evidence collected by the teachers about their teaching, and the hypotheses about teachers' personal change were helpful guides to the tutor's enabling role.

John Elliott's comment about the HCP makes an important distinction:

It was [the teachers'] professional responsibility to realise a worthwhile curriculum process for their particular pupils. The 'outsider's' task was to enable teachers to reflect about what constituted such a process and how it might be realised in their practical situation. Here we have a distinction between the curriculum development role of the insider and the teacher development role of the outsider.

(Elliott, 1989: 212)

Applying this to the primary science course, the role of the tutor would be as an outsider to the teachers' development of their science teaching by facilitating their reflection, and as an insider to the curriculum development of the course. As the course tutor, I used action research to enable me to carry out tutor development of myself. Just as teachers learn from their pupils, I learned from the course members and based my findings heavily on their perspectives. They are all provisional, personally controversial and changing. They are expressed in their state of gradual becoming, not in their final state. The non-personal value of the book is the support it may offer to other's existing ideas and, at the same time, the tests and criticisms it brings to bear on those ideas, within the area of study called action research for professional development.

Outline of the Course

In its original form, the course had three interrelated parts.

1   Looking at primary school science (the science part): The aims, processes and products of science education; aims, objectives and evaluation; science knowledge and understanding; integration of science into the primary curriculum; investigative ways of learning; resources; and children's scientific concept development.
2   Developing primary school science (the general, theoretical professional part): Ideas about pupils' development of scientific concepts, scientific attitudes and skills; analysing learning activities for pre-requisites and outcomes; differentiation – observing a pupil's development to influence the choice of learning activities to achieve the most effective learning, classroom organization; and the teacher's role.
3   Professional research into primary school science teaching and learning (the teacher's personal integration of the various components): An investigation into a professional aspect of science work chosen by the teacher; studying her/his own class; studying research by other teachers; and methods for the collection of evidence.

This outline reflects my beliefs at that time about continuing professional development courses as equipping teachers with theoretical ideas, which were learned mainly through abstract presentations, group discussions and exercise types of practical experience at the university, to guide their practices. Theories were to be *applied* in the classroom. A separation of theory from practice, which I subsequently overcame, is evident in this view.

The duration of the course was two and a half terms. Course sessions included:

1   Practical science workshop sessions to give direct experience of suitable starting points for pupils' investigative activities.
2   Experiential tasks and mini-lectures, which dealt with a broad range of topics and themes within the science national curriculum and beyond, to strengthen teachers' science knowledge.
3   Practical professional workshop sessions to give either direct experience (simulated or role-play activity) or a recorded version (such as videos or transcripts) of a teaching/learning event that has relevance to a practical, professional issue, as a basis for discussion.
4   Tutor-led presentations followed by a discussion of pre-planned inputs on key issues of theory or policy, and a review of progress of the individual study.
5   A visit by the tutor to each course member's classroom to observe their science teaching, discuss the issues arising and also discuss any relevant aspects of the teacher's more general participation in the course.

The assessment of course members' achievements was through two written assignments: one about a piece of their own science teaching, called the curriculum assignment, and another about the teacher's action research study, called the classroom-based study.

Characteristics of Course Members

Each cohort comprised about fifteen course members, mostly women, and usually between a half and two thirds of them were teachers of Key Stage Two classes. The age profile was usually fairly wide, several were fairly newly qualified, most had five to twelve years of experience and a few had twenty years or more experience. There was nearly always representation of a range of school types with regard to the age of the buildings, the predominant social group of the pupils and the type of location. Also, there were invariably representatives of a range of teaching styles and viewpoints, including some who appeared to match the following crude stereotypes:

•   knowledge-oriented subject specialists who were male, science graduated, Key Stage Two teachers, and
•   progressive, child-centred teachers who were female, Key Stage One teachers.

There was diversity also in their motivation for wishing to take a continuing professional development course in science. Some aspired to become the curriculum co-ordinator for science in their present or a future school, and so career advancement was significant to them. Others already held this responsibility, sometimes having had it thrust upon them, so they joined the course either out of 'conscious incompetence' or the demands of their head teacher. However, there was always a sizeable group, sometimes about half of the cohort, for whom overt career ambitions were not a significant motivation. They tended to be women with ten or more years' experience, and their motivation could be summed up in the phrase 'job satisfaction'. People in this group tended to show a particularly independent approach, and were most often the ones to express their satisfaction with the course at the end of the year by claiming that they were not as concerned about receiving the award as the worthwhile experience of participating in the course, which was the main gratification for them.

Pedagogical Principles of the Course

1   A commitment to support the teachers' improvement of their teaching as the central focus of continuing professional development.
2   Coherence between the way the tutor teaches the teachers and the way the teachers are encouraged to teach their pupils.
3   Both kinds of teaching are investigative and learner centred to draw out the highest human learning capacities.
4   Therefore, each teacher's action research should be into the aspect of the teacher's practice which appears to her/him to be the most immediate obstacle to the achievement of investigative learning.
5   Consequently, a significant part of the course (about a third) is allocated to individual or group teacher action research projects.
6   The main intrinsic enabling conditions within the teacher are a strong professional curiosity and a commitment to the evolution of her/his own practice through an open-minded approach.
7   The main extrinsic enabling conditions created by the course are support for teacher self-monitoring and pupil monitoring, and for the discussion of findings and the exploration of as wide a range of ideas as possible about the improvement of practice.

The Personal Context

As the holder of a degree in science, trained to believe in objective knowledge, I found myself inquiring into the nature of professional knowledge as part of the responsibility of supporting teachers' development. Also, having begun my career as a secondary school teacher who was trained to be an 'infallible expert' (Schön, 1983), I found myself running a continuing professional development course for primary teachers, facilitating their capacities to be 'reflective practitioners', while my own aims and practices were being challenged.

> Facilitators of teacher-based action research need to be constantly deliberating about their own practice and its relationship to the nature of the activity they are trying to facilitate. If they do not engage in this kind of second-order action research they will succumb to pressures to control teachers' thinking, and thereby distort rather than enable the processes of first-order action research.
>
> Submission to such a discipline is essential if academics are to avoid perpetrating ideas which misrepresent and distort action research in order to legitimate the hegemony of academics in their relation to teachers.
>
> (Elliott, 1989a: 2)

Originally, my image of professional inquiry had been something largely impersonal, detached and rigid, so that the product could be, like a scientific theory, something with predictive potential across context and time (see also pp. 150–7). But I have come to believe that a professional inquiry is something which the inquirer creates, which is not a *product* in the sense that it is external to or indifferent from the nature of the person who produces it, instead it is an *'activity in an objectified or congealed form'* (Bernstein, 1972). For this reason, it is important for an inquiry to include information about the inquirer which can assist the reader in understanding why the inquiry has certain characteristics. Each of us carries a particular load of cultural baggage, and each of us looks to find their way with particular conceptual spectacles. This inquiry has enabled me to unpack and repack parts of my baggage, and also to examine and reshape my spectacles. It now seems obvious that I could not in any real sense have started from some kind of detached beginning in order to do bias-free research. This realization is responsible for a sceptical attitude towards research on education which pretends to be objective.

As a school pupil I was fairly open-minded as to what might interest me, although I had established for myself a penchant for gathering and organizing facts, particularly about 'wonders of the world', cars and other forms of transport. Science subjects were the ones that I began to feel a commitment towards. Also, my appreciation of artistic experience tended to be biased towards the literal kinds of expression, for example I liked pieces of music such as 'The Sorcerer's Apprentice' or 'Fingal's Cave' which represented something to visualize. I chose A level GCE courses in Physics, Chemistry and Zoology, and went on to take a combined studies degree in Zoology and Chemistry.

The dominant belief about the nature of knowledge that I now think my secondary school education had endorsed was that firm and definite knowledge exists 'out there', in teachers' minds and in books, and the pupil's task was to learn it in what I now regard as a submissive and unquestioning way. Sciences had special appeal, partly because these were the subjects where the firmness and definition of the knowledge appeared to be best developed. The economy and power with which science knowledge is expressed as laws and definitions held the attraction that when they had been learned, they conferred an authority upon oneself. Although I was able to interpret and apply my knowledge, and to this extent had understanding which included a limited kind of creativity, the understanding was of an entirely unquestioning and uncritical kind. I have no recollection at all of holding in my mind any doubts or questions about the certainty of the knowledge 'out there', but only of being aware of the incompleteness of my own recall or grasp. This was a difficulty that I knew I had to resolve for myself by re-reading my notes or the textbook and learning them, in an accepting, passive way – my mind 'adapted to' the structures of knowledge rather than 'adapted with' them (Elliott, 1990). Writing the notes mainly involved copying phrases and sentences from books for two reasons: my own expressions would lack the required accuracy, and also it seemed to be part of the scientific tradition of faithful replication of evidence to put one's own interpretations to one side. Consequently, I found writing to be very difficult indeed when it is outside the mode of factual description or re-presenting existing ideas and information.

The phenomenon of 'learning for later' (Ebbutt and Elliott, 1985) also applied to my school learning. The possession of a good set of notes felt like learning. If they were in a well organized form for memorization later, they were good, regardless of their real comprehensibility now. In this sense, learning was not *knowing* as a part of engaging in productive thought within the *being* mode, it was *having more knowledge*, like the possessive satisfaction of a materialist, acquisitive instinct, as in the *having mode* (Fromm, 1976). I entertained no reservations, let alone outright criticisms of the science I learned, nor did I learn to use my initial ignorance or misunderstandings as a means of learning in a social context, since ignorance was something to be ashamed of and to be rectified in private. There were rare instances of having to learn standard criticisms of particular ideas, but I learned about them like other parts of the subject knowledge in an uncritical way and did not enter into debates. I became more sceptical about non-scientific kinds of explanation, and more narrow-minded towards non-scientific kinds of thinking. For example, I tended to expect representations of experience and knowledge to be factual and literal. I grew to devalue those which were imaginative, evocative or poetic. For example, I derided the ballet and scoffed at abstract art.

When I entered teaching, Nuffield curriculum development projects dominated school science education, and I became an uncritical adherent. Learners had to take an active role in their own learning, and I believed that the appropriate pedagogy was that of 'stage-managed discovery', that is, the teacher selects knowledge aims beforehand and sets those practical tasks which will lead the learner's thinking, during a planned series of experiences, towards grasping the desired knowledge. My school teaching experience gave me a growing awareness of the social and cultural influences on learning, an increasing interest in moving on from the Nuffield pedagogy of stage-managed discovery and an appreciation of the difficulty of achieving curriculum change.

When I became a higher education tutor, most of my students were preparing to be primary school teachers, so I learned much about primary education through classroom experience and further study. I also joined the then Classroom Action Research Network (now the Collaborative Action Research Network) which had grown out of the Ford Teaching Project (1973–5) at the University of East Anglia. I mounted a short course which aimed to assist primary teachers committed to the Science 5–13 Series (1972–5) pedagogy of investigative teaching and learning to develop their under-standing and practice of it. The work of one of the teachers in this group, Jane Ryan, gives an example of the course process and achievements (Ovens and Ryan, 1986). By this time, I was beginning to realise that the individu-ality of each teacher as a professional person, and the uniqueness of his/her professional context meant that when they used a self-reflective approach to their own development, they were creating a unique, professional inquiry. Until this time I think I had supposed that there were very few specific routes of professional development that any teacher could go down as part of their working towards the achievement of 'good primary practice'. In other words, I tacitly believed that the Nuffield science curriculum develop-ment projects' theory of 'stage-managed discovery' applied to teachers' professional learning, as well as to science learning. I was passing through an intermediate stage of accepting that every teacher had a different starting point, but that the ultimate goal, good primary practice in teaching science, was a fixed end point that was 'out there' for every teacher to converge upon. It could be visualized as a periphery-to-centre model, in which teachers start somewhere on the circumference of a circle, and progress to the fixed and pre-set centre where *the* ideal is realized.

The Conceptual Context

The academic and professional field of primary science education can gener-ally be seen as having been influenced by dominant ideas of primary education and of secondary science education. Where there are important issues about which the two traditions offer conflicting ways of thinking, the ideas origi-nating in secondary science have not always taken enough account of, and have tended to overwhelm the relevant primary perspective in their influence on much writing about primary science. A prominent example of this is the usage of the concept of *process*. Meanings of process originating from secondary science education are usually to do with inquiry methods associated with scientific research. When attempts are made to reduce these methods to their components, the result is to define constituent *process skills* (for example, Harlen, 1996) or *procedural knowledge* (as in Gott and Duggan, 1995). It can be helpful to focus attention upon components in order to deepen awareness of the whole process, but with two conditions. First, the analysis should be done on the understanding that the whole is still regarded as more than the sum of the analytical components which are identified, and, second, that identifying components that make sense analytically does not mean that the components have an independent existence. They are mutually inclusive. Different authors offer different analyses at different times, but none has gained universal agreement as a complete account. One danger among several is that these analyses are used as more than an approximate guide to a complex phenomenon, and are allowed to assume undue importance in their own right. In secondary science this led to the so-called *process approach* being used by some curriculum materials which were designed to focus on the separate processes of science individually and in isolation from science content. In primary science a similar approach can be seen, apparently in ignorance of a primary education tradition with the same name but much deeper meaning.

In general, there is too little formal recognition in primary science education of the primary education meaning of a *process approach*. The science version of a *process approach* has been justifiably criticized (see, for example, Driver and Millar, 1987), but without explicit acknowledgement of the significance of the primary education meaning of this term to understanding the curriculum.

Primary education has long held the aim of enabling children to learn how to learn as one which is overarching. The processes of learning are integrated with, but are more important than the products. There are various roots to this view, not least psychologists' interest in metacognition.

However, the main origin lies in an epistemology which denies the unquestioning acceptance of knowledge as having a separate, objective existence, but emphasizes the process by which 'knowers' search for and develop personal knowledge. This position is extensively explained and justified by Geva Blenkin and Vic Kelly, notably in their book *The Primary Curriculum* (1987). Rationality resides in the process as much as the knowledge product. Therefore, education is seen to be a process of enabling learners to develop and extend all of their own learning powers, including scientific ones, to the full, with less emphasis on what is learned or how much. Educators who reject a rationalist philosophy are cautious about the intellectual level of the response, which can be educed from any particular learner in any particular context, but are certain about one thing: what is valued above all else is the learner's own learning purposes and processes, and how these interact with learning experiences and the enabling functions of the teacher so as to provoke the strongest development of the learner's ability to learn. The work of Stenhouse (1975) has contributed a theoretical understanding of a process approach to curriculum (drawing on Peters' (1966: 159) reconceptualization of educational aims). Stenhouse also provided the practical embodiment of a process curriculum in the form of the Humanities Curriculum Project. Instead of aiming mainly or exclusively for specific knowledge as the product of learning, a process curriculum aims for the quality of the learners' learning process to match that specified as principles of procedure. Applying this to a primary science curriculum, the learners' scientific inquiry process is not valued instrumentally to the achievement of prespecified learning aims, but it is valued intrinsically.

So it is the experience of scientifically investigating objects, materials and phenomena *together with* the inseparable, interim, tentatively held personal knowledge (which is *part of* this ongoing process) that is valued in the process approach, as meant by the primary education definition of this concept. This represents a strong justification for 'whole investigations' in science education, and it is consistent with constructivist principles of learning. In the terms of the national curriculum for science, this indicates a clear way of integrating attainment target 1 with other attainment targets which specify desired knowledge and understanding. (Attainment target 1 is the common-usage term for the part of the science national curriculum entitled 'Experimental and Investigative Science', which requires that pupils should be taught the abilities to plan experimental work and to obtain and consider evidence. The contexts for such investigative learning are provided by the statements in what are commonly referred to as the three other science attainment targets – 2, 3 and 4.)

Applying the process approach to the task of planning a curriculum of a continuing professional development course requires the defining of principles of procedure which create the enabling conditions for teachers' processes of professional learning to be maximized. Stenhouse emphasized that the whole approach is a tentative and dynamic one which is constantly open to critical and empirical development. Therefore, a tutor responsible for a course (or other initiative) aiming for the professional development of teachers would also be expected to engage in the learning task of monitoring her/his own practice as a tutor, in the light of CPD principles of procedure, so as to be able to reflect critically on both and improve them. Insofar as the tutor is also a teacher (of teachers), there should equally be 'a commitment to systematic questioning of one's own teaching as a basis for development' since 'there can be no educational development without teacher development; and the best means of development is not by clarifying ends but by criticising practice' (Stenhouse, 1975).

These are the conceptual foundations for the work described here. The process of learning can be thought of as being an inquiring person. Inquiry is a way in which a person links her/his desires to know more things and to do more things (and better things) on the one hand, with her ideas of herself as a distinct person with particular abilities, interests, values, beliefs and ideals on the other hand. This applies equally to all three levels at which the learning of the participants in the course described here took place.

The children:	achieve science learning by *being scientific* in taking an inquiry approach to materials and phenomena with the support and guidance of other children and their teacher.
The children's teacher:	achieves professional learning by *being a teacher researcher* in taking an inquiry approach to her/his own teaching of science and the children's scientific learning, with the support and guidance of other teachers and an enabler – in this case the course tutor.
The teachers' tutor:	achieves professional learning by *being a teacher researcher* in taking an inquiry approach to her/his own tutoring and the teachers' professional learning, as well as the children's scientific learning, with the support and guidance both of the teachers themselves and of other tutors.

At each of these levels, carrying out inquiry as her/his process of learning led each learner to show the following qualities:

1   Curiosity, through questioning and criticising, to learn more and to learn better.
2   Confidence, at least in taking the next step in the inquiry process, that one is likely to be successful in one's own terms.
3   Courage in seeking improvement by taking risks of various kinds because one may experience disappointment or failure in one's own terms.
4   Trust that other people taking part will be encouraging towards oneself, and will also be constructively critical when necessary.
5   Attentiveness to significant details about events and actions in one's experience which are the subject of reflection and discussion, and might contribute to one's learning.
6   Empathy with others to appreciate their perspective on significant events and ideas, to offer constructive criticism and to be a member of a community of inquirers.
7   Open-mindedness, yet also a critical and self-critical attitude.

It gradually became clearer that professional development is a dynamic learning process which is represented by a person's own reflective dialogues between the following three aspects of the person's professional thought and action shown in Figure 1.1.

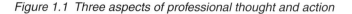

Figure 1.1 Three aspects of professional thought and action

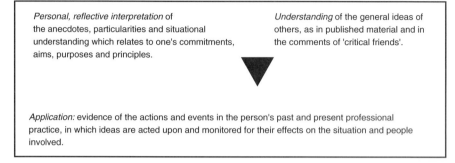

Personal, reflective interpretation of the anecdotes, particularities and situational understanding which relates to one's commitments, aims, purposes and principles.

Understanding of the general ideas of others, as in published material and in the comments of 'critical friends'.

Application: evidence of the actions and events in the person's past and present professional practice, in which ideas are acted upon and monitored for their effects on the situation and people involved.

There is no fixed starting point to any particular episode of professional development. Each of us may find a different point at which to make a conscious entrance into the interconnected parts of the triangle, and begin to set up the interactions between the three kinds of component activities. Changes in application may be more likely to prompt changes in interpretation and understanding than vice versa.

The ambiguity in the title *Reflective Teacher Development in Primary Science* is meant to convey that I have not only advocated a reflective approach to the professional development of the teachers taking part in a continuing professional development course, but also used such an approach to my own professional development as a teacher educator. Learning is not finding out what other people already know, but solving our own problems for our own purposes by questioning, thinking and testing until the solution is part of our life (Handy, 1988).

Primary school science

Almost all of the major curriculum development projects in primary science education, and in some ways also the first version of the science national curriculum, have been philosophical successors to Nuffield Junior Science (1967), which had the following basic belief:

> We concluded, and believe very strongly, that a child should raise his [sic] own problems, partly because isolating a problem is an important part of scientific thinking, partly because the ever increasing body of knowledge makes it increasingly ridiculous to prescribe what any child should know, but mostly because we do not believe that anyone can ask a completely significant question for someone else. This would demand a complete appreciation of the person's ability, and the extent and

quality of previous experience, and only the individual himself can ask a question which takes all that into account.

(Wastnedge, 1968: 640)

The more recent drive has been to prescribe certain subject knowledge and to give it growing emphasis as the most significant product of children's learning. This is in contradiction to the views about the nature of science and the nature of children's learning which are encapsulated in this statement. The Nuffield Junior Science (1967) philosophy does not regard knowledge aims of primary science to be unimportant. Children's investigations need to be about objects, materials and phenomena which have scientific as well as personal significance, and the conceptual understanding gained is part of the investigation rather than a separable product of it. There is no priority of investigative processes over the knowledge that is gained by them, but there is a priority of the investigatively derived knowledge (which cannot be pre-specified with certainty) over pre-specified knowledge outcomes which, if they were taken as aims, would in some way have to be imposed on an investigation. Such a prioritization distorts the 'investigations' into 'stage-managed discovery'. It was the latter version of the 'heuristic method' that dominated most of the Nuffield curriculum development projects which related to the secondary school science curriculum. It was rightly criticized by Paul Atkinson and Sarah Delamont (1977) as an unscientific form of the 'information game' which takes place in the 'management of knowledge' in teaching. By contrast, the Nuffield Junior Science Teachers' Guides (1967) provide many examples of children's scientific understanding of their investigative work, which show good conceptual understanding (knowing that), as well as procedural understanding (knowing how). In *whole* scientific investigations, which ideally would be primary school children's main kind of science learning experience, the development of scientific concepts would be the result of interaction between children's past experiences and current questions with their interpretations firstly of the data they collect, secondly of the texts they consult and thirdly the teaching they receive. The whole process is driven by their curiosity and guided by the inquiry purposes negotiated with the teacher. It is equally important for the teacher to foster the children's investigative abilities so as to encourage them to take seriously the conventional scientific knowledge about the objects, materials and phenomena under investigation. The supposition that *knowing how* is separable from *knowing that* is not supported by several kinds of study, including some psychological theories which claim that:

it is the norm in mental organisations for knowledge and skill to be stored together, in purpose-built packages, which have evolved to meet the range of demands which can be expected in a particular type of familiar situation or 'scenario'. This combination of content, context, purpose and process into flexible bundles of localised competence is the primary format of the mind. Far from being the neat, coherent unitary sort of theory to which science proper aspires, the mind-scope of the child is patchwork and piecemeal. It consists not of an integrated theory but of an assembly of 'mini-theories', each generated to provide successful engagement with a particular kind of scenario.

(Claxton, 1991: 86)

Therefore, it would depend upon how the teacher judges the changing context and the children's needs, whether s/he decides to tell the children about a particular item of scientific knowledge, and, if so, when to give it, withhold it or use it in the form of asking leading questions, and so on. As in Stephen Rowland's (1984) interpretive model of teaching, subject knowledge is used by an inquiry-oriented teacher in various context-dependent ways, and, only when it is judged to be appropriate, is it used as the basis for an episode of transmission teaching.

Some aspects of an investigative approach to primary science advocated by the course depicted in this book are informed by a critical evaluation of some dominant features of secondary school science. Guy Claxton (1991) characterizes secondary pupils' experience of science as:

- fragmented, lacking purpose, with results only being sought to conform with theory,
- a carelessness because of a lack of 'feel' for science,
- a difficulty because of the conceptual load,
- a boredom caused by lack of excitement and relevance to every day concerns, and
- the impersonality of subject matter, and a sense of 'learned helplessness' in the face of the 'infallible expert' of subject knowledge.

Following Claxton (1991), the investigative primary science advocated here:

- is cautious in its treatment of counter-intuitive ideas,
- requires investigations to be only as precise as necessary to answer immediate questions,
- is cautious in its use of terminology (which is grounded in experience),
- utilizes a playful, exploratory approach to learning,
- isolates problems that link with real life,
- seeks or constructs solutions pragmatically through messy ambiguity and with reflective exploration, and
- takes care not to overemphasize the rationality and articulacy of science, or its tendency to be authoritarian in its reliance on the arbitration of the teacher or the textbook.

Most recently, there are suggestions for science education to examine and adopt approaches derived from the social constructivist view of education as enculturation derived from the work of Vygotsky (see, for example, Hodson and Hodson, 1998a; 1998b). Here, the role of the teacher in sustaining pupils' learning processes as 'apprentices' includes the notion, familiar to primary education, of scaffolding as one of the means by which learners' autonomous learning is supported. There are other features of the kind of primary school science advocated by this course which appear in this approach (Hodson and Hodson, 1998b), such as modelling, learning the language of science, learning science through language and the importance of group work.

Action research for professional development

Professional learning through action research has some similarities to learning science through scientific investigation. An adaptation of Ron Wastnedge's words, as quoted on pp. 14–15, provides parallel beliefs about teachers' professional learning: A teacher should raise his/her own professional problems, partly because isolating a problem is an important part of professional thinking, partly because the ever-increasing body of professional knowledge makes it increasingly ridiculous to prescribe what any teacher should know, but mostly because I do not believe that anyone can ask a completely significant professional question for someone else. This would demand a complete appreciation of the teacher's ability, and the extent and quality of previous experience, and only the individual him/herself can ask a question which takes all that into account.

However, there are also clear dissimilarities between scientific and educative approaches to curriculum development and educational research. A scientific approach is unsuitable, mainly due to the inapplicability of scientific methods to the complexities of educational situations. The sustained series of attacks upon attempts to create scientifically based educational knowledge, not least that of Carr and Kemmis (1986) in *Becoming Critical*, have argued convincingly for the different character of professional knowledge. This is captured by Barry MacDonald's statement about the uniqueness of each educational situation: 'No two schools or classrooms are so alike in their circumstances that prescriptions of curricular action can adequately supplant the judgement of the people in them.' (MacDonald and Ruddock 1971: 166).

Having rejected the logical possibility that research or curriculum prescription based on scientific procedures can tell a teacher precisely what to do, the need remains for teachers to develop the capacities to adopt and adapt any such prescriptions, which are relevant to their pupils and their classroom and school contexts, for themselves. Such capacities could be used to generate a teacher's own 'practical knowledge'.

Teachers are currently faced with fulfilling the teaching requirements of a national curriculum which has a growing emphasis on subject knowledge at the expense of inquiry abilities. There are also other pressures on teachers, such as Standard Attainment Tasks (SATs), for them to possess more subject knowledge and to teach it in a transmission manner. The initial teacher education national curriculum has introduced even greater demands for the possession of subject knowledge by teachers. This is tending towards the use of the same 'pot filling' as opposed to 'fire lighting' (Ovens, 1989) methods for the teaching of science to teachers. In both national curricula, problems of content overload and external assessment targeting concept knowledge are having seriously distorting effects on the image of science being learned and the kind of learning demanded. The policy of this course has been to regard teachers' acquisition of subject knowledge as serving the professional purpose of furthering children's science learning. The important issue here is how the knowledge is developed and the use to which it is put. Despite the claims from some quarters, there is no convincing research to show that the possession of greater science subject knowledge, in the general sense of being detached from its professional use, has a straightforward causal link with the improvement of teaching, learning and assessing. Such improvements are most likely to be achieved by the self-critical monitoring by a teacher of her/his own teaching in the light of reflection on discussion and reading about aims and methods of science education. For some teachers on the course, this might lead to a diagnosis which indicates the need for the teacher's subject knowledge to be increased in some general sense. However, it is more likely that the needs identified are for subject knowledge in those particular areas relating to specific topics or themes being taught at the time. It is more likely still that the needs are for strategies and tactics for applying the subject knowledge to the investigative teaching being done. Subject knowledge is most appropriately gained in the context of its immediate professional use. The fundamental aim of a continuing professional development course therefore is not to transmit subject knowledge in a non-specific way, but to help teachers to develop their abilities to learn how to obtain and apply subject knowledge for themselves as and when it is needed for their investigative teaching. This should ensure consistency between the way in which teachers are taught science and the way in which they are encouraged to teach it.

The inquiry methods

The inter-relationships between action research done by the teachers for the course and my own action research are indicated in Figure 1.2.

My action research was symbiotic with that of the course members. My tutorial and action research aims coincided in seeking improved professional learning of teachers, which in turn meant the improvement of the scientific learning of pupils in classrooms. The methods of collection of evidence

Figure 1.2 *The inquiry methods*

	The course members' use of action research	My use of action research
The practice being studied	Teaching in primary schools.	Teaching teachers on a continuing professional development course at the university.
Subject taught	Science.	The teaching of science.
Purpose of the action research	To improve an aspect of the teaching which relates to each teacher's professional needs.	To improve the course and my teaching of it, particularly to strengthen teachers' autonomous professional inquiry.
General methods of evidence collection	Make observational notes and take photographs of teaching/learning action, tape discussions, interview pupils.	Make observational notes of teaching/learning action, tape discussions, interview teachers, etc.
Evidence analysis	Write analytic reviews, present interim reports to critical friends.	Write analytic reviews, present interim reports to critical friends.
Subjects of reflection	Their own teaching of science, pupils' learning of science, critical friends' feedback, science education literature.	My own teaching of the course, teachers' professional development, critical friends' feedback, science education and action research literatures.
Critical friendship groupings	Study groups of course member colleagues and possibly others.	Staff seminars at the university.
The value of the tutor's visit to the classroom	Receive my support with evidence collection, and discussion of issues, both methodological and substantive in their action research.	Development of my theories of primary science and of teacher professional development through action research.

about course members and of involving them in giving me critical feedback were coherent with the course rationale whereby the tutor and teacher are jointly responsible for the teacher's development. Course members were informed of my intention to do some action research at the beginning of the course, and were reminded when appropriate. I sought permission to collect evidence afresh on every occasion, turning off the audio recorder during sensitive stages of discussion when requested to do so. All my written accounts of course members' personal involvement, and the names under which they are written, were cleared by them before any public use.

The various course components yielded evidence for my research in the ways shown in Figure 1.3.

The collaboration between myself and course members involved was based upon values of democracy and respect for persons and for evidence, and with the aim of fostering professional autonomy. Since the pedagogy of the course is one that corresponds with Stephen Rowland's (1993) 'interpretive model', it entails a view of knowledge as a social construction and 'recognizes the importance of the critical engagement of individuals as they struggle to develop shared meanings' (1993: 32). Therefore, the role of the tutor includes a dimension of inquiry. 'This enquiry is something the tutor does as a central part of teaching, not in addition to it.' (Rowland, 1993: 32).

Figure 1.3 Research evidence was gathered in these ways

Course component	Evidence	How the evidence was to be used by my research
Application form	The course member's reasons for applying to the course and her/his description of present approaches to the teaching of science.	Inferences about her/his expectations of the course and her/his espoused theory of science teaching and learning at the start of the course.
Course sessions at the university	My observational notes of course teaching and learning action, my tape recordings of my discussions with course members and of discussion between course members.	Indirect evidence of her/his theory-in-use of science teaching and learning. Evidence of my theory-in-use of teaching the course.
Visit by the tutor to the course member's classroom	My observational notes and tape recordings of the course member's teaching, and our discussions before and after.	Direct evidence of her/his theory-in-use of science teaching and learning. Evidence of my theory-in-use of teaching the course.
Course assignments	The assignments and my comments on them.	Evidence of development of her/his theories of action.

2 Stories of Teachers' Development

Introduction

The purpose of writing case studies of teachers' participation in the course was to know more about individuals' experiences and learning, to be able to understand teachers' professional development in a more general sense and, therefore, be better able to enable it to take place.

The choice of any inquiry method must be made in relation to the purpose of the inquiry, its subject and context. Initially, I had an implicit belief, derived from my rationalist, scientific background, that patient evidence collection would give the foundation for certain knowledge. Some technically sophisticated form of analysis or esoteric abstraction of some kind would inductively erect theories which I had not anticipated. So I attempted to apply schematic and formulaic methods of evidence analysis, such as grounded theorizing (Glaser and Strauss, 1967). But I found that these methods created a distance, by which I mean: a loss of meaning between the analysis and the evidence with which I started. The act of wrenching an item of evidence from its context in order to place it, like a brick in a new wall, into an attempted theorization took on the mantle of a pointless game. No new insights emerged of any significance – only affirmation that existing interpretations had correspondence with recorded information. This situation compelled me to try to test my interpretations as fully as I could. It led me to adopt validation procedures which referred back to the participants in the situations I was analysing, including those who had taken or witnessed actions under consideration, and to provide my evidence and my interpretation of it for their comment.

The general method of analysis which seemed to work was:

- giving close thought and extended reflection to the evidence,
- writing a 'first level of interpretation',
- having 'internal conversations' between me and the accumulating material,
- doing further, more reflective writing,
- having 'external conversations' with significant others, and

- redrafting accounts in the light of the alternative interpretations discussed, the re-examination of evidence and deeper, more focused reading.

Instead of trusting a depersonalized method which alludes to objectivity, my approach has been to trust my own and others' capacities to be open to tests of our interpretations against each other and against evidence. Another lesson of experience was to accept that the research would not enable me to really *know* in detail each teacher's professional progress in terms of every precise cause/effect development along the way. I had hoped that it would be possible to reveal how each little step contributed to producing the main kind of development pathway which teachers generally used. If there was not one such path, then there would be only a small number of alternative paths. The value of such a mental map would be in more easily recognizing which pathway a future course member could choose (or be directed) to take and where it would lead them. All such assumptions were gradually refuted by the experience of writing these studies. The uniqueness of each teacher's development impressed itself on me more and more. Rather than gain knowledge of 'the path', the research has shown the kinds of choices people make when finding their own way, whether it is on a recognized pathway or (more usually) not, whether they easily get lost, have good maps, or are observant of clues to find a destination, and so on. As well as being interested in creating a map of pathways, I have gained insight into the nature of travellers and travelling. Having abandoned the use of a uniform set of detailed learning objectives as an expression of course aims for all course members, and adopted principles of procedure to guide the course planning, organization and pedagogy, the achievements I was looking for would not necessarily conform to an explicitly prescribed set of categories. Therefore, the case studies needed to be as open as possible to all reactions to the course which might be relevant to building an understanding of personal professional development. The studies are more descriptive than evaluative so as to provide the basis for the cross-case study analyses that follow.

A copy of her/his case study was sent to each teacher prior to my validation interview (see Elliott, 1990: 26) with them. I anticipated that any issues which emerged from the interviews would then be incorporated into a redrafted study, but no significant revisions proved necessary. I emphasized to each teacher that my reason for writing the study was to enable me, as the tutor, to increase my personal understanding of each teacher's experience of the course, to test this against the perspective of the teacher, and simultaneously to reflect back on my role and the course as part of my own professional development.

Angela

Profile of Angela

Angela had taught Key Stage One children for seven years at the school, recently obtaining a responsibility for science. She had studied chemistry at degree level and worked for ten years, mainly in scientific and technical posts, before becoming a mature student on an initial teacher education course. Here she obtained distinction grades in Mathematics and Professional Studies, as well as a commendation in the Practice and Principles of Education. She wanted to take my course to learn 'how to put it over', and how to fit 'meaningful science' into the rest of the teaching day. She appeared to see science as being about scientific concepts. The head teacher had asked Angela to join her in writing a science policy for the school. Angela shared a bay with one other teacher and two classes of Year Two children. The school had a distinctive approach to integrated curriculum planning.

My initial impressions of Angela were of a somewhat intense, very conscientious person whose personal and professional reasons for joining the course were strongly motivational. I initially assumed that her extensive science education would have led to a narrowly academic understanding of science, which was borne out at her interview.

Angela's Concerns

At the beginning of the course, her account of her team teaching indicated that the pupils were given opportunities for practical exploration separately from the teacher-controlled science elements of the curriculum, which tended to be purely observational. Therefore, she was concerned about whether the science learning could go beyond observational work. She posed a range of questions to herself which reflected an inadequacy that she saw in the achievement of matching pupils to tasks, and getting pupils to hypothesize and record.

At this stage I felt able to offer plenty of ideas about her concerns, and wanted to be as positive as possible because Angela seemed to lack confidence in her capacity for professional development. I tried to work on her ideas about the nature of science, for example by encouraging her to think through her own question: 'Is it necessary for all children to have the same experience?' Also, I encouraged her to look for examples of children's hypothesizing, and discouraged her concern for children to record their science where this seemed to be negating their interest in scientific thinking. Her conception of science as certain knowledge was becoming fairly clear. In this respect, I felt secure in my previous experience of the course that it would help Angela's idea to develop towards an appreciation of science as investigation, as well as towards increased use of investigative science in her teaching (my main concerns as course tutor). I felt less secure about how to understand her working context and about how I could support development there. I felt that she wanted me to tell her (my) answers to questions she raised about her teaching. My own direct experience of teaching infants is limited, so I found it difficult to identify with her situation. In such circumstances I am inhibited from making suggestions based only on reasoning for fear of them being seen as 'out of touch' and 'impractical'.

My Visit to Angela's Classroom

The work I observed was a little out of the ordinary for Angela because she worked mainly with one group in the open-plan situation. I saw the session falling into two distinct stages. The first part went as Angela had planned – giving encouragement to pupils' exploration, with their acquisition of her preconceived knowledge as the aim in view, to which her interventions were directed. Things began to get chaotic, and she was tempted to end the session prematurely. However, she noticeably relaxed, allowed them more freedom, and they continued to show total engagement with their exploration, which they took in various unexpected directions over a considerable period of time. The pupils had not previously shown such intense interest or extended perseverance with their explorations. Angela and I agreed that this was due to their own strong intrinsic motivation rather than a consequence of some aspect of the teacher's role acting as a stimulus. She agreed with me that the two stages of the session could be characterized by an earlier emphasis on teacher pre-planned knowledge objectives and teacher direction, followed by the dominance of pupils' own questioning, much of it implicit and indirect, together with teacher responsiveness. A more detailed account of this session can be found on pp. 85–92.

My impression of the children's science achievements was positive. In my notes for Angela, I emphasized the children's ownership of their exploration, referring to their implied questioning and hypothesizing, and the range of ideas about which they were gaining experience. I attributed this to their natural scientific learning powers, as well as their having enjoyed the good provision of resources and freedom from constraints. I saw this as a potentially very valuable experience for her – she had done it for herself – and despite the abnormal aspects of this context, she would possibly be able to adopt the approach, more or less entirely, across all future science sessions.

I believed that through this experience Angela had 'proved' to herself that:

- the children could 'be scientific' in a full sense,
- she could be enabling and facilitating, and
- she could recognize the scientific exploratory learning that had occurred.

Yet, she seemed not as able to exploit this development as immediately and as fully as I had anticipated. She seemed to be held back by the habit of seeing science as teacher-imposed knowledge, and therefore the urge to impose more structure on pupils' work to lead to the desired knowledge outcome, as well as by inhibitions about the working context.

Nevertheless, some further sessions in her subsequent teaching did show her that the same strength of pupil motivation could be released by investigative work, and that she could become less directive towards them, without any disadvantage, than she had been previously.

Angela submitted her curriculum assignment as a report on this work. It was well written, following the discussion and notes closely, and made good use of the guidance provided by the course handout for the structure of the assignment. The barrier to further professional development at this point appeared to be a difficulty about how to incorporate some of the characteristics of this work into more routine teaching situations. Her own questioning seemed to provide a promising basis for further reflection, although to me it seemed to be a bit diffuse. Throughout, she expressed apprehension that the pass/fail standards of the course might exceed her own performance ability. I gave reassurance based on an honest confidence that she would be successful.

Angela's Participation in the Course

In general, her contributions to whole group discussions were comparatively few and brief, but they often showed perceptive and critical views. Her participation in small group work seemed to be much more extensive. Among her regular criticisms of the course were: my tendency not to answer her questions, but to refer them back to the group; and the suggestions made by her (course member) critical friends about developing her own teaching appeared to Angela to underestimate her difficulties.

She seemed to experience pressure from the course assessment, as well as a lot of perceived pressure from the school situation to conform to a system of which she felt increasingly critical. She was also afraid of failing.

The classroom visit in the autumn term had proved to her that she *could* enable pupils to achieve good science learning. Much of the rest of the course saw her wrestling with the incorporation of this achievement into her routine teaching. She became defensive towards severe criticism from course members of the school's philosophy which inhibited investigative approaches. They advised her to exploit either the practical thematic work or the practical maths elements of the curriculum to develop opportunities for science. Subsequent small group discussions that Angela took part in were supported by my tutorial colleague, Pat, not me, so I lost touch with the details of Angela's work. However, there appeared to be an almost impenetrable barrier, set by the school's system of organizing the curriculum, to Angela's development of her science as she wanted it. Discussions about how to achieve a way through or around this barrier seemed to recur, and were accompanied by tense and frustrated accounts of the school constraints. I felt my help was limited to providing a framework of support (seminars) rather than making specific suggestions.

In her classroom-based study, Angela gives an account of the development of her science teaching which acknowledges an early preference for science knowledge aims rather than investigative skills or attitudes. She tells how her revised ideal of science learning came to be open-ended investigation. In her action research she began to open up the children's learning opportunities, from restricting them to observing and talking to enabling holistic exploratory work. She moved away from teacher dominance towards pupil independence, and teacher as support rather than as instructor. Her appreciation of children's abilities to be scientific, through exploration, clearly grew considerably. For example, she no longer talked about how to fit the science into the curriculum, but about how the science approach should be integrated with everyday work in the classroom. The study makes no explicit references to the anxieties she expressed at university, but is written in a very balanced, confident, rational and organized way. It isn't possible to guess exactly how the seminar discussions enabled Angela to develop her study, but, overall, they were a useful resource – as she acknowledges. The study was rewarding for me to read because it shows much progress towards my twin ideals for course members: pupil-centred science teaching and independent, professional development by the teacher.

An Overview of Angela's Professional Development

She achieved considerable progress – away from a view of science as knowledge towards an excellent appreciation of science as investigation. Her strong scientific background did not appear to have inhibited this change as strongly as in some (past) course members. In line with changes in ideals, her classroom practice has also changed in a very encouraging way towards pupil centredness. Her initial expectation (that the course would 'tell her the way to do it') was gradually overcome. She initially lacked self-confidence and was defensive about questioning her own practice. She grew in confidence to try out ideas and view them objectively rather than fearing inadequacy, drawing on support from my visits and discussions at university. She felt much more confident than at the beginning of the course about her task of working on the school's science curriculum. Her concluding remark is that she believes she has learned far more by self-evaluation than if she had been told what she should do (in the way she had expected she would).

The course seems to have provided a valid, enabling experience to achieve things of relevance to her, both personally and professionally. She was able to come to terms, to a fair degree, with her worries about the school system through expressing them at university within a context that stimulated both her criticism of the system and also her courage to enter into accommodation and assimilation with it. These were Angela's course achievements. A pretty respectable series of aims that became clarified at a specific level as the course progressed.

Figure 2.1 Map of progress in substantive aspects of personal professional development as expressed by Angela

A – Interview (June)

How do I put it over? What is meaningful science for young children? How do I fit it into the day? How do I write an outline science curriculum for the school?

B – Beginning of the Course (September)

Is it necessary for all the children to have the same experience? Can the science go beyond observational work? I now assess my pupils' present science learning as mostly observational in character and lacking hypothesis testing.

C – Classroom Visit by the Tutor (November–December)

Beforehand, I had selected 'pupil co-operativeness' as my main learning aim for the pupils for this session. Afterwards, I reassessed this as less important than the improvement of the higher skill of scientific thinking. I assessed the following things about the session: 1) the pupils' achievements were fully scientific, that is they included higher scientific thinking skills; 2) my role (in the second part of the session) as an enabling one; 3) pupils showed almost unprecedented levels of sustained interest – because of 1 and 2.

D – Course Sessions (December–May)

I am concerned that pupils should have more *direct experience* and less teacher demonstration. I feel *more confident* about science and my own ability to evaluate children's scientific learning. I am wrestling with the general constraint I perceive to be imposed by the school's organiza-tion of the curriculum, which prevents me from allocating additional time to expand science teaching in the way that I have indicated. I feel particularly constrained by: 1) the need for more fruitful collaboration with my team-teaching colleague; 2) the classroom organization, which needs improvement, to enable most children to experience activity.

E – Statement of Personal Professional Development (June)

The integration of my personal developmental aims with the school system seems to have progressed well. I acknowledge that my own attitude towards the system may have worsened my view of the constraint it had imposed.

Angela wrote strong statements about the value of children's self-sustained holistic scientific exploration and her personal confidence in her own ability to achieve this.

Figure 2.2 Diagram of practice/theory interactions in Angela's personal professional development

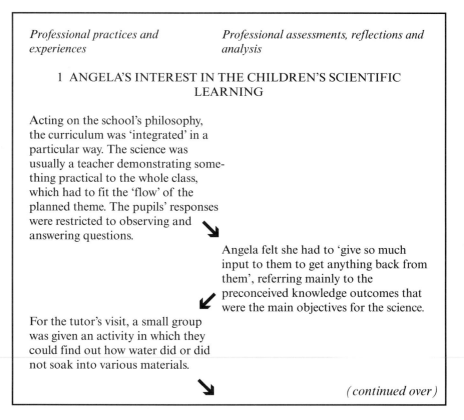

Professional practices and experiences

Professional assessments, reflections and analysis

1 ANGELA'S INTEREST IN THE CHILDREN'S SCIENTIFIC LEARNING

Acting on the school's philosophy, the curriculum was 'integrated' in a particular way. The science was usually a teacher demonstrating something practical to the whole class, which had to fit the 'flow' of the planned theme. The pupils' responses were restricted to observing and answering questions.

Angela felt she had to 'give so much input to them to get anything back from them', referring mainly to the preconceived knowledge outcomes that were the main objectives for the science.

For the tutor's visit, a small group was given an activity in which they could find out how water did or did not soak into various materials.

(continued over)

Although Angela said the aim was pupil co-operation, in fact she was looking for knowledge objectives, which the pupils did not at first seem able to attain.

Angela allowed the session to become more open and investigative, and the pupils set off on a varied and productive series of explorations into many aspects of the behaviour of the materials with water.

Angela said she had never before seen these pupils persevere for so long with a task and display such engagement with it in such a self sustained way.

Similar sessions were tried out with similar results. However, the school's choice of topic often seemed to reduce the opportunity for what Angela wanted to see as science learning.

Angela was ambivalent about what her aims really were – although she changed her practice by trying out more investigative approaches, she became aware that she was still judging their success mostly by preconceived knowledge objectives.

Angela became more confident about trying out practical ideas. Pupils became more confident in their responses to the science as they were encouraged to think that less importance was attached to the rightness or wrongness.

Angela became more concerned about developing pupils' attitudes and skills, realizing their importance to the better sessions she ran, and allocated more time for pupils to explore things of interest to them.

Angela started an 'interest display' made up of things brought in by the pupils. One such, on metals, was still the subject of pupils' fascination two to three months later.

(*continued over*)

Angela expressed clear commitment to an investigative approach to science learning.

2 MANAGING THE TENSIONS WITH THE SCHOOL SITUATION

Angela and her team-teaching colleague were required to plan thematic work so that *all* aspects of the curriculum and daily work in the classroom followed carefully predetermined lines of logical development.

Critical friendship discussion at university added to Angela's scepticism and frustration about the disadvantages of this philosophy. She found the proposals made by course members 'much more realistic'.

At school she felt unable to discuss or make any impact on the procedures and practices in operation, and was only able to modify her teaching experimentally to a very limited extent.

Other course members became very critical towards the school philosophy, causing Angela to be defensive about it and to claim that she was powerless to alter the situation.

Using certain of the positive suggestions from university, she introduced some gradual changes that created confidence in the value of change for both pupils and Angela.

Angela repeatedly raised this difficulty until she felt that her critical friends understood her situation intimately enough to be able to make suggestions that were realistic.

She gave her classroom-based study, containing her action research into

(continued over)

developing more investigative learning, to the head and deputy who said they liked it. Angela was able to negotiate adjustments to the planning procedure to make science something that was integrated into routine activities, rather than the subject of contrived demonstrations.

Angela became better able to assert her personal professional judgements about her teaching to impact on her professional context.

In the following year, Angela moved to a different bay where she did not need to team teach. She also began to look for a new post!

Brenda

Profile of Brenda

Brenda had twelve years of teaching experience, almost all with Key Stage One pupils, having obtained qualified teacher status (with distinction in Principles of Education) almost twenty years ago. She had recently attended workshops and short courses about science, and wanted to take my course to obtain 'guidance and stimulus to help me develop science teaching throughout the school and be able to offer more assistance and leadership to my colleagues'. Her post included a science curriculum responsibility for her large open-plan infants school, where she team taught a group of seventy pupils. The school seemed to have a good professional ethos of mutual support in the development of the curriculum. It is situated in a prosperous area where parental expectations are high.

Brenda had some science background, and felt that her previous experience had provided plenty of ideas for pupils' science activities. Although she felt confident about her own science teaching at the start of the course, she was a little frustrated and concerned by the similarity of the pupils' responses to the group activities they were given. Her other concerns related to school curriculum development. She wanted to know how to arrange (through the school) progression in pupils' science learning, in place of what she feared to be a haphazard and piecemeal kind of science learning.

My own initial impression of Brenda was of the self-confidence in her manner. She showed independent and perceptive thinking, and could contribute positively, critically and humorously to discussion. I felt her professional and intellectual strengths would be an asset to the course, and a stimulating challenge to me in the sense that here was someone who wanted and expected a good course and would be willing to contribute constructively to it.

Brenda's Concerns

The striking thing for me about Brenda's first analytic memo early in the course is the fundamental level and breadth of the questions she was asking herself about the nature of science, and her own teaching. She showed her willingness to redefine science as investigation rather than 'facts', and to regard her science teaching in the past as having been too prescriptive and teacher centred. In contemplating a more pupil-centred approach, she identified the following concerns:

- 'leaving pupils to pursue their own paths of inquiry cannot be the complete answer',
- overcoming the organizational problems,
- the difficulty of justifying it to parents,
- what questions to put to pupils to develop their thinking, and
- the need for a structure to 'science sessions' for pupils.

Clearly her open-minded yet critical approach had enabled her to make an extensive response to the early stages of the course, not least Brian Hewitt's talk about the nature of science. (Examples of the kinds of ideas and the style of presentation used by my colleague can be seen in the articles he has written for *Primary Science Review*, issue numbers 2, 3, 5 and 11. See, for example, Hewitt, 1986.) Brian's session dealt with induction and deduction, as well as its classroom implications. At a subsequent session Brenda asked herself: 'Have my children been the recipients of facts without understanding, or have they been convinced of the correctness of my logic and not their own?' She clearly wanted the children to have their own understanding rather than 'blind acceptance'. Later, she added: 'Accepting logically correct but "inaccurate" interpretation of facts by children goes against all my previously held ideas about science. It is a new viewpoint I can accept, but which could prove difficult to justify to parents.' Brenda's feeling was one of confusion, but intellectually she was engaged in a significant reassessment of her professional understanding and practice. She showed careful thought and questioning during course sessions, and at school she began to alter her science teaching. The other major enabling factor was the existence of an interaction between her own professional experimentation in her teaching and the dialogue about her experience with colleagues both at school and at university.

Brenda changed her thinking about the aims of her science teaching, and began to explore the practical implications for her planning, organization, teaching strategies, interaction with pupils and her justification for these developments to parents.

My Visit to Brenda's Classroom

I usually asked a course member if there is a focus they would like me to take for my classroom observations, and Brenda's request was unusually specific. I felt encouraged by this, not only because it might simplify my observational task, but also because I felt more confident that my notes would be relevant to the concerns that she had about her teaching. She wanted more evidence about her pupils' attitudes and their acquisition of information to show if the science was 'working'. In discussion after the session, I provided her with the copious notes I had made, describing what I saw as the extensive scientific exploratory play that the pupils had engaged in, searching for scientific patterns of understanding. Brenda agreed it was a good session in this respect and that it had somewhat exceeded her expectations. During our discussion about the repetitive nature of some pupils' activities, I said I felt this was justified as a learner's scientific pattern-seeking behaviour. But Brenda saw this differently, calling it 'skimming' or 'frippering', switching fairly rapidly from one object to another, or from one way of manipulating materials to another.

An example of this was the 6 year old child who was using the interactive display of 'shiny things' to gather experience of reflections. There were many kinds of foil, paper, plastic mirrors, silver cutlery and other reflective objects and materials. This child picked up and played with many things, and her use of the plastic mirror seemed to suggest pattern seeking. She repeatedly held it straight out in front of her, looking at the reflection of her own face. Sometimes she would turn the mirror one way and then the other, and sometimes she turned the mirror through 90 or even 180 degrees. It was as if she expected that turning the mirror to all these different positions would cause her own image to turn, as it would if the mirror were the same as a photograph. On other occasions she held the mirror above her head, looking upwards at it, and then held it below her body, looking downwards. Perhaps she was by now becoming accustomed to the stability of the image, but wanted to test it in yet more angles and positions. All of this took place in between other pieces of 'skimming' behaviour with other items. Presumably, her previous experience had been of fixed mirrors which did not permit this kind of exploration.

This was interpreted by me as the child's wish to gather experience across the breadth of possibilities which the situation contained, testing out ideas from one bit of experience in another context. Brenda's interpretation was that the child had not seemed to be behaving in the more deliberate and cumulative ways which she had expected to signify learning. Our clash of interpretations arose from our different beliefs about the manifestations of children's science learning. I felt apprehensive at the time that I was imposing an 'expert' view which was vulnerable on two grounds. First, my own limited experience as a primary teacher, particularly of infants, led me to feel open to the criticism of over-interpretation. Second, I was afraid that she would accept my view uncritically, and thereby become more dependent upon my views rather than less dependent.

My observational notes and photographs show the pupils engaged in a very wide variety of spontaneous activities with the rich resources available. They discovered that it is possible to see through metallic shiny paper if you hold it very close to your face. A large variety of images was obtained by looking at both sides of spoons held at different angles and different distances from the face. At one point, Brenda intervened to summarize their observations and said 'I wonder why?' They suggested it was magic. They made some bold attempts to produce a pictorial record of the lateral inversion of images, etc. Plane mirrors generated just as much interest, both singly (looked at from the side, below, above, at different angles to see round corners, etc.) and in pairs (to get multiple images of different kinds). Pupils watched one another, showed one another, repeated experiences over again, sometimes apparently with a different purpose, and co-operated with one another to see new effects. Brenda taught them the new words, 'concave' and 'convex', and responded encouragingly to their explorations.

Brenda's comparisons between the session we had shared and the norm showed that small group work in science had tended to be 'party tricks' that depended for success upon the teacher 'feeding them with the prompts' (her terms). But this session had depended very little on teacher prompts because the pupils' strong interests kept them totally engaged in their exploration. The artificiality of the tutor's visit quite often causes the host teacher to depart a little from normal practice. I find that, as on this occasion, the departure often has positive outcomes which lend encouragement for the new practice, and also the idea of experimenting with one's own teaching. The teacher seems to be stimulated to 'let go' a little, even though this appears to contradict the more understandable (and the more general) tendency to 'play safe' when being observed under conditions which feel like a test.

Brenda's objective for the session had been for the children to define a good reflective surface by reference to the objective physical properties of the materials provided. The pupils' criteria on the other hand were related to the degree of interest, value and fun which they subjectively saw. To them, a good surface was one that gave surprising and/or amusing reflections. Since they didn't produce the definition she wanted, she would have assessed that they hadn't learned anything. With my interpretations about pattern seeking in mind, she said that it was possible that much had been learned. A week later, I asked her if there had been any further evidence to support my interpretation. She described subsequent events which strongly suggested that pupils had been scientific rather than 'frippering' or 'skimming'. They went on to sustain a thoughtful, inquiring involvement in the topic throughout the following period of several weeks. During a later visit, Brenda said: 'But they've talked a lot since. Even now they're bringing things in, three and a half weeks later. It seems to take this long. After three or four weeks, the teachers are fed up with it, but the children are still bringing things in. They're still coming up with things they can do with those mirrors which they've related to the things they'd done in that session. So I think that maybe they *tested the water* then, and the thinking hasn't stopped.' This gave reassurance to me about Brenda's autonomous approach, because she had not taken my interpretation uncritically, but as a hypothesis for testing against her own experience.

The visit had been very useful, I felt, because Brenda and I had witnessed what I regard as good scientific learning, and Brenda's role had been that of enabler. Brenda was also positive about it: 'I thoroughly enjoyed it. It seemed to fit in to me with what we were discussing at university. It was confirmation, and it worked and it was fun. I felt very happy about it.' Although it had apparently been slightly atypical of Brenda's usual sessions, I hoped that she would regard this session as a useful yardstick for future ones. In other words, I hoped that she would continue to evaluate science in this way. However, I felt some tension when Brenda returned to her belief in the total dependence of pupils on the teacher's intervention for the learning to succeed. I believe that much valuable learning takes place within pupils' independent activity. She admitted feeling under pressure to ensure that the pupils 'achieve' something every lesson. I construed that Brenda was continuing to look for science knowledge outcomes, albeit from investigative exploration, as the mark of success, and her expectations about the science investigation which infants are capable of were too sophisticated. This entails more teacher imposition than I believed necessary, and meant for Brenda that there was a big problem in getting sixty to seventy pupils through the same science activity, since she felt she must be with them for so much of the time. She began to give greater credibility to children's capacities to learn for themselves, saying at a seminar:

> I think we try too hard sometimes with what we do. We feel we've got to be putting things in to the children all the time. Whereas if you sit back and let them do it, it all comes out of them. But it does need a teacher there some of the time. We did try it again throughout the rest of the week, with and without groups. For some children it worked whether the teacher was there or not. It depended on who they were and who they were with. But the most value of the teacher's presence was with the language – drawing out things they said, and highlighting them for everybody's benefit.

After Brenda had read this case study, we had a meeting (the validation interview) to discuss it, and she confirmed my interpretation of this point, saying: 'This is very true. I am still finding that I attempt and expect too much from the children, especially this year with a younger group.'

Brenda's Participation in the Course

Brenda made fairly frequent contributions to discussion. They were often perceptive and helped to develop the issues being considered by the group. After the work on 'shiny things', Brenda hoped that the next topic would yield comparable responses from the children. They carried out practical explorations of flour and water, but some children lost interest, merely making 'mud pies'. When we discussed Brenda's disappointment, she willingly considered several hypotheses for their response, all based on children's natural and understandable interests, and ways of responding to tasks at school. But she was finding it difficult to accept their response in such terms because she regarded it as a failed opportunity for them to learn.

Peter: Because that kind of response could recur, it's down to having an organizational strategy which tries to allow for some variation in the children's response.
Brenda: And accepting it.
Peter: Yes.
Brenda: I think that's the difficulty. Accepting it. You feel you've got to achieve at every session.

Brenda was a strong critic of some aspects of my role and some aspects of the course which had not operated well enough. For example, she voiced the frustration experienced by several others about my habit of replying to their questions with my questions, and never giving an answer of my own.

Brenda: It's become a joke that to ask you a question, you get a question back, and it's frustrating. We could argue about your answer if you gave us one, but if we get another question, we can't develop our own argument. We've got more answers from one another than we have from you.
Brenda: The LEA courses tend to be 'what to teach' or 'resources', and I felt I wanted to know 'how to teach' science.
Peter: Do you feel this course is doing that?
Brenda: (eight second silent pause) Yes. If I know I'm doing it. I've nothing to judge it by yet. Um … it's made me think a lot, which is obviously what it's meant to do. … Children have said things to me in the past few weeks which perhaps I wouldn't have noticed earlier, or I wouldn't have given the value that I now ascribe to

them, that this course has made me aware of. Are those the sort of things this course wants written down?

Peter: Yes.

Brenda: So when we're looking for big, earth-moving questions and answers to put in this reflective diary, are we perhaps looking for things that are ... and trying to philosophize rather than ... when nine out of ten times it would just be at the level of things that children have said. ...

Brenda was referring to the process of her adaptation to an autonomous role as a course member and showed a growing appreciation of this. She valued the self-questioning which the course provoked, but suggested that the course requirement for teachers to keep records of their own professional development should be clearer, for instance that what is to be recorded can be (and usually will be) things that course members probably at the time regarded as relatively mundane and anecdotal. There had been a common perception that 'big, earth-shattering questions' or abstract philosophizing was what the course considered as appropriate in their reflective diaries.

Near the beginning of her action research study, Brenda's concerns were stated to be mainly: How to manage the inclusion of science in a crowded curriculum so that all pupils have the same experience. Brenda expressed a new appreciation of the need for children to 'work through the processes rather than merely observe a demonstration or teacher-directed activity', as well as a reduced anxiety about having to 'feed information to children'.

Brenda adopted a systematic approach to the study, making close and detailed observations and records, then evaluated her teaching at intervals by writing lists of positive and negative aspects of the work done. As an example of her style, here is an extract from her action research report at the point where she was evaluating one cycle of action in anticipation of the next action steps to try.

Positive points arising:
1   The children were able to work independently and at their own level without constant teacher supervision.
2   Different levels of thinking were possible.
3   Recording skills were well matched.
4   They learned from one another, and the quality and complexity of their thinking increased with time.

Negative points arising:
1   As with the sand-clock activity, the whole group did not have hands-on experience before the activity was changed, but there was more opportunity for 'informal' investigation in between sessions, etc.

2   I decided my next action step should be a modified repeat of step 4, that is: an activity within the practical number session, but without any written recording so that more children could be included.

The study is therefore highly progressive in that each unit of teaching draws upon reflection about how the previous unit was taught and how the pupils responded. As an outsider, I cannot see a very strong justification on some occasions for some of the links between one unit and the next. I think Brenda herself did not feel that she was getting closer to 'the' solution to her concerns. At the end of her study she said the following:

> The CBS did not reveal any absolute solutions to my problems, but gave me greater insight into the needs of the children and the direction in which my teaching and organization needs to move in order to allow my pupils adequate opportunities for science learning. I intend to continue to follow the pattern of action/reflection in order to move more closely to a classroom which provides opportunity for rapid science learning within the constraints of the class routine.

An Overview of Brenda's Professional Progress

In her statement of professional development, at the end of the course, Brenda wrote that she had found the course to have been useful, and she listed the professional gains she believed she had made, including the ability to justify the new approach of her teaching to her colleagues and to parents.

> The course has provided both the encouragement and the necessary stimulus to develop my science teaching, and has been an enlightening experience.

It is difficult to know if Brenda's self image as a professional person changed. She had appeared to be autonomous in many ways at the beginning of the course, and yet throughout the course discussions and reports of classroom developments, Brenda's self-directed and inner-motivated professional developments were accompanied by indications that she still regarded the locus of control as outside her. An example occurs in the final part of her statement:

> This course has been like no other I have attended, with its emphasis on the process of professional development. At times it has been difficult to appreciate in which direction we were being led, but, on reflection, I appreciate that my attitude to, and understanding of, the teaching of science have undergone great change since the beginning of the course.

She acknowledged that her study did not yield 'absolute solutions', as if to imply that this had been her hope.

Brenda saw her biggest professional developments as having occurred near the beginning of the course rather than during the classroom-based study. I agreed with this in part because Brenda's responses then were very thoughtful indeed. But there were some insights which needed time to become securely established in Brenda's practice, and, in so doing, caused her to reconsider and re-experiment, for example, her insistence on the teacher being there with the children in order to ensure that the science learning is successful. Brenda grew more relaxed about this as her appreciation grew that children need more time than she had previously allowed in order to work through the investigative processes themselves. She also changed her view about the necessity for a tangible end product in every session, saying that this is not always necessary or desirable. She said at the end of the course that she felt far less anxious about having to 'feed' the children information because she saw how much they were able to learn without teacher intervention.

Perhaps Brenda has gained some professional *emancipation* – for which the *Oxford Illustrated Dictionary* (1962) definition is: 'setting free from intellectual or moral fetters' – in realizing that some of the constraints, which she perceived earlier, were related to her own beliefs more than externally imposed demands. She wrote:

> This has made me reflect on my previous attitude to science teaching, and recognize that many of the constraints which I believed prevented me from including more science were cerebral rather than practical problems.

The flow diagram of the lines of professional development evident in Brenda's participation in the course is shown in Figure 2.4.

Figure 2.3 Map of progress in substantive aspects of personal professional development as expressed by Brenda

A – Concerns Expressed at Interview (June)

I am concerned about the similarity of pupils' responses to the small group science activities assigned to them. I see the main constraint on my teaching to be the number of pupils (70) in the bay (open-plan) and consequently the problems of organization. I am concerned about the need for progression in pupils' science learning through the school, rather than being piecemeal or haphazard. I need to support colleagues at school to develop this.

B – Beginning of the Course (September)

I regard the idea of pupils deciding their own path of inquiry is not the answer to my problems. How do I organize *investigational* science? How do I justify it to parents? How best do I ask pupils the right questions – those that will develop their thinking? What structure do I need for 'science sessions'?

C – Classroom Visit by the Tutor (November–December)

What I regarded as 'skimming' or 'frippering' by pupils I now see as exploratory scientific learning. When they are *really* interested, pupils do not need repeated prompts by the teacher to be engaged in their learning. A narrowly conceived lesson objective can prevent a teacher from appreciating other kinds of learning achieved. I feel under pressure for pupils to achieve something every lesson. I believe the teacher must be involved with the children during their science activities. So for 60–70 pupils, it takes too long for them all (in small groups) to have a turn.

D – Course Sessions (December–May)

I am growing to appreciate the value of pupils' *own total* investigation rather than them merely observing a demonstration or doing a teacher-directed activity. I am less anxious about the need to 'feed' the children information. I am seeing how much they are able to learn without the teacher's intervention. To count as good science, I think that the focus of the pupils' activity must be explicitly scientific. How can I be sure that all pupils have the same kind and amount of science experience? How can I organize sufficient time for them all to have enough direct experience?

E – Statement of Personal Professional Development (June)

I have increased my knowledge and understanding of the investigative skills and attitudes involved in children's science learning, and increased my usage of the practical teaching methods which improve children's scientific learning. This has resulted in my increased awareness of the opportunities for science learning in the classroom, and has helped me to recognize children's scientific thinking. I allow more time for them to work through the necessary processes. There does not always have to be a tangible end product because the important things they are learning take more time than one session to achieve. I have more personal enjoyment in teaching science and a greater readiness to allow more time for science in an already crowded curriculum.

Figure 2.4 Diagram of practice/theory interactions in Brenda's personal professional development

Professional practices and experiences

Professional assessments, reflections and analysis

1 ASPECTS OF HER INTEREST IN THE CHILDREN'S SCIENTIFIC LEARNING

Brenda's own observations of the children's science prior to the start of the course.

The children's responses to small group activities assigned to them tended to be stereotyped. Children's 'skimming' behaviour (rapid movement from one object or way of manipulating objects to another) is not an acceptable kind of learning.

Brenda and I jointly observed children exploring a wide range of 'shiny things'. My interpretation of 'skimming' was that the children were gathering a lot of experiences to develop and test their ideas about reflection, etc. I called it 'pattern seeking', and claimed that it was scientific learning.

(continued over)

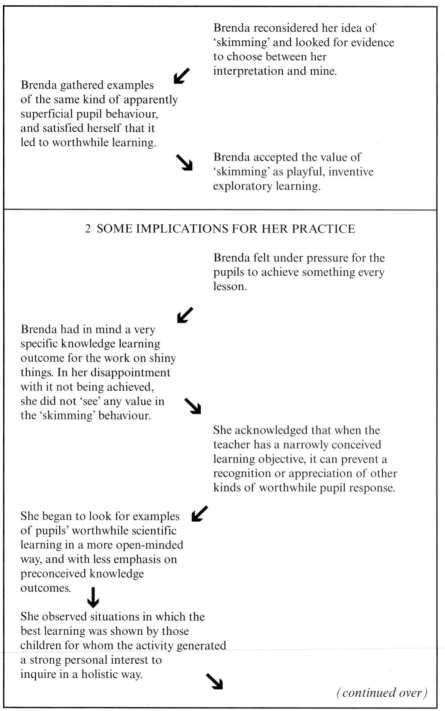

Brenda reconsidered her idea of 'skimming' and looked for evidence to choose between her interpretation and mine.

Brenda gathered examples of the same kind of apparently superficial pupil behaviour, and satisfied herself that it led to worthwhile learning.

Brenda accepted the value of 'skimming' as playful, inventive exploratory learning.

2 SOME IMPLICATIONS FOR HER PRACTICE

Brenda felt under pressure for the pupils to achieve something every lesson.

Brenda had in mind a very specific knowledge learning outcome for the work on shiny things. In her disappointment with it not being achieved, she did not 'see' any value in the 'skimming' behaviour.

She acknowledged that when the teacher has a narrowly conceived learning objective, it can prevent a recognition or appreciation of other kinds of worthwhile pupil response.

She began to look for examples of pupils' worthwhile scientific learning in a more open-minded way, and with less emphasis on preconceived knowledge outcomes.

She observed situations in which the best learning was shown by those children for whom the activity generated a strong personal interest to inquire in a holistic way.

(continued over)

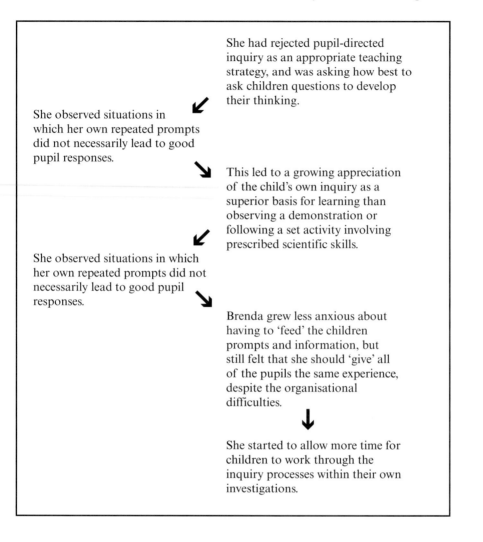

She observed situations in which her own repeated prompts did not necessarily lead to good pupil responses.

She had rejected pupil-directed inquiry as an appropriate teaching strategy, and was asking how best to ask children questions to develop their thinking.

This led to a growing appreciation of the child's own inquiry as a superior basis for learning than observing a demonstration or following a set activity involving prescribed scientific skills.

She observed situations in which her own repeated prompts did not necessarily lead to good pupil responses.

Brenda grew less anxious about having to 'feed' the children prompts and information, but still felt that she should 'give' all of the pupils the same experience, despite the organisational difficulties.

She started to allow more time for children to work through the inquiry processes within their own investigations.

Chris

Profile of Chris

Chris had taught for seven years, initially as a secondary school French teacher for four years and subsequently as a Key Stage One teacher. She had obtained her qualified teacher status thirteen years ago. She was teaching Years 3 and 4 mixed at a junior school where she had the role of science co-ordinator, and was consequently involved in the development of the science policy.

Chris's scientific background did not include any GCSEs, but professionally she had taken some short courses, and believed in the importance of direct, practical experience for good science learning. I didn't get any impression at first about how Chris saw herself as a science teacher, but there were several aspects of her previous experience which suggested to me that her self-image as a professional person was strong. For example, her participation in the LEA project to promote co-operative group learning seemed to have been valuable, not only because of the progress in her teaching, but also because of the developmental process of having observed pupils and being reflective. The school situation seemed to be an encouraging one in that Chris felt she could count on the head teacher's support for her participation in the course, for instance by covering her attendance at afternoon sessions. Also, Chris saw the staff as 'very committed', and I got the impression that Chris saw this as a stimulus rather than a daunting demand on herself as co-ordinator.

Chris's Concerns

Chris's way of approaching science drew upon her experience of the co-operative group learning project, which used a list of skills and attitudes as a guide to the planning. Chris allowed pupils to choose their own working groups, which then moved round a 'circus' of set science tasks once a week so that, over a half term, each group has tried every task. For example, in relation to water, the tasks involved such things as: buoyancy, absorbency, soaking through things, the filtering effect of various materials and the effects of water on the visual appearance of materials and plants. Chris also reported a problem-solving lesson, which was of a different kind from the tasks already referred to, which she tried out during one of the afternoon sessions of the course during which course members made observational visits to one another's schools. Chris felt this was a very valuable experience for her because of what she learnt about the children.

Her initial views about the course sessions were mixed. She felt encouraged by the similarity between her ideas about appropriate science learning experiences and the ideas offered on the course. On the other hand, she expressed criticism about some aspects, notably the course requirements for teachers' written work.

> I think there is a need for a compromise course that doesn't necessarily have a certificate at the end. I came because, other than our local support service courses, there's no other course of any great depth. I'm quite prepared to attend the sessions, but I could certainly do without the hassle of written essays and things. To me it's a drag having to do this essay [the curriculum assignment]. I'm happy to do the classroom-

based work that I can see is being useful and helpful to me, and to talk about it. It's hard enough finding time to come, without having to. ...

I hadn't encountered this reaction by a course member before, so it shocked me a little, and I was concerned about Chris's willingness to continue the course. My feeling at the time was that her expectations about the demands of an award-bearing course had been too low. She also expressed concern about her lack of scientific knowledge, and was beginning to think more critically about how she set the pupils' tasks and asked them questions.

My Visit to Chris's Classroom

I sat next to one of the six working groups (see p. 44) to observe them, and made notes. Among various aspects, the following are extracted from my notes to highlight the children's development of ideas. The task for 'my' group was to compare the passage of water through various materials placed over the top of a jar. They knew before starting that PVC wouldn't allow any water through, and they began to make predictions about the number of seconds it would take a fixed volume of water to soak through each sample of material. They worked systematically and in a well organized way, but with little discussion of the task or their observations, speculations or reasons why things happened. There were some indications that their knowledge of the task, if not the outcomes, had come from observing previous groups carry it out. They knew more details about how the task should be conducted than was shown by either the work-card instructions or what they said to one another about planning what to do. As well as knowing the 'obvious' results (like the PVC not letting water through, which was known from life experience), they also seemed to know other results in advance of doing the work. I thought that this may have been linked to the apparent lack of pupils' theorizing, curiosity and enthusiasm. The only pattern seeking I detected was the obvious relationship between the time taken for the water to soak through the linen and whether it was single or double thickness. Almost all other talk was task-related, that is, concerning the following of the set procedure and the self-organization of tasks and equipment rather than their own ideas about the materials and phenomena. Their greatest excitement was shown near the end of the session, during reporting to the whole group, when at some points controversy arose from disagreements between groups over their conflicting results on the same task.

I felt that they were more 'task oriented' than 'investigation oriented', mainly because of the 'circus'-type organization which led to them not feeling that it was their very own work but an exercise. My preference is for pupils' questions to be the subject of their tasks, and I was unsure about projecting this view. I wanted Chris to assess the situation herself and determine a direction and pace for herself rather than follow my directions simply because I was the tutor. Although this may seem arrogant of me to assume that an independent-minded person like Chris would do this unwillingly, my caution generally leads me to try to avoid this kind of tutor direction. However, Chris said that she already had reservations about the 'circus' method, citing the tendency for boredom to become apparent near the end. She also said that she saw the organizational side as 'a nightmare', and wanted to keep trying out various methods in an experimental way. So, encouraged by this, I asked Chris:

- what she thought the pupils saw as the purpose of the task, and
- whether she thought that the pupils seemed to lack curiosity about the findings and, if so, what were the possible reasons for this.

My intention was for these questions to be a stimulus for reflection rather than to yield answers immediately. I suppose they contain implicit judgements, but I felt I had given more comment and asked more questions than usual, and also Chris had asked fewer questions of me than teachers usually do.

There was a follow-up discussion at university which took place after course members (as a group) had criticized my role for not giving enough clear feedback of an assessment type to them. During this discussion, I suggested to Chris that pupils' scientific skills would develop better within an organization that fosters separate developmental investigation rather than within a 'circus' organization. Chris said she wanted to know *my* preferences for organizational method, and so I confirmed that investigatory work *is* my preference. I think I may have given to Chris rather more emphatic kinds of assessment and clearer expressions of my personal professional preferences because I felt I had to respond to the course members' criticisms, particularly when speaking to someone who had expressed the criticism most strongly. Another contributory reason could have been that I felt that Chris would appreciate 'straight talking'. There was no feeling on my part that 'since she has criticized me, I'll criticize her'; it was more a sense that her preferred way of relating is for both sides to say what they think. So, on reflection, I think that for Chris this would have been a better approach for me to have used on my first visit.

Chris's Participation in the Course

By the following January, Chris had resolved to let the children plan their own work, and was concerned to develop her abilities to assess and record their learning. She no longer saw how she should plan their science as a concern, having moved away from the 'circus' method during the previous term. Apart from the particular issues highlighted in this case study so far, I tended to be less aware of Chris's professional development issues and concerns than I was for some other course members. Chris had been, and continued to be, less forthcoming about such issues in an explicit way, or perhaps I was less perceptive towards her comments. I never felt anxious about her development because her contributions to discussion were often perceptive, thoughtful and positive, but they didn't seem to reveal specific lines of concern.

In her classroom-based study, Chris referred back to the classroom visit and my view that pupils showed independence in that they organized themselves well, but did not display *intellectual* independence in devising their own investigations or questioning or theorizing about their findings. The study describes how one group showed independent problem solving within a practical task. Then, during the next topic, another group with similar pupil membership was undertaking an investigation they had proposed, when they came up with a surprising idea. Working on taste, using pieces of fruit, they decided to count taste buds! They arrived at an apparently firm number of taste buds for each pupil in the group, though some pupils found it hard to recognize and count the surface features ('craters') on the tongues. This pupil talk seems to show holistic, scientific exploratory learning in which the pupils raise their own questions and seek answer themselves.

Children were observing the effects of placing first salt and then sugar on the tongue.

J: It tastes worse at the back [of the tongue]
P: It tastes more at the front and it's nicer [sugar]
D: Can we put sugar on our tongue and look at it instead of tasting?
Ch: Look at it and see how it tastes.
Ca: No, see how it *looks* what happens when you look [she looks]?
D: It's liquidized.
P: It looks like an ice [sic] on your tongue.
J: It's all changed to water.
Ch: My hands are all sticky.
D: It gets wet and changes into water. That might be how it does it. We taste it by turning it into water.
P: It dissolves.
T: What do you mean?
P: When you look at it, it goes littler and littler.
Ch: Salt doesn't go quickly.
Ca: Which one goes quicker? Salt? Salt is disgustinger than sugar.
J: Salt is stronger than sugar.
C: It's harder. It's bigger.
T: How do you know? [D puts salt and sugar side by side.]
D: Sugar is bigger, definitely. Salt is like circles. It might be harder to get into the taste buds. Let's look carefully. Put it on a plate.

P: No. Something black. We haven't got black. We've got brown. [Returns
            with some brown paper. D isolates a small amount of each. Others
            agree they can now see it better.]
D: Sugar is like squares. Salt is round.
Ch: Sugar looks like chips in glass.

They theorized freely and imaginatively, notably D's idea that the sense of
taste depends upon the substance being dissolved by saliva. This contrasts
powerfully with the evidence collected from the classroom visit, which shows
a much more limited scientific response. There were no grounds for
attributing the contrast to any other significant differences, such as the identity of the children taking part, because in each case the evidence used here
was seen by the teacher to be representative of the general class level of
response on each occasion.
    Chris analysed this and other evidence for signs that:

*   independent thinking was developing,
*   this was not only in one or two dominant children within a group, but
    more generally, and
*   validation for these assessments could be obtained from her 'critical
    friends'.

In her study, Chris characterized her role as changing from 'director' to
'onlooker', and attributed the insecurity she experienced in the early stages
to not feeling totally in charge. She credited some easing of the situation to
the course task of keeping notes during initial and feedback discussion
periods, which I regard as an example of the use of an action research
evidence gathering technique that is entirely in harmony with good teaching,
and therefore becomes synonymous with it. Chris did not explicitly refer to
'action steps' or use other action research jargon. Her account of the process
of her professional development through her conscious reflection on
evidence within a systematic, progressive framework is not reported as
action research. However, it is alluded to and the overall development is
consistent with such an approach, albeit 'on the run'.

An Overview of Chris's Professional Development

A significant feature of Chris's participation in the course, for me, was the
relative lack of awareness I had of the fairly specific nature of her professional development. Obviously at the points of the classroom visit, and
reading her interim statements and completed study, I was 'put in the
picture'. But, whereas with some course members, I could see the questions
or comments they made as specific professional development 'lines of
progress', this did not happen very much with Chris. I don't know if this is

an indication of my lack of awareness and perception, or if it is a fair reflection of what Chris's professional development really was like – less explicit. Chris showed herself to be an independent, critical thinker with strong professional commitments and self-confidence at the beginning of the course. It is difficult to say if her professional self-image changed. It is possible that the successful experience of developing her teaching had enabled her to be more confident in her ability to develop through the closer examination of her practices and the responses of the pupils. She never made any statements near the end of the course about her early objections to written course work. Her classroom-based study can be used to infer that in writing it she gained clarity of self-awareness and satisfaction in documenting the progress that was achieved. I felt sure that Chris had successfully been able to use the course as a resource for her individual developments. On pp. 34–5 of her classroom-based study, Chris wrote:

> My role as teacher changed from being 'director' to one of 'onlooker' and intervening as I thought necessary. This can be quite frightening at first. As a teacher who had hitherto planned a unit of work carefully, knew exactly where I wanted the children to be, and why, I experienced great feelings of insecurity when confronted with a situation of not feeling totally in charge: not knowing from one session to the next where a certain group was leading. I eased the situation [and my mind!] a little by making notes during initial and feedback discussion periods – my own record of what each group was investigating.
>
> The children's independence was, I feel, further enhanced by the change in the relationship between myself and the pupils: 'I plan, the children do' became 'We plan together.' Everyone was involved, everyone asked for ideas. This sort of planning requires the children to think through possible actions. Eventually, these young Year 3 and 4 children will be able to think through *alternative* approaches to an investigation and then select one most likely to lead to a successful result.
>
> I see my role as one of helping the children to become proficient at learning independently by providing opportunities for the groups to plan, to make choices and decisions; to guide the children where necessary and by discussing the original plan after an investigation and considering, alongside the children, how the original plan could be improved.

*Figure 2.5 Map of progress in substantive aspects of personal professional
development as expressed by Chris*

A – Interview (June)

No explicit concerns were evident at the interview from my records. Obviously there were implied concerns, such as the development of both her own teaching and also the role of co-ordinator, but these were not expressed in specific terms.

B – Beginning of the Course (September)

An internal debate: on one hand wondering if my own scientific knowledge is an inadequate background for effective teaching, whereas, on the other hand, wondering if it could be an advantage. I am encouraged to feel that I am on the right track. I am thinking more critically about the tasks I set and the questions I pose to the pupils.

C – Classroom Visit by the Tutor (November–December)

Accountability to parents is a pressure on me to get pupils to produce written records of work for display. In a 'circus' organization I noticed that the pupils tend to become bored, but at least they all have access to the same experiences for learning. I am beginning to reconsider this as a priority. Organization is my 'nightmare'. I want to experiment with different methods. I also want to try to elicit more prediction and fair testing from pupils.

D – Course Sessions (December–May)

I am abandoning my desire to direct their planning, and am adopting pupil-centred, investigative work in which there is not the same experience for all. I am concentrating now on how to assess and record their scientific learning. I see this now as 'an obsession' and 'so structured it could be inflexible'. I am focusing on pupils' intellectual independence in devising their own investigations, and succeeded in 'letting go' of my control over their work, releasing their investigative ability. I am evolving my understanding and skills to become an enabler.

E – *Statement of Personal Professional Development (June)*

Chris wrote a direct, factual account. The initial emphasis of her teaching had been on planning as an activity belonging only to the teacher. Organization also had been teacher-controlled with emphasis on all pupils having the same experience. Evaluation took place at the end of the topic, and was conducted by the teacher. Now, she has 'more questions than ever before' which force her to be 'constantly looking at what I am doing and why'. Planning and organization are now pupil-determined (as is content). Evaluation of the process shows all pupils are developing the skills. Chris is able to concentrate on enabling this much more. Feedback sessions are more meaningful: 'I have changed and developed, not just in my science teaching, but in my teaching generally.'

Figure 2.6 Diagram of practice/theory interactions in Chris's personal professional development

Professional practices and experiences	*Professional assessments, reflections and analysis*
	Chris planned science using a list of skills and attitudes and devising a range of set tasks around a theme or topic. As she later called it, her method was 'I *plan*, the children *do*'.
During the autumn term the theme was water, and the tasks were organized as a 'circus' arrangement. I observed one session and commented on the pupils, whom I judged to be very co-operative and well organized, personally, but lacking interest, intellectual independence and a sense of ownership over their learning.	*(continued over)*

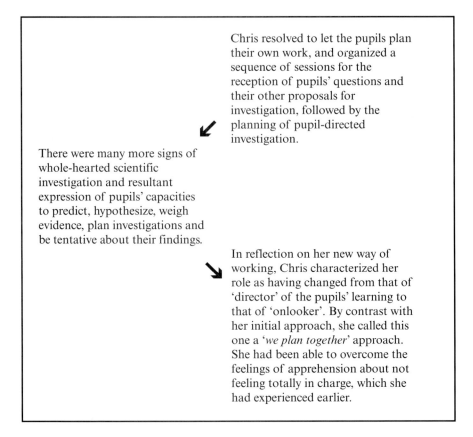

There were many more signs of whole-hearted scientific investigation and resultant expression of pupils' capacities to predict, hypothesize, weigh evidence, plan investigations and be tentative about their findings.

Chris resolved to let the pupils plan their own work, and organized a sequence of sessions for the reception of pupils' questions and their other proposals for investigation, followed by the planning of pupil-directed investigation.

In reflection on her new way of working, Chris characterized her role as having changed from that of 'director' of the pupils' learning to that of 'onlooker'. By contrast with her initial approach, she called this one a '*we plan together*' approach. She had been able to overcome the feelings of apprehension about not feeling totally in charge, which she had experienced earlier.

Kay

Profile of Kay

Kay had seven years teaching experience across the primary age range, having obtained qualified teacher status as a mature student seven years ago. She wanted to take the course to 'increase knowledge and understanding, so as to enhance my expertise as a co-ordinator both for myself and for the benefit of the whole school'. Kay's science background was limited to a Biology O Level GCE and a sixth form course in physiology and hygiene.

Kay's overall teaching pattern for science was to provide materials for direct exploration, and to ask the children questions to encourage them to find out more about the materials. She said that she usually elicited an enthusiastic response from the children. When she first taped herself teaching, it had caused the usual combination of self-critical and uncomfortable feelings. Her overall organization of science-based topic work was to begin with class work and move into small group work. The examples given by Kay at the beginning of the course were of activities that were largely teacher selected, and which directed the pupils to some aspect of the overall topic. I regarded Kay as a sensitive, caring person who would contribute constructively to the ethos of the group. My image of her, professionally, was that she had a less self-confident manner than I considered appropriate to someone who also was so perceptive and insightful. During the validation of this case study, Kay made the following comment:

> I think I've crammed quite a lot into the ten years I've worked now. I've been in two schools, had three heads, taught every age across primary 4–11, done remedial, class teacher and support teacher – so I've learned from other teachers as well. So I think it's my personality more than my lack of experience.

Kay's Concerns

Kay felt that her knowledge of the science learning being achieved in her classroom was still largely 'intuitive'. She believed in and could see the benefits of holding back from too much directing or leading the children, but was clearly thinking through this aspect of her practice when she raised the question: 'Do we *never* give facts to children?' She commented very favourably upon all of the early stages of the course, including the ethos of the group which made her feel 'able to speak without feeling embarrassed'. Also, she appreciated the visit to another teacher's classroom as a reassurance because she saw science content that was similar to content she had taught. At this stage, I felt very optimistic that Kay's experience of the course would be worthwhile because of the similarity between her philosophy and that of mine for the course. Taking advantage of this, as well as the established nature of our professional relationship, I decided to request that the first visit by a tutor to a course member's classroom would be to Kay's. The idea was that in jointly presenting an account of the visit to the group, they would have a better introduction to this aspect of the course than would be given by an abstract account. Knowing that the visit is a threatening experience for course members, I believed that they would gain more reassurance from comments by the teacher who had been visited than the views of the tutor. Kay agreed to this willingly.

My Visit to Kay's Classroom

Kay worked with half of the class doing science-related tasks on a theme of writing secret messages. The rest of the class was doing routine, scheme-based work which needed less teacher support. Working in ones, twos, and threes, the children explored the effects of applying different kinds of substances to try to make marks on paper, and to make the marks disappear or reappear. The task that Kay had set was to solve a problem, to which not all of the pupils were attending closely, to do with secretly sending messages from a desert island. Kay had wanted them to keep this problem in mind whilst exploring and classifying various materials, and therefore be able to use the knowledge thus obtained to solve the problem. Kay's first comment after the lesson was that she should have made the lesson purely exploratory. She began to doubt whether pupils had valued the problem and seen it as their own. Also, she wrestled with the dilemma between giving too much direction, which risks the stifling of originality, and giving too little direction, which risks creating doubt.

I felt very satisfied by this visit because of several things. Despite Kay's criticisms, which I agreed with, I regarded the pupils' science exploration as a fine achievement for their age since it showed creativity, high-level thinking skills and strong individual purpose. I thought I had successfully worked with Kay to clarify her theory-in-use for that session, compare it with her espoused theory (Argyris and Schön, 1974) and discuss them both in the light of our observations. Also, the discussion identified some professional issues which I thought were significant and likely to lead to valuable professional development for Kay. She had obviously been nervous and had shown her insecurity, mainly in her excessive self-criticism and self-doubt, but she had also been very open, and readily agreed to the positive, encouraging and gratifying aspects of the exercise.

Kay's Participation in the Course

My overall view was that Kay was not a frequent or extensive contributor to whole group discussion, but her contributions were often insightful and always constructive. In small groups she seemed to participate more in discussion – about as much as the others. During an early discussion about what should be the aims of science education, it was Kay who proposed 'the enquiring mind' (and explaining what she meant by this, emphasized its depth of meaning) after others had suggested separate science skills. This was another way in which I felt we were on the same wavelength. I dislike the reduction of science aims to atomistic skills.

During a session when course members were asked to give their assessment of course sessions, a dominant theme was the course members' expressed need for more tutor direction and assessment. Kay argued that although some teachers are confident enough to 'dispute and express dislike for a tutor's assessment comment', others would be 'very easily squashed by it'. She added:

> I feel that most teachers feel insecure, and therefore the method of support in this course is ideal – we need positive comments on our teaching so we can feel that we are choosing the right direction. We tend

to know instinctively when things go wrong. We never feel satisfied with a lesson. One can always do better!

This tended to confirm my image of Kay as having many of the qualities of a reflective practitioner (Schön, 1983).

Kay then became very interested in pupils' intellectual independence. She had shown during the classroom visit a well-developed awareness of the variation among her pupils as regards independent thinking, calling it 'adventurousness', and believed that there was a clear need for development among many of the pupils. Examples of what Kay saw as lack of pupil independence given on p. 18 of her classroom-based study include:

> anxiety about writing on the wrong line, they cannot take a message without asking for someone to go with them, a generally 'over-fussy' behaviour such as children saying things like: 'Do I write on the top line?', 'Can I start?' and 'I don't know what to do.'

For Kay, independent thinking in science meant that pupils would 'think scientifically ... develop their own powers of reasoning ... increase their ability to solve a problem in a scientific way ... interact with new experiences on their own terms'.

At the beginning of her classroom-based study, Kay wrote about the classroom visit of the previous term in strongly self-critical terms: 'I realized I was initially unintentionally over-directing and constraining the children. ... I was sending them down one track and supplying blinkers.'

She decided to strengthen the 'partnership' aspect of her relationship with pupils. She introduced her class to brainstorming for collaborative planning of science, giving four positive 'steps', which I recognized as principles of procedure (Stenhouse, 1975), for encouraging their activity and thinking to guide her interactions with them. They were:

1 Appreciating a pupil's effort whatever the result.
2 Avoiding the 'right answer' syndrome.
3 Accepting pupils' answers as correct provided that evidence and reasoning have been used.
4 Encouraging pupils' own interpretations of their observations rather than imposing adult interpretations.

She exploited a spontaneous expression of one pupil's independence (he brought in his own 'ice balloon' (Ovens, 1987) after Kay had told the class the previous day about the ice balloon session at university), which led to a good response from the pupils. She then organized the class to select their own stimulus for investigation from a range of possibilities, and to determine the investigative questions themselves. This worked well, but Kay wanted to try another approach so she gave each group in turn the same opportunity to explore some white powders. She initially regarded the second group's response as disappointing because they had been unable to find out things which Kay had anticipated they should. The first group explored systematically (and Kay was very pleased), discovering that one powder caused the cork to be blown off the container. The second group had observed this, and when it was their turn with the powders they only wanted to recreate the popping effect that had excited the first group so much. Kay was disappointed, writing ' ... my usual feelings of inadequacy. I took the blame for their lack of interest in finding out whether the powders dissolved or not'. However, in discussion at university she reassessed their learning as having been a valid exploration, albeit in an unexpected direction, under the circumstances. Kay resolved to ask more open questions 'to make the children think and come to their own conclusions'.

Returning to the strategy of encouraging groups to select their own focus of interest, this time within the topic of the school grounds, Kay described how the pupils' demands for resources to meet their chosen lines of inquiry show much more independence than before. Also, the ability of the groups to organize themselves clearly advanced, albeit more for some pupils than others. Tracy was heard to say: 'We will need something to dig with. Get a spade from the sand pit in Mrs Chesters' class.' Kay 'marvelled' at this as she had seen Tracy as 'a little mouse' a few months previously (classroom-based study, p. 16).

Michael prepared for his visit to the school grounds by preparing a 'tick chart' listing the mini-beasts he hoped/expected to find, using a tick to record each individual mini-beast. This was entirely his own initiative. Michael had sat through the first ten minutes of a handwriting lesson, several months earlier, without a pencil because he 'didn't like to ask'. Now he was hypothesizing that smaller slugs would move faster than larger ones, attempting to test his hypothesis, and when he encountered difficulties, modifying his method of testing – all independently.

Kay gives several other examples of independent thinking in subsequent work. Her classroom-based study concludes by saying that there is 'no real conclusion ... because it is an ongoing process'. It summarizes on p. 22 the developments for Kay of her abilities:

- to observe closely ('incidents I normally would have missed'), and
- to reflect on her teaching ('I have learnt more about my class and myself').

I think that a teacher like Kay, who is able to empathize with the pupils so strongly, is very likely to be responsive to their needs and to adapt her teaching to them. I certainly felt pleased that her teaching was successfully using pupils' investigations. Kay did not show as much explicit understanding of the procedural side of action research method as some other course members showed in their writing, but, in her reflections and discussions with critical friends, she was open to others' ideas and was self-critical in sustaining her own strongly felt philosophy through fairly systematic advances in her practice.

An Overview of Kay's Professional Development

I made assumptions about 'where Kay was' at the beginning of this course based on my contact with her on a previous course. I think I was accurate in my view about her professionalism – taking an inquiring approach to her practice – although I underestimated her lack of self-confidence. But, more significantly, I also overestimated the extent to which the previous course had enabled her to develop investigative learning. This may be because I kept forgetting how gradual are the changes involved, and also because I was somewhat overlooking the differences between the courses. I suspect that in having a classroom visit, this course has a major stimulus to self-assessment which the previous course did not have.

Kay showed emphatic progress in the areas she defined as growth in her:

- self-confidence in her classroom teaching, in discussion with professional colleagues and in her role as co-ordinator,
- understanding of scientific learning, and her abilities to encourage and assess it,
- professional skill in creating rich opportunities for pupil-centred investigative learning,
- ability to reflect on close observations, and experiment with her teaching.

Figure 2.7 Map of progress in substantive aspects of personal professional development as expressed by Kay

A – Interview (June)

Kay was not interviewed because the functions of an interview – the exchange of basic information between the course tutor and applicant – had been achieved during Kay's participation in a previous, different course.

B – Beginning of the Course (September)

I need to build up my self-confidence. I need to pick out and define the science which I feel intuitively is going on in my classroom. I am sensitive to my tendency to lead the children towards my expected outcomes. Do we *never* give facts to children?

C – Classroom visit by the Tutor (November–December)

I feel that my own intuitive grasp of science is not matched by my ability as a teacher to use it as a way of learning. I also feel it is a problem not being able to observe pupils enough – to know what is going on during a lesson. I doubt that pupils valued the teacher-imposed problem (as compared with one they raise for themselves). Therefore, I question problem setting as a strategy for eliciting exploration. I recognize the dilemma between too much and too little teacher direction. I want to develop pupils' independent thinking.

D – Course Sessions (December 1987–May 1988)

I have greater ability to recognize scientific skills of hypothesizing, etc. in pupils. I am still concerned, but better able now to notice pupils' ideas. I am using this as evidence not only for my own reflections on teaching, but as feedback to colleagues during my visits to their classes (as co-ordinator of science at the school). I think it is possible that not giving every pupil the same experience may be an advantage. I am still concerned with pupils' independent thinking, and recognize that this may mean accepting some responses from pupils that are unexpected and, at first sight, disappointing. I am developing strategies and tactics for encouraging individual thinking.

E – Statement of Personal Professional Development (June)

Kay's statement contrasts in emphatic terms her initial enthusiasm for science with her lack of self-confidence at the start of the course. Her ideas for adapting her teaching came from other course members, and the confidence to experiment with her teaching is attributed to the course, as is the confidence to work alongside colleagues at school, and visitors from the LEA support team.

Figure 2.8 Diagram of practice/theory interactions in Kay's personal professional development

Professional practices and experiences	*Professional assessments, reflections and analysis*

Kay's usual way of teaching was to lead the children the achievement of pre-set knowledge aims.

Kay felt she had an intuitive grasp of the science learning happening in her classroom, but felt the need to be able to pick it out and define it.

During the tutor visit, Kay's lesson contained an opportunity for scientific exploration within a problem-solving framework. The children's responses were encouraging in some respects, for instance in their thoughtful hypothesizing, but in other ways led Kay to critical reflection.

The response of many children made her doubt the value of setting artificial problems for the children compared with them identifying their own. She acknowledged the presence of hypothesizing and other 'higher-level' scientific thinking skills in a way she had not recognized before.

After the visit, Kay continued to express concern about not being able to observe the children enough, to understand their thinking, but felt this was improving. She voiced her observations during discussions both at university and during her visits to colleagues' classrooms (as co-ordinator).

Kay continued to be concerned with children's independent thinking, recognizing that this may mean

(continued over)

During the tutor visit, Kay had held back from giving the children direction to some extent, but saw many of the children fail to use their exploratory behaviour to solve the problem she had set. She recognized the dilemma between too little and too much teacher direction.

accepting some responses from pupils that are unexpected, and, at first sight, disappointing. She saw a need to build up her self-confidence in her science teaching. She was sensitive to her own tendency to lead the children to the outcomes she intended for them.

Kay interpreted this as inappropriate lesson planning rather than too little teacher intervention.

Kay began to question the apparent necessity to give every child the same experience. This was over taken as a priority by the wish to observe the children more.

Discussion with other course members gave her ideas for experimenting with her teaching, as well as the confidence to do so.

Kay developed ideas to try out various tactics and strategies for encouraging independent thinking.

Teaching thematically about the environment, Kay elicited impressive examples of children's independent investigation.

Kay claimed to have much improved self-confidence to develop her own teaching, to work alongside colleagues at school and visiting advisory teachers.

Lesley

Profile of Lesley

Lesley had been a primary school teacher for nine years, having obtained her B.Ed. degree followed by a Diploma in Primary Education. Prior to this she had five years experience as a nursery nurse. She was currently teaching Year 5 and 6 children at an inner-city primary school in a socially disadvantaged area. She held a post of responsibility for English. She did not hold any science qualifications, and not one of the numerous continuing professional development courses she had previously attended had been about science.

Lesley's reasons for coming on the course were mainly personal, 'to become more knowledgeable about science teaching and learning in order to increase my effectiveness in the classroom', but her reasons also related to school developments. She sought 'good professional guidance' that would enable her to make her contribution ('based on sound knowledge') to the formulation of a school policy for science since she hoped to take a leadership role for science. Talking about her own teaching, Lesley said she liked to get pupils to ask their own questions, to discuss how to get answers, and to evaluate their learning. She said that project work is 'boring' if it is entirely imposed on the pupils. She gave them written instructions for experiments on work cards, and she allowed the pupils 'to go off at a tangent'. She saw experiments that 'don't work out as planned' can be used as a basis for thinking scientifically.

I felt optimistic that Lesley's participation in the course would be successful because she appeared to have a strongly committed, professional approach that was characterized by a controlled, business-like manner, direct and clear self-expression, and an ability to engage in reasoned discussion.

Lesley's Concerns

Lesley described her teaching as based upon small group work with practical tasks and discussion-based learning, using her own work cards with 'a few teaching points on each'. She expressed dissatisfaction with the school's use of science-based topic organization because it did not lead to enough science learning by the pupils.

At an early course session, based on 'ice balloons', I observed Lesley's reaction to the invitation to explore these large lumps of ice. She was reluctant to handle the ice and seemed inhibited from exploring it in a free and playful manner. However, she then selected one of the questions or hypotheses about ice, which had been brainstormed by the group earlier, and began to design a controlled experiment. It was as if Lesley felt more able to apply what she knew to be a scientific way of working with the new object rather than to react more spontaneously and informally as most of the others did. During the case study validation interview, Lesley wrote: 'Not being used to working in this way I saw the activity as somewhat demeaning to my self-image as a teacher.' When she used ice balloons with her own pupils at school, Lesley found that there was a somewhat limited reaction. The younger pupils said very little, which was attributed by Lesley to their limited vocabulary. Several course members, including Lesley, had noticed an absence of questioning raised by their pupils about the ice when they tried out ice balloons with them in their own classrooms. Lesley volunteered to organize bringing in pupils from her own school to the university for an afternoon course session at which the course members supervised and observed pupils using ice balloons as the stimulus. In this context, her pupils gave a rewarding response overall, making a range of observations *and raising questions and hypotheses*. Lesley was surprised and delighted by how well they had responded – it had been beyond her expectations (see also pp. 110–14).

At this stage (mid-autumn term), I had collected only one specific professional concern expressed by Lesley herself, which was about the limited response to science which she felt she was obtaining from her pupils. In my reflection, I felt that Lesley's teaching was less child-centred than had appeared to be the case earlier because I felt that Lesley used much more teacher-set structure. I wondered if this had been having an inhibiting effect on the pupils. There were already indications, not recorded but perceived by me, that Lesley was reviewing her ideas and practice in a critical way.

The Tutor's Visit to Lesley's Classroom

I was not the tutor who visited Lesley's classroom. My colleague's report of her visit showed that the lesson had been successful in eliciting pupils' scientific exploration during the making of cardboard spinners, with different groups of pupils showing the freedom to adapt the overall task as they wished. A brief summary of the tutor–teacher discussion of the session suggests that the lesson had achieved 'satisfying progress' in the development of greater responses from the children to Lesley's science teaching. It was agreed that Lesley could have restricted her use of scientific terminology to the term 'friction' and allowed more time for children to participate in discussion (and less time for teacher introductory talk). Instead of allocating tasks, she would allow the children to investigate their own interests, with support for those who were unsure in this situation. It was agreed that the next step in this development would be the encouragement of children's self-organization. In her report to the course members at a subsequent course session, Lesley said she had used terms like 'inertia' and 'momentum' in her pre-lesson planning, and had anticipated that fair testing of spinners might be possible. The task had been to make the best spinner (the one that spins for the longest time). It had been clearly understood and yielded a variety of ideas and practical tests. However, friction was the only relevant concept for the children, and the phenomenon had been too complex for the application of fair testing procedures. Lesley told how it was firstly her recognition of the pupils' own ideas and suggestions for the activity, and secondly her expansion of the resource base which had subsequently enlarged her own thinking. She said: 'I could have let more come from them.' She also said: 'I think I put them down a lot.'

This seemed to have been a valuable series of experiences for Lesley. Coming after her experiments with practical problem solving and other fairly new ideas in her teaching, Lesley appeared to have reached a secure basis for reflecting self-critically and constructively about her growing awareness of pupils' independent thinking and her own ability to elicit and support such thinking. This interpretation was endorsed by Lesley at the case study validation interview for which she wrote the following: 'I was imposing my ideas of what the children should get out of the activity rather than allowing children more freedom to experiment initially.' So, although my monitoring failed to give me much more than one major focus for Lesley's professional development, such development was proceeding very profitably under Lesley's control and in the direction she chose.

Lesley's Participation in the Course

Lesley made about an average number of contributions to whole group discussion, and they were often quite penetrating with strong relevance to the course. At the beginning of the spring term, Lesley wrote about her 'preoccupation' with her own lack of scientific knowledge and skill, which led her to consider 'a programme of learning for myself over and above what I'm doing on the course'. This is consistent with the information about the classroom visit which showed how Lesley had felt she needed to consider concepts such as inertia and momentum in her preparation, even though the pupils did not need to use them in thinking about spinners. It suggests that although Lesley did not have science qualifications at, for example, A Level, she was working hard to be aware of the science knowledge relevant to her teaching. Lesley wrote:

> A lack of knowledge and/or experience of particular aspects of science teaching can lead to a lack of confidence in presenting such aspects in the classroom, therefore leading to an imbalance of scientific learning on the part of the children.

Later, she wrote again about this saying:

I am much more aware of the analytical aspects of my science teaching now. The first analytic summary was concerned with very practical aspects, such as the investigative table, topics I had introduced, whereas now I am much more concerned with what I need to know in order to achieve a balance of science presentation in my classroom.

Lesley's self-assessment clashed with my assessment of her levels of scientific knowledge and skill. In comparison with other course members, I had noticed that she had some relatively advanced scientific ideas (for example, momentum and inertia) and that she could use them effectively in the conduct of investigative work, for example, with ice balloons. I wrote a comment to this effect on Lesley's analytic summary.

Lesley selected pupils' observation skills as the focus of her classroom-based study. She wanted to find out:

- about observational skills as a 'tool for learning',
- how to offer appropriate experiences and activities, and
- how best to introduce them in the classroom.

I saw the three aspects of Lesley's intentions as having the potential of yielding a good example of seeking development in understanding and practice interdependently. Lesley saw observation as a purposeful activity leading to what she referred to as the 'development of cognition'. Lesley read about the significance of the learner's existing ideas to his/her selection of things to observe (and also to the kinds of further ideas which it would be possible to develop). She inferred that good observation had to serve a purpose in the mind of the learner. This led to a question in Lesley's mind at this stage, which shows the extent of the development of child-centredness in her thinking about scientific observation. She asked: 'Is it *observing* if they're noticing what the teacher tells them to notice?' In the first stage of her study, Lesley set out to make more 'open' interventions in her discussions with pupils. Her self-monitoring evidence shows that she did this effectively. Her evaluation of the session says that the children's interest in one another's comments had been impressive and better than their normal interaction, which tended to be argumentative and 'shouting one another down'. In the second phase, Lesley tried to encourage them to observe better by eliciting their questions, predictions and hypotheses. The preliminary discussion about these went well, but it did not lead to better observation as hoped. Lesley attributed this disappointment to there being too many variables for the pupils to cope with. Therefore, in the next phase, where the activity was to perfect a hot air balloon, Lesley felt that she had a more specific task within which alterations that pupils could make to the balloons would depend upon their observations. Monitoring at one point showed that

Lesley needed to draw the pupils' attention to the toppling behaviour of the balloon in order to enable them to progress. Lesley wrote:

> I think the most significant thing to arise regarding observation was the boys' inability to link the overturning of the balloon with its top heaviness. Just because the action of the balloon was observable did not mean that it had been observed.

Lesley regarded the pupils' lack of understanding of 'how air behaves' as the cause of their failure to observe. I would agree that this possibly was a case of the absence of appropriate conceptual frameworks preventing an observer from noticing what was significant. However, I suspect that the conceptual deficiency was more to do with ideas about balance than about how air behaves.

In the fourth phase of the study, Lesley attempted 'to see how children's observations develop when given "free time" in which to make observations'. She did not impose her own ideas for classifying the collection of things which accumulated in the classroom brought from the environs of the school. Instead, she noticed instances of pupils discussing their own categorizations of observations and measurements, and examples of strong curiosity, detailed observation and vivid communication, both formal and informal. Lesley provided the following evaluation of this stage of the study: 'Given time in which to observe, the children showed an evolutionary development in their ideas of sorting and classifying.' The next stage focused on the use of models to encourage observation of daisies, and, in the final stage, following the environmental theme, Lesley encouraged the children to focus their observations to see if it enhanced their gain of knowledge. They concentrated on the organisms living on the sycamore tree, and learned a great deal about them.

Although the study is organized into sections entitled 'Action Step 1', 'Action Step 2', etc., Lesley did not use the term 'action step' in quite the same way that is defined by John Elliott in his practical guide to action research (Elliott, 1991b: 69–89). For Lesley a shift in focus to a new action step was justified implicitly, rather than explicitly, by her desire to explore various strategies in turn rather than by her findings from the previous action step. This raises the question of which should take priority in such circumstances. Should there be an action research methodological requirement for action steps to have a rational justification, or should the teacher researcher be free to explore action steps that s/he justified for her/himself by personal interest? (See also pp. 114–21.)

Overall, I felt that Lesley's study was interesting because of the enlightened way in which observation was dealt with, integrating it with the wholeness of the children's scientific inquiry learning. It was conducted in a systematic and organized way, and it showed valuable developments in Lesley's teaching.

An Overview of Lesley's Professional Development

Although I felt that I knew enough about Lesley's work on the course to believe that she was progressing professionally, I did not have specific information about which particular professional concerns or focuses she was working on. For example, I was aware of only one specific concern during the autumn term. During the spring term, I knew about the overall focus of her classroom-based study, and in the summer term I read the report and became fully informed. I am highlighting this because I felt I should have had a clearer picture of Lesley, and I wonder why I didn't. I think it would have been mainly because I did not visit Lesley and observe her teach and meet her pupils, thereby gaining an image of her professionally to which I could relate and keep in mind when Lesley spoke during seminars. This was reciprocated by Lesley's view of her relationship with me. At the case study validation interview, Lesley wrote this comment on the study:

> I too felt that because you did not observe my classroom teaching there was a 'distance' between us that I felt did not exist between yourself and colleagues who you had visited. I felt you lacked a 'complete' picture of me!

Lesley's own statement of professional progress clearly showed that her self-confidence and self-criticism professionally had grown during the year as she had made important developments in her teaching. She wrote: 'What now emerges is that I am much more confident of being critical of how and what I teach!' During discussion at one of the concluding course sessions, course members said that they had remembered their early impressions of Lesley, at the beginning of the course, as being someone with a lot of confidence. It emerged that although Lesley was aware of lacking background science knowledge which some other course members possessed, she gave the impression of being knowledgeable and confident to the other course members in other ways. Brenda said: 'That just shows how much you've changed because you were quite confident about what you were doing. Now you're questioning.' To which Lesley replied, amid course members' laughter, 'I'm more open-minded now.'

Figure 2.9 Map of progress in substantive aspects of personal professional development as expressed by Lesley

A – Interview (June)

I wish to become more knowledgeable about my science teaching and the children's learning to increase my effectiveness in the classroom. I also want to be able to contribute to the formulation of the school's policy for science.

B – Beginning of the Course (September)

I feel dissatisfied with the amount of science that children gain from my science-based topic work. I feel that pupils are relatively unresponsive to the science opportunities. How can I understand teaching and learning science? I am learning to acknowledge the value of the teacher taking the role of observer of pupils' learning. Previous school curriculum development initiatives had *begun* with the formulation of policy, and this had not been successful – what shall I do instead?

C – Classroom Visit by the Tutor (November–December)

I can see progress in the improvement of pupils' responses to science. This has occurred in association with greater flexibility of my organization and teaching, which seem to elicit greater independence in the pupils' thinking.

D – Course Sessions (December–May)

I feel 'preoccupied' with my own lack of scientific knowledge and skill. In this sense particularly, I am becoming more analytical about my own teaching. How do I use more open types of teacher interventions? How do I get pupils' questions and hypotheses to improve their observation?

E – Statement of Personal Professional Development (June)

My ways of presenting work to pupils and my ways of encouraging them have both changed to give pupils more control over the content and structure of the work. I recognize pupils as more resourceful and creative than I had previously given them credit for. I have greater confidence to be critical about how and what I teach. I am providing advice and collections of ideas and resources for colleagues at school to support the development of science within cross-curricular topic work. I have greater confidence to perform this role, which has been enhanced over the year.

Figure 2.10 Diagram of practice/theory interactions in Lesley's personal professional development

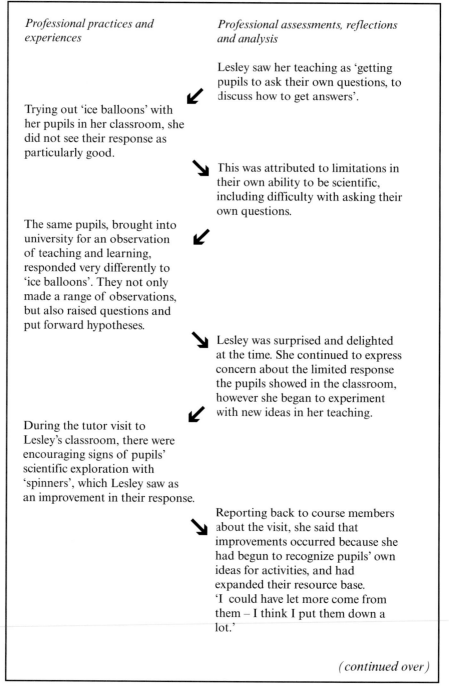

Professional practices and experiences	Professional assessments, reflections and analysis
	Lesley saw her teaching as 'getting pupils to ask their own questions, to discuss how to get answers'.
Trying out 'ice balloons' with her pupils in her classroom, she did not see their response as particularly good.	
	This was attributed to limitations in their own ability to be scientific, including difficulty with asking their own questions.
The same pupils, brought into university for an observation of teaching and learning, responded very differently to 'ice balloons'. They not only made a range of observations, but also raised questions and put forward hypotheses.	
	Lesley was surprised and delighted at the time. She continued to express concern about the limited response the pupils showed in the classroom, however she began to experiment with new ideas in her teaching.
During the tutor visit to Lesley's classroom, there were encouraging signs of pupils' scientific exploration with 'spinners', which Lesley saw as an improvement in their response.	
	Reporting back to course members about the visit, she said that improvements occurred because she had begun to recognize pupils' own ideas for activities, and had expanded their resource base. 'I could have let more come from them – I think I put them down a lot.'

(continued over)

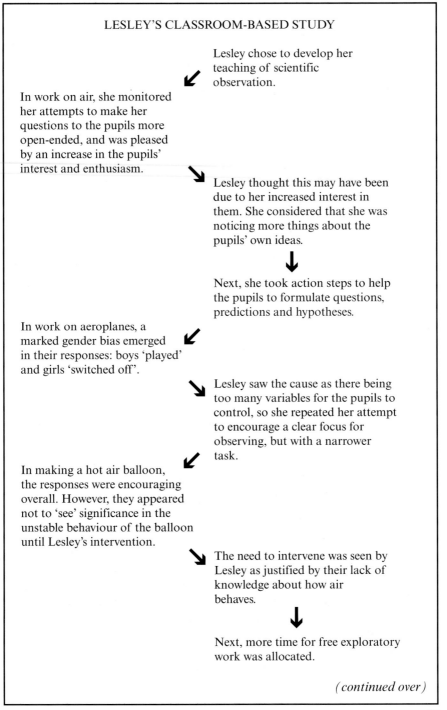

LESLEY'S CLASSROOM-BASED STUDY

Lesley chose to develop her teaching of scientific observation.

In work on air, she monitored her attempts to make her questions to the pupils more open-ended, and was pleased by an increase in the pupils' interest and enthusiasm.

Lesley thought this may have been due to her increased interest in them. She considered that she was noticing more things about the pupils' own ideas.

Next, she took action steps to help the pupils to formulate questions, predictions and hypotheses.

In work on aeroplanes, a marked gender bias emerged in their responses: boys 'played' and girls 'switched off'.

Lesley saw the cause as there being too many variables for the pupils to control, so she repeated her attempt to encourage a clear focus for observing, but with a narrower task.

In making a hot air balloon, the responses were encouraging overall. However, they appeared not to 'see' significance in the unstable behaviour of the balloon until Lesley's intervention.

The need to intervene was seen by Lesley as justified by their lack of knowledge about how air behaves.

Next, more time for free exploratory work was allocated.

(continued over)

In environmental work, they devised their own categories and schedules for observation and collection of specimens, and made inventive use of various methods, such as models, to show what they knew about the objects through their observations.

Lesley was bringing to bear several new strategies during this stage, and felt that this was the most successful example of the children's observational abilities.

Steve

Profile of Steve

Steve had been a police constable for three years between taking his A Levels and entering university, where he obtained a BA and PGCE (Primary) qualifications. Since then he had taught Year 4 and 5 children for two years, and recently obtained a science curriculum responsibility. Steve's science background did not include any A Levels, but his recent PGCE science course and his LEA course in science led him to join this course to obtain 'valuable resource ideas, knowledge and practical learning activities'. His course application was supported by the head teacher and also the LEA science adviser. Steve's involvement with the school staff in encouraging their science teaching had been at an informal level, focusing on *their* existing topics and giving them practical ideas.

Steve seemed to be a talkative, positive and an energetically enthusiastic person with a strong sense of humour and a serious commitment to teaching. I felt that he would be successful on the course both personally and as a group member. In the past, I had found that some course members, more often men, have a rigidity of self-image regarding both their teaching and their knowledge of science which, in my view, had been a disadvantage both for their development and their contribution to the course. Not so with Steve, he seemed open-minded to new ideas to set alongside his own views, and confident in experimenting with his teaching.

Steve's Concerns

At this point in his career, Steve was adapting to several new challenges (a new school, teaching in an open-plan area and being science co-ordinator) with apparently no reduction in his cheerful enthusiasm. Of these three, the open-plan situation appeared to be his main concern early on, coming to terms with new practical problems and developing successful professional relationships with his colleagues in the team-teaching organization. Steve saw these concerns as taking priority over 'working on the children' (developing his teaching). His understanding and practice of what he called the 'active learning', which he saw the course advocating, had to be fitted into what was feasible within the open-plan constraints.

My Visit to Steve's Classroom

Steve set up two groups with candles and some work cards he had made which contained open-ended questions aimed at encouraging their exploration of various aspects of the candles. I sat between the groups and noticed that the group I called 'A' seemed to be more able than group 'B' to handle the materials, and to talk about and be interested in them. Steve made regular visits to both groups (in between attending to the rest of the class) to encourage progress. With group B he was unable to elicit ideas from them, so he offered one that he said he had collected from other pupils the previous day. He asked them: 'Do you think the colour of the candle makes any difference to the colour of the candle flame?' He wrote this on a card and left it for them to think about how they could find out. Group B continued to function in this way, 'aloof from the investigation'.

By contrast, group A had sorted out a question they agreed to try to answer concerning how fast a candle would burn down in relation to its thickness. Some had hypotheses about this. When Steve intervened, he did not discover this, but fed in further ideas for investigations and asked questions about their observations of the candles, neither of which related to their own investigation. Group A had organized the burning of the candles one by one, for a fixed time period, measuring each candle before and after to know how much it had burned down.

S: [Steve, as he arrives to intervene.] What's going on here?
R: [Pupil] We are measuring how fast they burn.
S: Why is there sand in the candle? [The pupils had put the candles out quickly at the end of the time set by touching the end against the sand.]
R: It's gone hard.
S: There's a candle that's been lit. What's happened to the wax? Is it hard or soft?
Group: Hard.

S:	Is it the same as it is when it's lit?
Group:	No.
S:	How has it changed?
A:	It's melted.
S:	What does it look like when it's melted? What does it remind you of?
R:	Plasticine – you know – like when you can push it in.
S:	You mean it's more pliable and softer?
R:	Yes.
S:	Now you've done that (pointing to sand in the candle wax) can you get it out?
C:	No.
R:	It's stuck in.

On the basis of my observational notes, I talked with Steve afterwards about his intentions for such interventions, and he had already begun to question their effectiveness. I left the audio cassette with much of this talk recorded on it for Steve to listen to, and he selected an extract and assessed it himself, writing:

> All very interesting and consolidated ideas on cause and effect, and change, but after reading through the transcript, bears no resemblance to what the children had been discussing and investigating because I had not witnessed some very important developments in the formulation of their thoughts.

This led to one of the main questions to emerge from the visit as follows: 'Do my interventions stunt the development of their investigations?'

Meanwhile, group B had tended to restrict their scientific learning to observing and noticing patterns, but had been much more productive than group A of written and visual records of their observations. I characterized their response as 'task-oriented' and using 'producer strategies' rather than autonomous investigation. I hypothesized that when he gave them the question, they had regarded that as 'what teacher wants' rather than 'a possibility (among others) originating from another pupil'. They had attributed to it an authority, which Steve had tried to avoid by quoting other pupils as the source rather than himself. This had been the obstacle to their expression of their autonomy.

Another major issue discussed at this time (though not arising from evidence collected during the visit) was the necessity for firsthand experience. We agreed that sometimes a pupil may need to repeat an experience to consolidate his or her understanding. In other cases, a pupil may be able to go ahead faster than the teacher judges to be appropriate, for example, when a pupil has learned by observation of, or communication with, other pupils and their investigation so that it is unnecessary for him/her to experience it directly for him/herself. The head teacher had joined the discussion at this stage, and the three of us discussed a shared preference for there to be suffi-cient flexibility in teaching to allow one group of pupils to learn from the mistakes made by another group who have previously worked on a partic-ular task. During a subsequent course session, Steve was talking about how he saw his professional development:

> The questions seem to arise more readily than the answers. But I can see myself able to reflect and improve. I've taped one or two sessions since the classroom visit because there were things in there I thought 'Blimey – I'd better get that sorted out.' I kept butting in on the children's talk and going over the top. It's just a trait I've got and it's something I've got to try and curb – that's my professional development!

Steve did not mention his concerns about his co-ordinator role, or his adaptations to open-plan and team teaching, but I saw evidence of shared interest and understanding, along with close collaboration between Steve and his immediate colleague who was teaching in the adjacent bay.

I felt this had been a highly successful visit in several respects. Mainly because I had captured evidence that had been a valuable resource for Steve, who, with little encouragement from me, had used it to considerable effect. Steve wrote, at the conclusion of his report:

> I must understand the ways in which I can help the children learn. There are many forms this can take of more or less directness, most of them appropriate at some time or other, whatever the form of organization in the class. I must get to know the advantages that each can offer, and when they are best employed in my own circumstances, with which I found the tape and transcript invaluable in evaluation.

His report shows gratifying use of the monitoring to develop his own insights, assess his practice and anticipate developments in an autonomous manner despite his lack of experience. Steve said: 'When you say we need to assess our own professional development, we haven't necessarily got the experience to fall back on. I haven't. I have to build it up as I go along.' He had reconsidered his strategy for intervention by questioning the appropri-ateness of offering suggestions for investigations, and, instead, trying to develop ways of discovering the pupils' own ideas for investigation.

> I thought science (teaching) was 'showing children science' – having prescribed investigations and set explanations. Now I'm more concerned with the thought processes than getting correct (scientific) results – proving Newton all over again!

He found children's ideas to be an acceptable basis for their science learning as he now conceived it. This raised for Steve important new concerns about how such learning can be monitored and assessed by the teacher.

Steve's Participation in the Course

At this stage in the course, Steve appeared to have entirely adapted to the open-plan situation and team teaching, and was not apparently under pressure from his co-ordinator responsibilities. He had become 'less guilty' about pupils not recording their science at every opportunity, and instead was concerned about assessing and adapting to pupils' needs and achievements. Steve's self-awareness was enhanced by the co-operative aspects of his team-teaching work. One of his school colleagues was a retrained secondary science teacher. I wondered if this person's perspective influenced Steve because he began to be more concerned about pupils' 'right' answers and correct scientific understanding. He was also still struggling with this problem in his own thinking. In the context of a whole group discussion about the course expectations of and framework for course members' professional development, he said: 'Throughout my educational career there's been a right and a wrong. I've come up for the first time to being neither, and it's up to me to decide. That's the part I'm finding a bit tough at the moment.'

Two constraints which Steve perceived at this time were:

1   The lack of space which prevented more pupils from working independently on diverging lines of interest.
2   The need to be seen to be working in harmony with the rest of the staff meant using the school-selected scheme, and its associated emphasis on concept development.

In discussion about his classroom-based study, Steve began to argue strongly for the teacher's responsibility to correct pupils' scientific misconceptions. He accepted that some value lies in the development of process skills when pupils pursue their own hypotheses, but insisted that they must also learn scientifically correct ideas. Steve referred to the knowledge and understanding components of the national curriculum in support of his position. These views were expressed in the face of other views within the group, such as:

1   Can any teacher be confident about the complete accuracy of her/his own scientific understanding which s/he wants to project to pupils?
2   Doesn't this clash with Steve's declared aim for pupils to 'form minds of their own'?

I suggested that in his study Steve could therefore collect evidence about either pupils' own investigations which appear to enter conceptual blind alleys to explore possibilities for teachers responding to this profitably, or carry out a closer assessment of what pupils' meanings are. Steve expressed some reservations about monitoring one or two pupils as the basis for developing his teaching on the grounds that this is artificial in a class-teaching context. This seemed to contradict claims by Steve about the value he saw in taping.

Steve's practice of conducting plenary discussion at the report back stage of working was developing into a useful source of feedback information. He claimed that:

> It is paying off not only in their scientific thought, but they are encouraged to retell in sequence. This feedback time fuels thoughts for planning subsequent activities. I say things to them like: 'How could you help tomorrow's group start their investigation?' and 'If you had the chance to start again would you change anything?'

But he became dissatisfied with it when he noticed that reports did not always do justice to the quality of science learning achieved, writing:

> I also became aware through the tapes that some of the children had formulated and discussed with their groups some excellent observations and discoveries. But when they shared them with the class, they were lost, either because of limited time, or because the child thought they were insignificant, or they had forgotten!

So he considered some kind of written record whilst being wary of destroying the pupils' enthusiasm. He decided to introduce a science notebook as described by Jos Elstgeest, Wynne Harlen and David Symington in *Children Communicate* (Harlen, 1985). Steve helped the pupils' organization of their records in the notebook by giving them printed record sheets for specific recording tasks linked with the topic (weather). The sheets were stuck into the notebooks. In his own reflective diary he wrote: 'I feel at this moment I am on the brink of exploring a freer and more meaningful approach to science teaching, but must be careful not to be so radical as to make changes for changes sake.'

Steve organized a rota for each group to take a turn at recording each aspect of weather to encourage interdependent use of one another's records. His interventions were now based upon his assessment of how to intervene the previous term, for example:

> I joined the group to hopefully provide guidance rather than interference, keeping my intervention down to a minimum. I listened intently to

their problem, which was how to count the rotation of a yoghurt pot anemometer which rotates too quickly. Together we had the idea of fitting a clicker made from a nail and a piece of card and I left them to it.

Steve also saw the value of enabling the different pupil groups to be a problem-solving resource for one another. He continued:

> The nail caused a shift in the balance of the rotor blade so that the arm with the nail in it tilted downwards a little and so the nail stopped against the card. When presented to the larger group, R said: 'Put a nail in the other side to balance it up.' Steve said 'That will make the clicker click twice.' R replied: 'Make the nail point up, not down.' This made it work.

Steve was listening to recordings, reading transcripts and keeping a detailed reflective diary, with occasional note making about his observations of group interactions. Standing back from the developments taking place and remembering his previous teaching style, he wrote that it had been 'acting in many ways as a strait-jacket to some of the children' (p. 25). He then became more aware of the importance of co-operative interactions within the working group to successful learning by all its members.

Steve was searching for a framework for his teaching that would harness the pupils' investigative ability and, at the same time, ensure that important scientific ideas were learned and understood. The framework would have to be one that enabled Steve to feel in control of the conceptual development and to know about its progress. Steve drew justification for this partly by quoting from his reading and partly by referring to his perception of the needs of his school colleagues, and his role as co-ordinator to meet their professional needs. He wrote:

> I am fast drawing the conclusion that in order to develop skills in a cumulative way so that some important skills and concepts are not entirely disregarded, there is a need for a scheme of work or syllabus to assist the logical development of the children's learning. I say this as a co-ordinator in my school with my colleagues in mind, some of whom are not as convinced about developing their science teaching as I and who are not as confident in formulating their own starting points.

Using the topic of 'Vikings', Steve produced work cards aimed at giving the majority of his pupils 'the direction and framework … in aiding their planning', and to introduce the basic concepts he wanted them 'to become aware of'. His study provided transcript material as evidence of the cards acting 'as both stimulus and safety net'. The system enabled Steve to feel more in control. He wrote: 'If they were all finding separate lines of interests and tasks, the teacher's task of monitoring progress would be almost impossible.' Steve concluded his study by returning to the focus of teacher–pupil interaction, saying that this is where he saw his major professional progress. He wrote: 'I can see a contrast between my initial role as "authoritative instructor" to that of guide responding to specific needs seen in children.'

An Overview of Steve's Professional Development

In his statement, Steve gave emphatic support to the belief that his self-evaluation skills had grown a great deal, and that they were now an integral part of his professional self-image.

> I have answered many questions about the 'whys' of my own science teaching by using my reflective and researching actions outlined by the course, which will remain a major and integral part of my whole teaching strategy.

He had expected to discover a 'magic formula' to solve his professional concerns, and he had expected his professional progress to be a linear pathway following a straight line. Looking back, he recognized that the main gain was that of 'awareness', by which he meant: the knowledge gained from reflection on experience of a range of strategies and their effects, and greater skill in employing them. 'With which I am extremely satisfied.'

Steve's writing showed a strong sense of personal ownership of his professional development and a high degree of autonomy in determining the direction and pace of his experimentation with his teaching. Steve's writing, like his contributions to discussion, showed an enthusiastic commitment, but there also were signs that his thinking had made good use of the conceptual framework of the course.

His use of the action research framework was effective in that his monitoring provided an excellent basis for reflection and the modification of his practice. Some of the changes of direction in his zigzag path (for example, moving from pupils recording to intra-group dynamics to writing work cards, etc.) seemed inexplicable to an outsider, and they did not appear to match John Elliott's (1991b) notion of an action step as following preceding analysis in a logical sequence. He wrote: 'During this process of self-evaluation, I couldn't work out (and still can't!) whether it was Elliott's fault or mine when my study didn't follow the straightforward lines of development he outlined.'

This raised a similar question about the action research approach to professional development to that raised in Lesley's work. Does the most effective way of developing teaching consist of exercising the freedom to switch focuses, as Steve did, according to the perceived relevance or interest at the time, or should greater methodological discipline be applied in some way? By this I mean tutorial insistence that such changes of focus must occur only when *substantial evidence* for them has accrued as judged by the teacher and a group of critical friends. Steve's work tended to encourage the principle that teacher autonomy to switch focuses should take precedence over methodological 'rigour' because his progress was so good.

Figure 2.11 *Map of progress in substantive aspects of personal professional development as expressed by Steve*

A – Interview (June)

I want the course to give me 'valuable resource ideas, knowledge and practical learning activities'. As science co-ordinator, I am supporting the science teaching of my colleagues by offering them practical ideas for activities to relate to their own topic work.

B – Beginning of the Course (September)

My pupils tend to give the same measurements ('cheat') out of a sense of competition to get the right answer. I am concerned about the practical problems of open-plan organization and my professional sensitivity towards colleagues in the team-teaching situation. I must solve these problems to do with 'the bay' before 'working on the children'. How can I fit active investigative learning into my open-plan situation? I give work cards to pupils because I do not consider that they are ready to make decisions to determine the path of an investigation.

C – Classroom Visit by the Tutor (November)

Do my interventions stunt the development of their investigations? How can my teaching achieve the flexibility for one pupil to repeat the experience so as to consolidate personal understanding, whilst another pupil can omit the experience, having learned through his/her observation of, or communication with, other pupils' investigations? I am increasing my awareness of different pupils' needs. Are they being scientific? How do I know? How can I record their progress?

D – Course Sessions (December–May)

If maths understanding can be assessed by pupils getting right answers, how do I assess science understanding? Can pupils' scientific recording aid their learning? I feel dissatisfied by not feeling in control of the pupils' learning, and feel the desire to ensure more concept development by pupils. I am searching for a 'framework' for my teaching, using work cards. I see science teaching not as 'showing and telling', but to do with the thought processes. It is more than getting right answers. As co-ordinator, I feel obliged to evolve ways of working which take account of: 1) the schools adopted scheme and 2) my perception of colleagues' needs for structure in their teaching.

E – Statement of Personal Professional Development (June)

I saw my intended development at the outset like a straight line, but, looking back, I now see it as having taken a zigzag path, looking at several side-issues on the way. I have increased my ability to 'get outside myself' and 'analyse the why and with what effect' in the changes in my teaching 'that were being done intuitively before the course'. I anticipated the discovery of a 'magic formula', but have experimented with many alternatives and I now understand their advantages and disadvantages. My main outcome is 'awareness'.

Figure 2.12 Diagram of practice/theory interactions in Steve's personal professional development

Professional practices and experiences	Professional assessments, reflections and analysis
STEVE'S SCIENCE TEACHING	
Noticed that pupils tended to compete with each other to get the 'right answer' in science.	
	Steve did not consider the pupils capable of making decisions to determine the path of an
	(continued over)

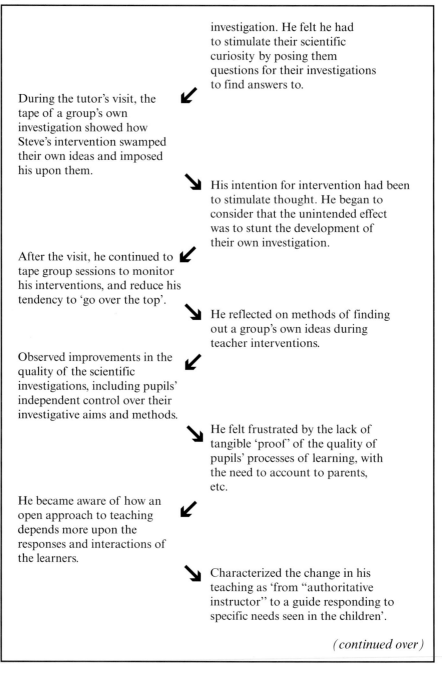

investigation. He felt he had to stimulate their scientific curiosity by posing them questions for their investigations to find answers to.

During the tutor's visit, the tape of a group's own investigation showed how Steve's intervention swamped their own ideas and imposed his upon them.

His intention for intervention had been to stimulate thought. He began to consider that the unintended effect was to stunt the development of their own investigation.

After the visit, he continued to tape group sessions to monitor his interventions, and reduce his tendency to 'go over the top'.

He reflected on methods of finding out a group's own ideas during teacher interventions.

Observed improvements in the quality of the scientific investigations, including pupils' independent control over their investigative aims and methods.

He felt frustrated by the lack of tangible 'proof' of the quality of pupils' processes of learning, with the need to account to parents, etc.

He became aware of how an open approach to teaching depends more upon the responses and interactions of the learners.

Characterized the change in his teaching as 'from "authoritative instructor" to a guide responding to specific needs seen in the children'.

(continued over)

STEVE'S PROFESSIONAL DEVELOPMENT

Listening to the tape of his
inappropriate interventions to
group investigations.

'Blimey! – I'd better get that sorted
out. It's just a trait I've got – butting
in and going over the top – its something I've got to try and curb. That's
my professional development.'

Seeking other aspects of his
teaching to consider for
development, he felt that his
own lack of teaching experience
was a handicap.

'Throughout my professional career
there's been a right and a wrong.
I've come up for the first time to
being neither, and it's up to me to
decide. I'm finding that a bit
tough.'

Steve continued to tape his
teaching and keep a reflective
diary to learn more from his
experience.

He characterized his personal
professional development as 'getting
outside myself to look objectively at
what I was doing intuitively'.

3 Individual Characteristics of Development

The professional development of the six teachers studied here is presented as personal journeys. The use of this metaphor is intended to offer a gestalt recognition of a common human experience which involves the whole person, not just as a narrow set of intellectual considerations.

Angela's Journey

Angela began her journey with a larger than average amount of knowledge about certain geographical aspects of the terrain, and wanted to concentrate on these during her journey. But she began to appreciate other aspects of the journey as it went on, slotting her specialist knowledge into a broadening appreciation of the countryside. When she began, she expected the journey to be controlled mainly by the journey organizer – as a kind of courier perhaps. The unusual features of the vehicle she drove, needing two drivers simultaneously, required a very particular driving style that she grew to dislike as it inhibited her from developing her own style, and limited the kinds of places she could visit and find out about. Allied to this, Angela was a nervous driver, tending both to underestimate her own driving skills and to lack confidence in her ability to complete the journey successfully. Consequently, her journeying tended to be dominated by concerns about how to manage these difficulties, and her thoughts often returned to this. However, this did not prevent Angela from finding out quite a lot from her journey, and making good progress towards her destination, though not as far as others. She also developed increased confidence in her driving generally, and got the vehicle modified through negotiation with its owners to make it better to drive and more able to get to places that Angela felt were important. She also gained confidence in her ability to control her journeys rather than assume that a journey organizer was the better person to do this for her. So her journey is characterized as much by the improvements in her journeying capacities as by her satisfactions derived from this journey itself. It is not unreasonable to imagine her taking over a different vehicle with owners who are more supportive to her journeying capacities, and Angela taking better advantage of such an opportunity as a result of what she gained from this journey.

Brenda's Journey

Although Brenda had not taken a journey quite like this before, she had already gained the ability to take the opportunities it presented for taking control of the vehicle to make it go where she wanted. She drove observantly, carefully and quickly, with a lot of confidence. The vehicle was a fairly difficult one to drive because it needed two drivers and had a lot of passengers to whom Brenda was very committed about ensuring an enjoyable trip. She had covered a great deal of countryside within the first stage of the journey, deriving much satisfaction from learning about some of the most important landmarks and kinds of country around, and so subsequent stages of the journey included becoming more familiar with them all to know her way around well. At regular intervals she paused to read her map, which was sketchy, to fill in details on it, take stock of the journey and carry out frequent checks on the enjoyment of her co-driver and passengers. Brenda appreciated having made the journey, and complimented the organizer, having been positive as well as constructively critical of the organization throughout.

Chris's Journey

Chris had been used to day-trips with a courier to lead the way and point out all of the significant things along the way. She began this journey expecting a similar experience, and was disturbed to find that she would be expected to create part of her own map of the journey herself, as well as determine more and more of the route. This took a while for her to adjust to. During this time she took the main road, believing that this was expected of everyone taking this particular journey, and was angry about the amount of traffic and other tedious aspects of the travel, blaming the journey co-ordinator. She sounded the horn a lot and flashed her headlights at others to warn them of her frustrations. However, she began to appreciate both the length of the journey, realizing that there were unlikely to be short-cuts, as well as its distinctive quality (that of exploration and discovery). Then, Chris began to work out her own routes more, and made her journey worthwhile for herself and her travelling companions. Her style of travelling became well organized, observant and thoughtful.

Kay's Journey

Kay had little difficulty in making her own choice of route using smooth country roads through beautiful scenery. She enjoyed the travel for itself and had a clear sense of making progress. She tended to get cross with herself if, and using a crude map, she seemed to get lost. However, she became better able to judge for herself when she was travelling in the direction she wanted, although it was difficult for her to make the reasons for her choices clear to her passengers. She regularly checked that they were liking the countryside, and they clearly found the ride enjoyable. The dominant impression of Kay's journey is one of serenity and pleasure. Having avoided appearing a flamboyant or racy driver, and erring on the side of caution, Kay became confident enough to give driving lessons to others, to contradict others' advice about driving and to feel secure in her own, well-established journeying experience.

Lesley's Journey

Lesley gave the strong impression of having fairly firm ideas about her preferences for how and where to travel. She expected to be in the driving seat and to control the speed and route of travel carefully. However, she reconsidered her direction of travel fairly radically after early experiences had suggested that a different direction held out the possibility of a more interesting journey. To accept such a serious review of her own choice of destination was a slightly surprising but very positive step. It was surprising to other drivers who initially had been under the impression that she was very clear and confident about this important aspect, but later they found her beginning to question them about which way to go, and in ways that revealed much less certainty than they had suspected. Her characteristic style of driving was steady and thoughtful, always within limits of safety and prudence, and with a dignified and somewhat serious image.

Steve's Journey

Steve had not travelled around much, so he wanted to see as much of the countryside as possible. Without losing sight of his chosen destination, and usually making steady progress in its general direction, he nevertheless chose a zigzag route, in a somewhat haphazard manner, to take in particular attractions that became available along the way. He was a speed merchant, willing to take risks and have accidents, but equally willing to admit mistakes cheerfully and seek advice about how to avoid making them again. Steve seemed to enjoy it all hugely as if it was some kind of 'treasure hunt'. Whilst retaining his enthusiasm, he developed the abilities to notice much more as he journeyed, to gain more satisfaction from the views along the way, and to form his own judgements about the best route to take. He maintained that he had seen much more of the important parts of the countryside because of his zigzag routes than if he had stuck to routes laid down in the visitor's guide.

Looking Closer at Individualities

Some significant and sometimes critical episodes in the teachers' developments are now examined in detail using a series of vignettes (Stenhouse, 1978) – short extracts of evidence about episodes which enable reflection on significant issues. They have been chosen to give attention to issues about the professional development process and also to aspects of science teaching, learning and assessment. Each episode is best understood in the context of the teacher's story of development.

Angela's Step in the Dark – Reconsidering Science Conceptual Knowledge Aims

During my classroom visit (see also p. 24) an opportunity arose for Angela to observe pupils' capacities to be independently investigative in a way that might not normally have arisen, or, if it had, she might not have given it any special attention because of her existing beliefs. Angela usually demonstrated something practical to the whole class, but, as often happens in this situation, at least to some degree, she 'put on a show' for me as the visitor, possibly by adjusting her practice towards what she perceived I would approve of. Therefore, she was probably treading near the boundaries of her confident practice (allowing for the norms of the school) within which events would be easiest to anticipate, and strategies existed to cope with most things that were likely to arise.

Extracts from my Observational Notes of the Session

A group of six 5–6 year old pupils sat in twos, two pairs of boys and one pair of girls, around four tables pushed together and covered with newspaper. Angela asked them to find out: 'What happens when water is put on things?' There was water in a dish with plastic spoons and supplies of dry sand, wet sand, soil, powder paint, leaves, foil, tissue paper and paper towel. Angela's declared objectives for the session were to encourage them 'to work co-operatively' and 'to develop the skills of observing closely what was happening, and to talk about it'. Angela got them to practise pouring drops of water from a spoon and said: 'Don't do everything at once.' She got them to name each material in turn, and repeated the task by saying something to emphasize that they should add a few drops and see what happens to each material, emphasizing her wish for them to work in pairs co-operatively.

John and Nigel reached for the magnifiers immediately. I observed Nigel and Ian most closely. They quickly tried dropping water on to each material, fulfilling the task as set with a little lateral exploration, such as when Ian touched the sand where it had been wetted. Nigel offered Ian the hand lens. Soon Ian asked Angela: 'What next?' She encouraged them to look more closely and to put more water into the sand 'to see what happens'. They pressed on with this, Ian telling Nigel that as he used the magnifier he looked as if he had a bigger face. Ian commented that the soil was 'waterproof'. They added water to powder paint saying: 'This is making real paint', and discussed things they knew about how to mix water with paint.

By this stage, quite a lot of the time allocated for this session remained, but Angela seemed to feel that its value neared exhaustion and she considered winding it up. Some co-operation and close observation had been evident, but things appeared to Angela to be getting a little out of control, unproductive and messy. However, Angela felt unable to do this because of 'wasting' my visit, and also because of the special arrangement that had been made with the other teacher in the bay. So Angela seemed to relax a little, and allowed the activity to continue with less teacherly interference. I think that Angela was experiencing some 'de-skilling', or a 'burden of incompetence' (MacDonald and Rudduck, 1971). I felt that the pupils had not yet shown a particularly good scientific response, but had seemed to be using 'producer strategies', giving more attention to the novel effects of the magnifier and the satisfying familiarity of mixing paint. However, what happened shortly afterwards *was* spontaneous and unpredicted:

Ian: The paint has dissolved.
Nigel: Soggy.

They compared the effect of the water on different materials and began to notice patterns about when water 'dissolved' the material or 'went under' and when it 'stayed on top'. Before turning to try this out on the leaves, Ian speculated that water would go into the veins of the leaf, and later he asserted that this had happened. Angela asked him if he could see if it had, and also suggested a development of his line of investigation – trying again on the reverse side of the leaf. (My notes do not record the outcome of this.) A little later, Nigel picked up a container of dissolved paint and moved it towards a leaf, then paused to look at Ian, then at Angela. As Nigel hesitated, Ian saw him and guessed what Nigel seemed to want to do, and Ian did it for himself. So then Nigel also went ahead and poured a few drops of paint on to a leaf, saying quietly to himself: 'See what it looks like with paint on.' Nigel looked at the drops of paint through the magnifier as he then spread them out over the leaf with the spoon. Others in the group began exploratory play, John using a leaf stalk to print repeated marks on paper. Nigel began to spread liquid paint onto the foil. Ian said to Angela (as if to provoke her to admonish Nigel): 'Look at what Nigel is doing.' Angela ignored this, so Ian joined in adding water with Nigel. Ian: 'It sinks through.' Angela: 'Foil?' Nigel: 'It doesn't sink through.'

There were signs that the pupils were a little tentative about investigating freely because of a degree of unfamiliarity with this kind of opportunity, and they wanted approval for their actions. Having received it, they went on to retrieve liquid paint from a piece of paper it had soaked into by squeezing the paper, but failed to get the same result from foil. They tried leaf printing the paint on the foil, comparing the results with paper, and also folding foil then opening it up to see if a symmetrical pattern was produced. They gathered a considerable amount of varied experience through making these comparisons about the behaviour of different materials. In their discussion with Angela after the activity phase, many ideas were elicited from the pupils about the capacity of various materials to soak up water, allow it to pass through, take paint, and so on. They could list those materials from the set provided which would or would not allow water to pass through. One pupil hypothesized that this was due to the presence or absence of little holes. Broad agreement existed about most items on the list other than leaves, which provoked some controversy. Angela and I were both delighted with these scientific investigative responses which demonstrated pupils' capacities to gather experiences in ways that superficially seemed like aimless play, but which were related in the pupils' minds with many justified personal theories which bore a good likeness to scientific ones.

Issues Raised by this Vignette

Reconsidering the Role of Science Knowledge in Teaching and Learning

During our discussion after the session, I asked Angela what her conceptual knowledge aims had been for the session. None had been mentioned beforehand, but it transpired that Angela *had* expected them to learn various things (for example: water tends to stay on top of certain materials, such as powder paint, and be absorbed by others, including leaves, as part of their developing knowledge about properties of water), and that the pupils' apparent difficulty in arriving at this knowledge fairly quickly had been one of the frustrations Angela had felt about the session, which had tempted her to end it prematurely. I suggested that in comparison with the teacher-controlled, demonstration type of session, which Angela and her pupils were used to, it was her apprehensions about not only the vagueness of the knowledge outcomes, but also the comparative lack of teacher control which might have caused her to feel dissatisfaction at that point. Maybe she then gave up worrying that they would pour water over everything! Angela considered this view, saying that whilst she would allow pupils to try something if she thought that they would learn something, at this point in the session, she considered that they had got all they would be able to get out of it.

I interpret this statement in the following way. As a teacher, Angela had expectations about what items of scientific conceptual knowledge and understanding can potentially be learned within a specific context (of certain pupils and their needs and abilities, the resources available – including time, and so on), and s/he may hold particular parts of this knowledge and understanding as 'objectives in mind' or intended learning outcomes. As long as the teacher's on-the-spot grasp of the situation suggests that these objectives may be achieved, albeit with further teacher intervention, then s/he will persevere with it. Her difficulty with this practice, as I saw it, was how to ensure an appropriate match between the chosen objectives and these particular learners with their distinct (and unknown) existing knowledge and interests. In this case, her theory-in-use was to think mainly about the objectives themselves, having made her best assumptions about the pupils from such things as knowing their preceding school work. In short, decisions about the match between pupils' needs and objectives are made externally to the pupils' responses at the time of the session and prior to the event, so that when pupil responses during it do not appear to match the objectives, the session may be aborted. The degree of freedom exercised by pupils is limited to those responses which approximate to the teacher's knowledge and expectations of understanding. This kind of theory-in-use could be called 'teaching objectives'. There are always such limitations to children's learning imposed by the teacher's planning which is too closely tied to knowledge objectives rather than aims which include knowledge gain within a broader conception of the science learning intended. No teaching plan can predict children's responses, except in very closely constrained conditions, which are more like a behaviourist kind of 'shaping' of children's responses than a constructivist inquiry situation.

What transpired next was a scene with a different kind of learning which was the basis for Angela to move away from 'teaching objectives' towards 'teaching children'. The kind of learning which came about was constructivist rather than behaviourist in character. The children's responses were ones resulting from their own creations of meaning from their experiences.

During the ensuing period, which could be characterized as exploratory play, pupils tacitly drew on what they already knew, and acted on what interested them about the things provided so as to develop new meanings for themselves by being scientific (as well as being aesthetic, literate, and so on) about the experiences. In doing this they were, in part, creating their own knowledge and understanding objectives for these areas of learning. One major advantage of pupils having some part to play in the determination of learning objectives for themselves is obviously that of the much closer match to personal needs and interests, which are important parts of the individual starting points. Many of the pupil-initiated activities were partially replicating things that they knew they could do, and might have done fairly recently in school, for example printing from a shape such as a piece of potato or getting symmetrical patterns by folding paper with ink or paint marks on it and opening it up. But, unlike the apparently mindless mixing of paint which they did during the first phase of the session, this seemed to have much more learning purpose in that they were testing hypotheses about the applicability to these new materials of known knowledge and techniques, and were extending their knowledge of the behaviour of these materials in contact with one another. They undertook other activities which applied existing, relevant knowledge about the materials, such as knowing that leaves have veins in them which carry water. They were behaving as if the session had been set up with an investigative purpose. It hadn't. However, the relaxation of Angela's control had allowed them, apprehensively at first, to subvert it to one in which the theory-in-use was more like what could be called 'teaching children'.

Another advantage of pupils having some control over their learning objectives is that the link between the knowledge learned and the process of learning it, is the one that seems most sensible to the learners at that time. The natural, that is to say uninhibited, learning process which young pupils often show is one in which there is intimate interaction between thinking and acting. This is not easy to see because of the speed and the variation in the sequences and directions of thought and action which they can take. When the teacher's approach is that of 'teaching children', s/he is acting as an enabler to such processes. This includes using public science knowledge to encourage pupils to discipline their thinking by stimulating them to consider alternative ideas, and to introduce fresh interpretations and concepts. But each pupil often needs, to some extent, to have his/her knowledge constructed out of direct experiences and dialogues *before* such challenges can best be met.

This is not to vilify and deny a place for a 'teaching objectives' approach as an espoused theory. Of course, a learner can gain much by following a linear path through certain experiences determined by a teacher so as to offer to the learner the ideas seen as justified by the teacher's conception of what is rational and valuable. But the learner's resources for benefiting from this mode include his/her active exploration of similar things and reflective thought about them prior to entering into a dialogue, and too often 'teaching objectives' can inhibit the achievement of real dialogue.

Figure 3.1 summarizes the two approaches as rival *espoused theories*.

In practice, there are undoubtedly many variants and intermediate versions of the alternatives juxtaposed here. Nevertheless, each depends upon a deeper set of values and beliefs which form two distinct ideologies of education.

Angela's original theory-in-use of teaching science, from her own account of it, could be characterized as a fairly clear version of a 'teaching objectives' theory, even to the extent of the teacher carrying out the active manipulation of materials by demonstration. But, for my visit to observe Angela in her classroom, she changed her practice. The course had probably been affecting her ideals of primary science, and she had begun to espouse a theory which moved away from the 'pure' form of 'teaching objectives', for example: she stated that her aim for the session was one quality of

Figure 3.1 Summary of the two approaches

A 'teaching objectives' approach	Components of teaching and learning	A 'teaching children' approach
Assessed and used before the session to determine objectives at a specific level and in a relatively fixed way.	Definition of pupils' needs	Assessed by the teacher before the session, at a general level, to guide the creation of open opportunities for learning. Possibly known tacitly by the pupils. Assessed by the teacher more specifically during the session.
The set of knowledge items and understanding selected by the teacher before the session as intended learning outcomes.	Knowledge objectives	Determined loosely beforehand by the teacher's choice of learning opportunity, and specifically by the pupil (tacitly) during the session as s/he responds to it autonomously.
The teacher's conception of the most rational sequence and the best form of activities and ideas for pupils to follow in order to achieve the objectives. Processes have an *instrumental* value to the teacher, as a means to achieve the chosen objectives.	Learning processes	Within the frame set by the teacher, the pupil selects her/his own version of a rational sequence, and chooses or creates learning activities as an expression of her/his personal capacity to be scientific. This is of *intrinsic* value to the teacher, who can challenge both the sequence chosen (and other parts of the process) and the knowledge developed (as the product).
Selected beforehand by the teacher to match the predetermined learning process.	Learning resources	Broadly anticipated by the teacher, but chosen specifically by the pupil during the session as part of her/his grasp of the inquiry.
Tasks are specified to establish the predetermined learning process, and the session should not be allowed to deviate from this or else unwanted experiential 'results' may appear and 'incorrect' learning may take place.	Teaching strategies	By close observation of the pupils' responses and discussion during the session, the teacher discovers at specific levels what are the pupils' needs and objectives. The teacher then creates an appropriate teaching response to this 'teachable moment', which aims to discipline their thinking with science knowledge.

A 'teaching objectives' approach	Components of teaching and learning	A 'teaching children' approach
This is assumed to be essentially the public knowledge of the concepts of science as an academic subject.	Implied view of the nature of science	Not only the conceptual knowledge, but also the procedural learning capacities and attitudes involved in being scientific.
This is used prior to the session to assist the teacher in determining the knowledge objectives.	The role of public science knowledge	It is used during the session to assist the teacher in disciplining the pupil's thinking *if* and *when* this is judged to be the appropriate teaching response.
By seeking specific evidence for the achievement of the pre-set learning objectives.	Assessment of the pupil's learning	By judging qualities of mind inferred from the pupil's response to this particular context whilst taking into account the manifestations of his/her perceived needs and objectives.
By seeking specific evidence for the achievement of the pre-set learning objectives (as if teaching can cause learning!).	Assessment of the teaching	By judging the extent to which the whole session constituted an enabling rather than a constraining context for learning to be scientific and developing pupils' science knowledge.

the learning process – pupil co-operativeness. Yet her theory-in-use during the first phase of the session was that of a 'teaching objectives' approach. Angela implied this when she recognized that her (unstated) knowledge objectives were not being achieved, and hence the session was seen to be failing with regard to both the teaching and the learning. In our debate about when accurate scientific knowledge is best used in teaching, we explored the teacher's perception of a dilemma between encouraging knowledge outcomes and strengthening investigative capacities. We used an example from this session: that of the leaf soaking in water. Angela believed that leaves do soak up water by immersion, and that this idea should be encouraged as correct scientific knowledge. I argued that there could be legitimate doubt about such a belief as a general statement, thinking about leaves with waxy coverings; and, even if it were true, might not the amounts of water absorbed be so small as to be difficult or impossible to observe or measure without special equipment or methods? So, in this example the teacher may wisely judge that a preferable strategy is not to stress 'official' science knowledge, but to leave the question open to encourage pupil investigation and logical debate about the evidence available at the time to arrive at a *justified* and *tentative* personal opinion, even if it temporarily appears to contradict 'official' science knowledge. This retains the integrity of the learner's own scientific learning processes, albeit with the expectation that there is room for further learning at some appropriate point in the future. Angela had some reservations about this initially.

I neglected to ask her, but presumably Angela had not intended the character of the second phase of the session, yet she tolerated its uncertainty and showed signs of practices which would form the basis for a more 'teaching children' kind of theory-in-use.

With the same vignette in mind, attention now turns to its significance for Angela's professional development.

Angela's Step in the Dark

In our post-session discussion Angela and I turned to the question of the pupils' investigative capacities. Angela said that she had never before seen these pupils persevere with a task and display engagement with it for such a long time and in such a self-sustained way. I asked her why she thought this had happened. She replied that the pupils might not have found previous activities as interesting as this had been. She did not regard her own interventions as having led directly to the learning which took place during the visit. I asked why the pupils had found this more interesting. Angela said she had been thinking more deeply and noticed that in the past she had felt it necessary to 'give so much input to get anything back from them', and she had feared it would be the same during the visit. The second phase of this session had turned out to be the opposite of this. Angela had not needed to 'give much input' at all, but 'got a lot back from them'. I think that this experience was similar for Angela to a point in Lesley's development (described pp. 110–12) when her pupils also showed unexpectedly rewarding scientific responses to an opportunity to be investigative.

The impact of such events can be called 'seeing is believing'. Until someone can see for themselves, in their own situation, events that are manifestations of qualities which have only otherwise been encountered indirectly, there is a natural doubt that they exist or that they can be achieved in one's own situation. This may be the only way in which the problem can be overcome of a teacher saying: 'That wouldn't work with my kids.' However, this is not a matter of 'shaping' a teacher's beliefs by changing his/her behaviour. This would be to try to by-pass the teacher's own generative capacities, such as that of constructing personal understanding of the processes she/he is engaged in. In Angela's case, she had created the context for the pupils' responses herself, albeit during the different circumstances of my presence and with some good luck that the pupils rose so positively to the occasion! Her willingness to tolerate the ambiguity and threat of the events at the time, and to respond to it herself in an adventurous way, was an example of 'stepping into the dark'. In other words, Angela acted in ways that were a departure from the theory-in-use she had appeared to use. The interactions with the pupils during the second phase did not show the same intention to guide them towards knowledge objectives as in the first phase, but was supportive of the more open investigation initiated by the pupils. More insight into this phenomenon is needed, but there seems sufficient evidence already from several manifestations of 'stepping into the dark' to regard it as a significant contributor to the value of a classroom visit of this kind to a teacher during a continuing professional development course. The presence of a stranger in the classroom quite often seems, at some point, to stimulate the teacher to be experimental and depart from usual practice, overcoming the opposite tendency to play safe and remain strictly within familiar practice. The direction in which the departure moves often seems to be one that tacitly reflects ideas that have been discussed during the course which the teacher is attracted to, but has never put into action before.

During the validation interview, eight months after the end of the course, Angela remembered the value of the visit in the following way:

Angela: ...we're kept on such a tight rein in this school, it's difficult for outsiders to understand the set up.

Peter: So do you think that limited the value of the classroom visit then?

Angela: No, it helped actually 'cos it meant I had to do something about it. With you coming in I had to do something. If you hadn't come in I would have had no reason to do something different. It made me do it and it was acceptable.

(transcript lines 152–9)

This corroborates the justification for such visits.

It seems certain that Angela 'stepped into the dark' to the extent that the pupils showed responses not previously recognized by her. Subsequently, Angela repeated the activity with other groups, which had a somewhat smaller resource provision, but produced similar results as far as the degree to which the pupils were self-motivated and showed high levels of curiosity. The school situation, with its tightly controlled curriculum planning and team-teaching organization, had made her feel unable to expand and develop her science teaching as she had wished. This proved to be an intractable problem which dominated the rest of Angela's participation in the course. Also, the topics chosen within the school did not offer as much science potential to Angela as she wished. For example, there was the activity of planting bulbs which put the pupils through a set routine that included counting, weighing, classifying, and so on. Angela cited this saying that further science opportunities were limited 'because they can't be really exploratory and, for example, cut them open and see the flowers inside'. Nevertheless, by the end of the course Angela had developed a very clear exposition of a 'teaching children' type of espoused theory which was largely consistent with her accounts of the theory-in-use evident from her action research.

The phenomenon of taking a 'step in the dark' is an antidote to the Machiavellian edict about change.

> It should be borne in mind that there is nothing more difficult to arrange, more doubtful of success, and more dangerous to carry through than initiating change. ... because ... men [sic] are generally incredulous, never really trusting new things unless they have tested them by experience.

This suggests that although change is difficult, a desired (but feared) change can be achieved by testing it in practice, seeking experimental experience of it in a context with minimal threat and maximum support whilst remaining within one's own sense of one's competence and knowing that, finally, one retains control over the decision about its value.

The Assessment of Angela's Personal Professional Development

Although she did not seem to me to have achieved the same 'amount' of professional change as some of the others by the end of the course, Angela produced careful and detailed descriptions of classroom events, reflected on them evaluatively and discussed them openly, honestly and thoughtfully with critical friends at university. In short, the processes of reflecting in action and reflection on action seemed to be operating for her powerfully, and there was no doubt about the strength of her commitment. Therefore, I attribute what I perceived to be the comparative slowness of her development to two main difficulties: first, the external one – the school-based constraints; and second, an internal one – Angela's inhibitions about taking more personal control over aspects of her practice where this would have been legitimate and justifiable. In her statement of personal professional progress, Angela wrote at the end of the course: 'Although the situation does place some constraints, my attitude had something to do with it. I have learned a lot from this course, not least about myself.'

At the validation interview Angela said:

> I think the hardest time on the course was when I was wrestling, as you say here, [reference to the case study] with my frustrations, because I

found it very hard to come to terms with what was being said on the one hand at school, and what people were saying at university, which I thought was much more realistic, and actually getting the two to knit together. ... But you have to work how you have to work. It really made me think hard about what I was doing.

I drew the following lessons for my practice from my reflections on this case:

1   The pace and 'amount' of a teacher's development cannot be predicted beforehand with certainty, but can be understood in retrospect by reference to the teacher's subjective experiences.
2   Ultimately only that person can act for her/himself. If a course values wisdom, then it must tolerate situations such as this wherein it takes time for the person to make that decision for her/himself.
3   Delays in arriving at a point when knowledge is freely and wisely acted upon may involve the development by the actor of the capacity to believe in her/himself as someone with the power to intervene in situations that are otherwise perceived to be outside one's own personal influence. The situation may of course prove *not* to be one that can be influenced, and therefore the wisest intervention may be *not* to act. However, an important factor in the overall capacity of a person to develop themselves professionally is having the self-image of someone possessing the confidence and ability to make a positive impact on appropriate situations. This seems to be similar to the notion of *cognitive initiative*, which is one of three clusters of abilities identified by Klemp (1977) and described by Elliott (1991b) as commonly exercised by above-average performers in diverse occupations which involve problem solving and decision-making in complex situations.

Improved Scientific Learning and Changes in Chris's Teaching

One of the distinctive features of Chris's participation in the course is the detail I have of two episodes of primary science which illuminate both the improvement of her pupils' science learning and the development of her teaching. The first episode is the work I observed during my classroom visit, and the second is reported by Chris in her classroom-based study. This section is based on comparisons between the two. I have selected them for close attention because of the value of comparing earlier and later examples of things which are claimed to have developed. In a hypothetico-deductive method of research an attempt to obtain a pre-test and post-test comparison would have been an important part of the study. But I am not a neutral, disinterested outsider who wishes to prove or disprove truths, therefore this material is not included. I was an insider to these events; someone with *interest* in them. Of the six definitions of 'interest' in the *Oxford Illustrated Dictionary* (1962), four are legal and/or financial in meaning. However, I am using the word here with the meanings conveyed by the other two definitions:

4   Selfish pursuit of one's own welfare; *make*, bring personal interest to bear (*with* person).
5   Concern, curiosity or quality exciting them.

My 'selfish pursuit' is my professional development in seeking improvement in my teaching of this course, and my 'concern' is to increase my understanding of teachers' professional development. Operating within this framework, as a tutor-researcher, I take Chris's claims, that her pupils' scientific learning and her own teaching have both developed, as statements that can be tested against the evidence available, subjected to our critical reflections as independent, self-aware people, and used as resources for my research. I am not applying preconceived and immutable categories of primary science and professional development as standards against which to test Chris's work. I am drawing on Chris's work and my evolving ideas to reflect on each other. Therefore, I wish to look more closely at the comparison between the earlier and later episodes to deepen my own understanding of the qualities of the teaching and learning that went on, and to consider the relationship between these things and my ideas about Chris's professional development. It is worth noting that this value position has been made explicit. A 'traditional' educational researcher might wish to make similar kinds of comparisons under the guise of an 'objective' approach in which there is no comparable statement of the value position taken by the research. For example, school effectiveness research may attempt to uncover some kind of mechanism and identify cause-and-effect relationships in teaching and learning. Such an approach to research has its own frame of values, which according to Elliott (1996) are to do with gaining knowledge as information to be used for control and to encourage orderliness, uniformity, adherence, hierarchical leadership and 'technical efficiency'.

'The search for the mechanism, the *efficient cause*, which enables one to predict the outcomes of schooling is shaped by a set of control values which define schooling as a coercive process of social induction' (Elliott, 1996: 210). What follows is not a search for a mechanism but an exploration of examples of development.

The Earlier Episode

During the classroom visit (see pp. 46–8), I observed one of the six working groups of five 7 and 8 year olds. 'My' group was comparing the rate of the passage of water through a range of materials as part of a 'circus' of activities organized around a topic on water. Before they began work it was evident that they already knew about some of the things which the task was intended to enable them to 'find out'. They knew that water does not pass through PVC ('It is used to make raincoats'), and that water goes through other materials more quickly the second time it is applied, that is, when the material has already been wetted. In the notes, which I discussed with Chris and left with her at the end of the visit, I wrote:

There was very little talk between group members during the session. They still tested PVC even though they were all absolutely certain that no water would pass through, and they dutifully followed the set procedure for the other materials, saying aloud their predicted time for a measured amount of water to pass through each sample of material. No one commented on the different thicknesses of different materials as a possible reason for the different times taken for the water to soak through. They were surprised by one material, Binka, when the water stayed on the top in a large globule for a long time before soaking in. No one in the group questioned or hypothesized about this, or suggested anything else to try. Almost the only talk was when someone felt it was time to take their turn with one or other of the tasks – notably operating the stop watch! After making individual predictions of the time it would take for the water to pass through each sample of material, the actual times were measured and recorded with no comment other than personal, competitive ones like S's: 'I told you it would be more than you said.'

They have practised a method for carrying out the comparison, showing a well-organized, co-operative approach, with an apparent appreciation of being systematic and accurate, which seems well developed for their age. They enjoyed the work. I'm not sure what they learned from writing their accounts.

How do they see the reports from the other groups about tasks they have already done themselves? The point at which strong interest was obviously aroused was when there was disagreement about the findings from a particular task done by another group. During the reporting back, one group gave an account of events which was disputed factually by other groups who referred back to their own previous experience of the task. Apart from this moment of controversy, which still did not broach theorization about the phenomena, there was a marked lack of expression of strong interest or curiosity.

The only explicit expression of a pupil voluntarily theorizing about the phenomena under examination in the task was S who drew attention to the relationship between the longer time taken for the water to soak through two thicknesses of linen as compared with one. When I asked S why he thought the water went through the blotting paper more slowly than through the linen, he said that the hole was smaller. It became clear that he meant the single hole which he believed exists at the lowest point of every conical piece of material placed in the conical filter funnel, not the many minute holes in all permeable materials.

These observations support the view that investigative and theoretical scientific thinking was largely absent from the pupils' learning. They were mainly concerned to fulfil the expectations of the task set by the card in a routine, unthinking way, having already gained an expectation about what was to happen from observation of other groups who had done the task previously. No doubt the varied experiences could have contributed to the erection of a network of ideas in a pupil's mind, but there was no externally visible indication that a pupil was constructing new meaning through seeking an answer to a personally held question or testing a personally held hypothesis. The scientific qualities of the experience were restricted to the techniques being practised and the use of the overall methods set by the teacher, without evidence of understanding the significance of either. Pupil progression and continuity did not seem to be dominant characteristics of this approach. The pupils' performance of a restricted range of technical, investigative processes was instrumental to the acquisition of the scientific knowledge about water chosen by the teacher. This led to 'task orientation' in which the pupils used 'producer strategies'. The pupils' constructive scientific learning at their own conceptual level was largely denied in this approach.

Having observed the other groups in the class at the same time, albeit much more superficially, I did not have any grounds to doubt Chris's assertion that the responses described in detail from 'my' group were typical of all of the others.

The general pattern of a directive style in primary science teaching has been called 'activitymania' by Moscovici and Nelson (1998), and is characterized by the following:

- a barrage of activities,
- a collection of pre-packaged, short, hands-on activities,
- each activity has a beginning, middle and end,
- the content and outcome are defined by the teacher,
- students follow procedures without questioning the reasons for their actions, and
- a disconnection between science and the students' real world experiences are often perceived.

These authors claim that this is not an adequate way to enable children to be scientific, and they propose the term 'inquiry' to denote a pattern of teaching, which they regard as much more consistent with constructivist principles of learning, with the following characteristics:

- student work which is related to *students'* interests and questions *from the beginning*,
- plans for a long-term process approach rather than short-term coverage of products,
- emphasis on 'students' higher order cognitive skills' (p. 16),
- tutor involvement which enriches the students' inquiry learning processes, and
- also peer and self-assessment as part of the process.

Some of these characteristics were adopted by Chris in her teaching (as the following episode shows).

The Later Episode

By comparison with the episode of teaching just described, a later stage in Chris's development is represented by part of Chris's classroom-based study. It provides the following transcript as an illustration of the kind of response routinely shown by the pupils at the later stages of her study. Children were observing the effects of placing first salt and then sugar on their tongues. My comments are in the column on the right.

J: It [salt] tastes worse at the back [i.e. of the tongue]	Observation presumably based on a question about the sensitivity of different parts of the tongue to the different substances.
P: It [sugar] tastes more at the front and it's nicer.	Observation in a similar vein.
D: Can we put sugar on our tongue and look at it instead of tasting?	Proposal for a change in observation implying a different question such as: What does sugar look like when it is being tasted on the tongue?
Ch: Look at it and see how it tastes.	An attempt to correct or clarify.
Ca: No, see how it *looks* – what happens when you look [she looks].	A rejection of this attempt in order to retain the impetus of D's idea for the investigation.
D: It's liquidized.	A close observation of dissolving.
P: It looks like an ice on your tongue.	An observational comparison between tiny crystals of sugar and ice.
J: It's all changed to water.	A theory-laden observation.

Ch: My hands are all sticky.

A less significant observation.

D: It gets wet and changes into water.
    That might be how it does it.
    We taste by turning it into water.

A theorization that the substance changes in contact with the watery covering of the tongue and turns into water in order to cause tasting.

P: It dissolves.

Alternative to 'turns into water'.

T: What do you mean?

Request for clarification.

P: When you look at it, it goes
    littler and littler.

Restatement of the observation of sugar crystals dissolving.

Ch: Salt doesn't go quickly.

Comparative observation.

Ca: Which one goes quicker? Salt?
    Salt is disgustinger than sugar.

Meaning of 'quicker' unclear, but possible to do with the relative speed of dissolving. 'Disgustinger' refers to the taste of the salt.

J: Salt is stronger than sugar.

Presumably a stronger *taste*.

Co: It's harder. It's bigger.

Meaning of 'harder' unclear. 'Bigger' may be relevant to an emerging theory about relative speed of tasting.

T: How do you know? [D puts salt
    and sugar side by side]

Request for evidence. Sets up a comparative observation.

D: Sugar is bigger, definitely. Salt is like
    circles. It might be harder to get into
    the taste buds. Let's look carefully.
    Put it on a plate.

Further observational comparisons. Development of the theory of how these substances are tasted is sought: if the particles have to enter the taste buds, their relative size may affect the ease with which they are tasted.

P: No. Something black. We haven't
    got black. We've got brown.
    [Returns with some brown paper.
    D isolates a small amount of each.
    Others agree they can now see it
    better.]

Suggested change in observational technique based upon the improvement in ease of observing small

	objects if there is a contrast in colour or tone between the object and the background.
D: Sugar is like squares. Salt is round.	Observation.
Ch: Sugar looks like chips in glass.	Comparative observation.

Much of the most impressive scientific thought in this excerpt is contributed by D who proposes and follows through a line of investigation involving an abstract theory of taste which is scientifically accurate. Substances depend upon their characteristic of being soluble in water to affect taste buds in the tongue and cause the sensation of taste. Therefore, both the degree of solubility and the speed of dissolving of any particular substance affect the experience of taste. D appears to be moving towards this view. Although the word 'dissolve' is not used in D's account, a fairly well-substantiated association of tasting with dissolving is expressed in: 'It gets wet and changes into water. That might be how it does it. We taste by turning it into water.' This is tentatively linked with the idea that the substance being tasted enters taste buds in some way as expressed in: 'Sugar is bigger, definitely. Salt is like circles. It might be harder to get into the taste buds. Let's look carefully. Put it on a plate.' More important than the comparison between D's theory and the conventional scientific theory of taste is the comparison between D's theory and its basis in D's prior thought and the observations carried out. Aided by some of the other pupils, and slightly hindered by another, D made good investigative progress and created an imaginative leap in understanding.

As before, Chris maintained that this typified the quality of the pupils' science at this stage. I am unable to draw on my own observations to comment on this claim, but have no reason to suggest that it is a distorted one. On the contrary, the openness and honesty apparent in course members' self accounts in the later stages of the course have encouraged me to have confidence in the accuracy of such statements. No doubt this was a particularly impressive example in order to warrant its inclusion in Chris's study, but I do not have any reasons to believe it to be an atypical example.

Review

I regard the comparison between the two episodes as suggesting the following hypotheses about science teaching and learning in primary schools (illustrative evidence is given in italic).

1   Young children who are learning scientifically are able to theorize imaginatively about their experiences, linking their existing ideas with new observations, creating new ideas and testing them by seeking further evidence.

During the later episode about taste, D questioned the behaviour of sugar crystals on the tongue and observed them dissolve, leading to the hypothesis that 'turning into water' is a necessary step by which the sugar causes the sensation of taste in the taste buds.

2   Children who are placed in situations where they are required to follow tasks set by the teacher do not tend to show the kinds of abilities referred to in 1.

During the earlier episode about water, there was no discussion of reasons for each pupil's prediction of the time before it was measured, or of the results afterwards. They seemed to make off the cuff guesses in a disinterested way, one pupil merely wishing to guess more accurately than another in a personally competitive way, without explaining reasons for the guesses.

3   The situations which foster good science learning are ones in which the children have intellectual control over the following main components of the situation:

   •   selection or preferably identification of the question or hypothesis to be pursued;
   •   selection or preferably design of the investigatory strategies to be used;
   •   selection or preferably creation of the answers to the questions and tests of the hypotheses.

The only intellectual requirements on D appear to have been to find out something about taste, therefore there was the freedom (and responsibility) to start from pupils' existing, relevant, personally held ideas. For S and the others in the water episode, there was very little intellectual control. Their thoughts were apparently confined to adherence to the set task, and opportunities to think scientifically were not explicitly taken.

This does not *prove* anything mechanistic about primary science or teacher professional development, and it is not intended to do so. It is part of the progress of my own understanding through searching for interactions between my existing ideas and careful interpretation of new experiences. I would argue that the comparisons above illustrate improvements in the quality of Chris's pupils' science learning, and I attribute this to development in her teaching of science. Pupil improvements could of course have been the result of a variety of factors, such as mental maturation which proceeded independently of her teaching and outside of her control. For my purposes, I need to know only about the extent to which she acted as an educator to such improvements, and in doing so developed her educative capacities. I believe that if Chris had continued to teach science in the same way as before and had not joined the course, the pupils' science learning would not have shown as much improvement as it did. This belief about all of the course members is impossible to test independently and exhaustively, but rests largely on my judgement which admittedly is subject to my bias. But my bias is exonerated to the extent to which the course members regard this to be true themselves when given the opportunity freely to express their views and substantiate them, as has happened.

Kay and the 'White Powders' Episode

This is an example of how a course member used her interaction with critical friends during university sessions to assist her development. (See 'Kay's Participation in the Course', p. 54.)

During one of the preceding course sessions, a practical workshop had included the exploration of a collection of 'mystery' white powders that are harmless and commonly found in the kitchen. One of the several scientific outcomes of the exploration by course members was the link between the comparative solubility in water of the powders and the strength of taste sensation they gave in the mouth. (This is because a substance has to be soluble in order to stimulate taste buds.) Kay took the idea back to her class-room, and gave a similar range of powders to the children hoping that they would notice the comparative solubility. For example, one of the powders, flour, is virtually insoluble, whereas another, sugar, dissolves quickly and in relatively large amounts, whilst the other powders showed intermediate levels of solubility. The first group had added each powder one by one to separate amounts of water, placing tops on the tubes to enable them to be shaken, and they had found out things about solubility which had satisfied Kay. However, at some point, there was a chance discovery that under certain circumstances one combination of the liquids effervesced which caused the top to be blown off its tube.

When it was the turn of the second group to repeat the same task, Kay wrote the following in her classroom-based study (p. 16):

> Instead of using any system, they each piled a bit of everything into a container with water and shook it. Their aim was to make the top pop off as they had seen the previous group do. When asked which powder had made the top pop off, they couldn't say because they had mixed the powders up. Even after discussing this problem with the group, and giving them a chance to observe the powders again, they still could not say anything about dissolving.
>
> I discussed this disappointment with my critical friends at university. Somebody said: 'Oh they weren't doing what you wanted, were they?' My initial feelings were the usual ones of inadequacy. I took the blame for their initial lack of interest in finding out whether the powders

dissolved or not. Yet, on reflection, they were very interested in the powders.

Kay was able to accept and give support to a divergence from her intended path for the activity, but, nevertheless she expected a similar knowledge outcome related to her main purpose for the session – to know about dissolving. She concluded that the surprising behaviour had been a manifestation of a lower level of scientific 'maturity' than that of the previous group. The task was interpreted as having required a kind of thinking that these children were not yet ready to carry out, and Kay wrote that: 'My previous methods of working had not brought this to light, but, through allowing myself to observe, I had made myself aware that there were some children who need more time to explore.'

This led to the action step that questions posed to pupils should not presuppose the right answer, but be open, to make the children think.

This vignette raises the following issues for me.

The Various Understandings of Educational Aims for Science

This analysis uses the typology which originates in the Ford T Project (Elliott, 1975). The purpose is to clarify communication and thought about the ways in which teaching and learning can happen. The three dimensions are as follows:

1   The overall degree of intellectual dependence which learners actually have upon the teacher's authority position – are they thinking for themselves? (*independent*) or are they thinking what the teacher wants them to think (*dependent*)?

2   The emphasis in the teacher's own aims upon preconceived subject knowledge (*subject-centred aims*) as against the way in which learners learn (*learner-centred aims*).

3   The degree of teacher direction of the learning activity to be performed is expressed by three terms along a single dimension. Where the teacher prescribes beforehand what the learners are to do, this is a *directed strategy*. Where tasks are set beforehand, but the teacher elicits any problems perceived by the learners in performing them, and responds to their questions or suggestions by modifying tasks accordingly, this is a *guided strategy*. An *open-ended strategy* is one in which the teacher avoids imposing constraints on learners' abilities to direct their own learning, and also seeks to remove any such constraints.

Kay had been looking *only* for the achievement of a knowledge aim. Even though she had been prepared to tolerate unexpected changes in the activity, she had not anticipated it could lead to the acquisition of different knowledge. She did not seem to appreciate at first that the pupils were less likely to learn explicitly about dissolving when their attention was attracted to solving the practical problem of recreating a fascinating experience. Perhaps it seemed to her that as long as the activity included the experience of dissolving powders into water then, regardless of the *child's* aim for his/her actions, an understanding of dissolving should be achieved.

Also, she had not yet begun to see product or knowledge aims as being interdependent with process or investigative skill types of aim. Subject to various factors in each context, principally the learners' interests, I began to see that the educational worthwhileness of an experience can be understood as a compound of the two kinds of aim, in which one kind may tend to assume a greater significance than the other, but never displace it. The first group must have accepted Kay's guidance as to what to do with the powders, and learned about dissolving as she had wanted. I suspect it had been a *formal/structured/guided* situation in which the children were intellectually dependent on the teacher. The aim was to learn subject knowledge and the strategy was interactive, yet under the guidance of the teacher. With the second group, the situation had changed to *informal/unstructured/open-ended* since the children were exercising intellectual independence, formulating their own problem-solving aim and devising their own strategies to achieve it. After expressing her disappointment at the failure of the second group to achieve pre-set knowledge aims, Kay then experienced a feeling of inadequacy in not realising that she had acted against her declared valuing of child-centredness. She arrived at an action step which seems appropriate to a growth of the investigative element of practice – asking more open questions.

The various aspects of this issue need to be confronted repeatedly across many situations in order to appreciate the interdependence of the two expressions of the aim of learning science – gaining scientific knowledge as a learning product and being investigative as a learning process. Kay felt guilty and self reproachful about what she perceived to be her failure to use logical thought. This might be an appropriate reaction if a teacher regards teaching as being about applying clear rules to any situation. But she was instead trying to do something much more complex and subtle, which was to interpret a guiding principle whose relevance to a particular context needed to be discovered through reflection on the principle and action in the context interdependently. Having had little experience of operating with these principles, it was natural for her to find it difficult. Kay assumed that to have acted rationally she should have avoided the difficulty by more rigorous thought beforehand, but in professional development, the most 'rigorous' *a priori* theorizing carries no guarantee of wise action because this has to be discovered as situated reasoning by reflection-in-action and reflection-on-action afterwards.

A Closely Associated Issue – the Use of the Idea of 'Levels' in Children's Learning

Kay was happy to attribute a surprising response in which one group was apparently unable to learn something that another group had done, to the explanation that the former were at a lower level of maturity than the latter. I feel that great care has to be taken with the use of explanations such as this. It parallels the way in which those young children, who are being hectored by a teacher (or researcher) to demonstrate scientific knowledge by giving an explanation for something they have observed, simply like to shrug their shoulders, smile and say: 'It's magic!' When faced with a confusing range of imponderables, we may feel the need for catch-all categories, such as 'magic' or 'levels', but they have their dangers. Assigning a child to a lower level may mean abandoning attempts to discover a different way of assisting the desired learning to occur because the child lacks the 'readiness' associated with a lower level. A saving grace is that there is a sense of not 'blaming' the child either for a lack of general intelligence, or for showing some kind of obstinacy. But it also avoids 'blaming' the teacher for misjudgement of one kind or another, and therefore dilutes a teacher's search for an explanation on which s/he could act more creatively. A natural consequence of assigning a pupil to a lower maturational level of ability is to allocate simpler tasks which are thought to be at the lower level in terms of demand, and this may be a self-confirming act.

In this case, my own hypothesis is that it was necessary for the second group to complete their search for the powder with intriguing powers of top-popping before the teacher should attempt to recreate the original situation designed to encourage learning about solubility. Only then would it be reasonable to compare their capacity to understand about solubility with that shown by the first group.

There are dangers in the idea of levels when teaching and learning situations are so complex. The concept alludes to a model of learning in which stepwise, incremental changes of a straightforwardly recognizable kind can reliably be observed in an individual learner's behaviour, and such an assessment can be used to decide in a rather general way what should be learned next. I propose that it should be confined strictly to the situation where a clear diagnosis of *need* can be made, that is, in a context where a learner's immediate and very specific aim appears to the teacher to be frustrated by the *need* for a particular piece of information, a certain idea, or the refinement of a specific skill or technique. Then it is much safer to talk about a lower level. It may be possible to discern a fragment of sequential progress in learning and therefore to talk about levels but only in the context of 'micro-cases'. This argument is one which is also relevant to the assessment of teachers' professional development.

The Development of Kay's Teaching of Science

In the story of the development of Kay's teaching, there is a strengthening of the teacher's role as an enabling influence on the children's scientific powers. Earlier, she had felt it necessary to supply significant parts of the overall scientific pattern of the work, notably the specification of the questions to be answered or the problem to be solved (for example, the secret message writing problem, see pp. 53–4). When things departed from the expected (such as with the white powders), Kay saw it as blameworthy, and herself as culpable. Having set up an activity to teach about the solubility of white powders, Kay saw it as a failure when one group seized upon their observations of the previous group's excitement about one powder in particular which made the cork blow off the top of the tube, and consequently showed no desire to learn about solubility! She did not at that point seem willing to regard their unexpected interest in a different phenomenon as an acceptable basis for their scientific learning. Later, she felt better able to 'let go' of the knowledge strictures she felt she had to impose on their learning and allow her own child-centred preferences to take precedence. During seminars at the university at which the progress of her action research was discussed, her critical community supported her in doing this by offering interpretations of her experience which Kay was prepared to be open towards, allowing her pre-judgements to be risked and tested (see p. 152), and to make concessions to different courses of action. An important aspect of the professional development which can occur in this way is the growth of what Marion Dadds calls the 'expert within' as a journey of professional growth which is:

> often unpredictable, often non-linear, often emotional as well as cerebral. It demands the capacity and strength to ask questions, to analyse and interpret feedback, to discipline the emotions generated by self-study, to change established practices in the light of new understanding, to remain interested and professionally curious.
>
> (Dadds, 1997: 37)

Thus, the main 'perspective transformation' (Holly, 1989) for Kay was probably the reconsideration of the meaning of scientific learning for young children. The phrase 'perspective transformation' denotes that this was not merely an intellectual change for Kay. It was not simply a matter of deciding to adopt a revised definition of science, and then adjust her teaching technique a little, as a consequence. This *might* be so if the relationship between knowledge and action were so simple. Also, this *might* be so if teaching were a technical task that did not involve the self in devotion to ethical goals. But Kay's dedication to the children's learning was such that it was necessary to be able to recognize improvements in the quality of their learning in order for the change to be an acceptable one. Her choice had been to pursue improvements in the pupils' independence, which is the sort of commitment to individual children's best education which Joseph Schwab (1969) calls the 'practical ethic'. The teaching described by Kay in the concluding stage of the course shows how the pupils were showing increased intellectual independence in determining for themselves their own learning aims, strategies and resources, and certain individuals had made particularly impressive progress in comparison with their recently observed learning difficulties (see, for example, Michael on p. 109). Again, a rationalist view of professional development is seen to be partial, misleading and potentially destructive compared with a holistic view of the growth of human capacities.

Pupil Independence in Learning Science

As early in the course as the tutor's classroom visit, Kay had experienced a dilemma between the pupils' need for teacher direction and her ideal of pupil intellectual independence. In response to this, she developed her approach, and by the later stages of the course, during a topic about the school environment, Kay created and then applied four practical principles to her teaching (see 'Kay's Participation in the Course', pp. 54–6).

The practical principles were:

1 Appreciate efforts, whatever the results may be.
2 Avoid the suggestion that the only worthwhile result is the 'right answer' in terms of correct fact and conclusions.
3 Accept what the children find from their investigations as the right answer, providing that they have used their evidence and their reasoning.
4 Allow the children to make sense of their observations for themselves without imposing explanations that are outside or beyond their experience and comprehension.

At the beginning of the topic, Kay wrote: 'Looking back at the methods that I have tried, I realize that the "best" work, the most scientific work, has arisen from self-motivation.'

She planned for her Key Stage One pupils to choose for themselves the size of their working group, the identity of its members, the part of the school field or yard to study and which aspect of it interested them. They responded with excitement, some asking for paper and pencils, others for magnifiers, jam jars, or 'something to dig with'. They were certainly keen to get going. This was especially pleasing remembering how timid many of these children had been six months ago when they would ask questions like: 'Do I write on the top line?' and 'Can I start?'; or would just sit there and say: 'I don't know what to do.'

'It's not until you look back that you see the development both in the children and in yourself. Class discussions were now a two-way thing rather than me talking at them' (Kay's classroom-based study, p. 18).

These developments are familiar to me from my observation of other teachers who were able to take a bold step with their teaching, and let go of some of their control over learning content in order to enable the children to contribute more of themselves to their own learning. Kay switched her attention to an enabling role by talking to the children about their planning and self-organization, aware that there would be variation in their abilities to respond to this opportunity. The range and quality of the investigations that were then carried out were fine examples of scientific learning by young children. An example referred to in the case study is worth quoting here at greater length.

> Michael predicted that the small slugs would be quicker than the large ones, and tried to test this out by placing them all at the one end of a board and trying to race them. It wasn't successful because they wandered to the sides. He then made something to keep them in straight lines. This was a success for me because Michael was hypothesizing, testing his hypotheses and modifying his test. He was thinking scientifically, working independently and gaining knowledge about animal behaviour. He had been a child who sat through the first ten minutes of a handwriting lesson without a pencil because he 'didn't like to ask'. Now he is planning an investigation knowing that he doesn't have to ask because I value his work.
>
> (Kay's classroom-based study, p. 21)

From the perspective expressed by Kay in her four practical principles, the major line of development in her teaching was to try not to be seen by the pupils as scientifically omniscient. Her success in reshaping these expectations was, however, closely linked to other changes which did not appear to receive her explicit attention, but which were, on reflection, also significant contributors to the improvements achieved. The most important of these was the change in the pupils' perception of an increase in Kay's trust in their efforts. Refusing to be omniscient was not merely an intellectual move, but also a personal and moral one that was motivated by Kay's ethical commitment to pupils' intellectual independence. As a critical example, Kay's determination to trust pupils' efforts had transformed her relationship with Michael. Second, as Kay withdrew from the role of science expert, she substituted it with the role of 'critical friend', which stimulated the pupils' capacity to learn for themselves.

Many other examples of the pupils' achievements, which leave little doubt about their high quality, are included in Kay's study. I had seen signs of the pupils' investigative potential during my visit six months previously, and other indications were visible in the 'White Powders Episode', but I doubt if Kay's teaching would have yielded such achievements had it not been under active development in the ways just explained. I am sure that such changes could not be attributed to, for example, the pupils' general maturation over this period.

In conclusion, I drew encouragement from this for my hypotheses about the kinds of conditions that are crucial for good science learning:

1   Pupils need to have confidence that the teacher will:

- value their interests and suggestions for investigatory subjects and methods,
- trust that their own attempts to make sense of what happens will be their best efforts,
- respect their individual and group thinking and working, and
- be interested in their ideas and, as far as possible, try to understand them.

As evidence of this, I would cite the critical example of Michael's development, regarding this as an insight into the enabling climate that also applied to the other pupils.

2   Pupils must receive from the teacher the kinds of assistance to both their thinking and their actions which in the medium to long-term foster the growth of independence without frustrating the progress of their investigation in the short-term.

An Early Aspect of Lesley's Development: Seeing is Believing

During one of the first few course sessions, I presented 'ice balloons' (Ovens, 1986) as an example of an everyday substance that could be investigated scientifically in many ways. Particular attention was paid to the large number of questions which can be asked about the large blocks of ice, and questions were analysed according to whether they are either investigable by young children, are stimuli to thought experiments, or are non-scientific in nature. The session is one that is usually liked by teachers on such courses as this because it is practical and easy to resource, consequently, it often leads to classroom trials. Lesley was one of the course members to try it out in her classroom. She reported that her pupils had not asked many questions, the youngest none at all. Lesley explained this experience as evidence of several limitations in her pupils' abilities – the youngest pupils had a limited vocabulary and others lacked scientific ways of thinking. Naturally, she was disappointed by this.

At the beginning of the course, Lesley had described the project work in her teaching as based upon pupils asking their own questions, followed by discussion about how the pupils could seek answers to their questions. She said that she regularly asked them what they wanted to know, and also asked them to evaluate their own learning. All of this had sounded impressively investigative, but she had referred to the use of work cards, which tend to limit the degree of investigativeness, even when the cards are made by the teacher, as were Lesley's. The view I had formed about her teaching was therefore an ambiguous one. Nevertheless, I guessed that the reasons for Lesley's pupils not offering questions about ice balloons might have been more a reflection of some aspect of her teaching than their lack of ability. The wish to make use of one's experience (and prejudices) as a tutor in challenging a teacher's perception of her/his experience can be strong. In my own experience of working with ice balloons, I have found the responses by pupils of all ages to be so lively as to believe that Lesley must have restricted the pupils' responses to some degree. But to claim to know a teacher's own pupils better than s/he does is inviting a serious misunderstanding at least! I did not do so, and had I tried, the disappointing experience might have been explained partly in relation to the inner-city location of the school, and partly in relation to the very poor home backgrounds of the pupils. In both respects, Lesley's situation was certainly the most extreme one represented in this cohort of the course.

Fortuitously, a golden opportunity to develop this situation arose very quickly. The course plan included an afternoon session to make it possible for shared observation of some teaching of primary pupils at the university, and Lesley offered to bring in some pupils from her own class. Working in groups of about five, they were given ice balloons to investigate, while groups of course members were asked to give light supervision (specifically *not* teaching) and to observe. I set the pupil task as: 'Find out as much as you can about the ice.' It was fortunate that the university situation, with all the strangers, did not inhibit the pupils from showing their interest. They offered a fairly large number of observations, questions and hypotheses, for example, they noticed and questioned the cause of the variations in the texture of the ice in different parts of the block, they hypothesized that the more granular ice was softer than the clearer ice, and they tried to test this by hitting samples of each with a hammer, and so on. Lesley, having warned us not to expect too much from the pupils, was also pleased that the course members had found the pupils' responses to be rewarding. She also expressed pleasure that the pupils had done so well.

The impact of Lesley's reflection about her pupils' unexpectedly good scientific responses on her teaching could be described as one of *seeing* that her pupils could be scientific, and meant *believing* that they had the abilities which she had previously doubted. No rhetoric from me, or a course member, would have been nearly as convincing. Having reached this stage in writing this summary, I sent a copy to Lesley and we discussed it over the telephone. She said that reading my account, it had been easy to recall events, and she was able to endorse this version as 'very fair'. She gave full agreement to my account of the events on the course as a major influence on her development at that time, saying: 'If I hadn't brought the pupils into university at that time, I don't think I would have developed in the same kind of way.'

She went on to explain that looking back, her view of science for young children 'had been clouded', and several things at this time helped to secure clarification. Mainly, it was the 'seeing is believing'. The presence of so many adult observers during the university session to give her feedback on her pupils' responses had been of considerable help. Also, she had been trying to work scientifically on the course, a point I had remarked upon in Lesley's story (p. 61), so she had projected onto the pupils this demanding, adult version of 'good science', which had caused her assessments of their achievements to be a little severe. Another factor was the encouragement which the course was giving to the acceptance of a different kind of pupil response – that of exploration and investigation as valid science. So Lesley was not only 'believing what she saw', but also 'seeing differently'. Yet another factor was the social context for the teacher seminar groups, which were emotionally supportive and intellectually stimulating.

After this episode, it was clear that Lesley's concern for her pupils' disappointing responses continued, but I think she was beginning to consider that changing her own teaching might help. By the time her visit by another course tutor took place, a few weeks later, she was no longer using work cards, but discussing ideas for science explorations with the pupils before the practical work began, and she was showing much greater willingness to take account of their thinking. In Lesley's own words, at a later stage in the course, when she felt able to speak freely about her past practice:

> Before I came on this course, I would almost invariably produce a set of work cards for the topic in hand and expect the children to work through these. My approach is now, I feel, more flexible and takes more account of what the children bring to the topic in hand; they are now expected to take a more active role in the learning process by helping to determine the content and structure of science work. The children have proved to be more resourceful and creative than I have previously given them credit for.
>
> ('Statement of Personal Professional Development')

Saying What you Mean and Meaning What you Say

A question to turn to now is the coherence of the accounts that Lesley gave of her teaching at different stages of her development. It seems clear that Lesley's practice prior to the course did not match some aspects of how she communicated it in the interview at the beginning of the course. Her claim that the pupils used to raise their own questions seems particularly odd in the light of subsequent events. Two explanations come to mind: either Lesley felt that this was part of the rhetoric of 'good primary science' that would impress the interviewer, or she believed that this was an accurate account of her practice. If the first explanation is correct, then there was a discrepancy between her espoused theory and her practice, which presumably did not concern her unduly, and which was subsequently closed, that is, her practice changed to match the unchanging theory. If the second explanation is correct, then she meant something different by the words 'pupils asking their own questions' when she used them in the interview compared with her different use of them near the end of the course, that is, her practice and her expression of her espoused theory both grew interdependently together, retaining their coherence. My hunch favoured the second account, and I tested it during the telephone conversation with her referred to on p. 111.

I offered Lesley the tentative belief that, in the interview, in saying that 'pupils raise their own questions', she meant that her routine practice in some way involved the children recognizing or taking on questions in a way which was coherent with the understanding that she then held about science teaching and learning for that class, and which would not too inaccurately be called 'pupils raising their own questions'. The form of her practice would have taken account of the doubts about the scientific abilities of her pupils which she then held. Since she doubted that they were able to question and hypothesize *in a mature way*, then presumably she did not mean that pupils raised questions freely and independently, but perhaps raised them within a framework or structure of some kind, which she supplied to take account of their perceived needs.

By contrast with this situation before the course, Lesley's understanding and practice by the end of the course was based on the belief that her pupils did, after all, have the ability to question and hypothesize, therefore her practice had changed to recognize this. It became a form of practice which did not include the structures or frameworks to compensate for a need which was no longer in evidence. My theory rests on the idea that Lesley's perspective at the end of the course had been transformed, such that, looking at her practice before the course, she would recognize a quite different meaning of the phrase 'pupils asking their own questions' in the two contexts.

Lesley confirmed this in full. After she had read the account of my theory, she reflected on her teaching at the earlier stage by looking at some work cards she had used at the time but not since. The cards were about 'sound', and they contained what Lesley herself came to describe as instructions for how to perform a fairly structured series of set activities of the type: 'See how many different noises you can make with your ruler by holding it against a table and twanging it … ', etc. She had used the cards to elicit pupils' accounts of what they did, plus their comments, which at the time she saw as 'asking their own questions'. At the time, the pupils' outputs were sufficiently different from her input to be seen by her as independent, but looking back, Lesley said that she saw herself 'leading them to make the connections in the work which I wanted them to make'. Lesley came to regard this form of practice as not being accurately described as pupils 'asking their own questions', but that at the time she had used such a description honestly. She would presumably have projected her own meaning onto the form of practice used by another teacher who used the same description. This theory–practice link in her mind was presumably challenged mainly by the experience of hearing another person's description of a teaching and learning practice, having observed it for herself so that she could consider the theory–practice links held by others about events they had both experienced together.

This is an example of the genuine difficulty of professional communication. It suggests that even an apparently unambiguous descriptive expression, like 'pupils asking their own questions', incorporates a complex cluster of interlocking pieces of a teacher's understanding about a certain form of practice, the aims in view, the nature of the classroom context, expectations of the pupils' responses and associated evaluations of them. An accurate communication of Lesley's meaning depends on the content of those constituent understandings held by her coinciding with those held by another person. Rationalist rules of discussion of teaching and learning tend to emphasize the separation of means and ends, whereas in action research, discussion is about instances of practice in which the whole complex of constituent meanings are considered interdependently.

Lesley attached considerable importance to the episode of bringing her pupils in to university. It is another instance of the power of the most favourable situation of all – one in which two people's views of the same shared events can provoke discussion which can have significant effects on the theory–practice understandings of the people involved.

Towards a Better Understanding of Action Inquiry

'Lesley's Participation in the Course' (pp. 63–5) tells how she did not use the term 'action step' in the same way as it is defined in John Elliott's (1991b) book (Chapter 6 of which was used as a practical guide to the action research approach to the classroom-based study). Although the shifts in focus from one episode of Lesley's monitoring and reflection to the next were not logically related to each other in a linear and progressive way, they nevertheless *were* related to each other in a *tacit* way. There were links which were consistent with Lesley's exploration of her own theory-in-use more fully, albeit in an apparently less rational way than Elliott's model appeared to demand. In highlighting this aspect in the case study, I hoped to clarify my own understanding and test it out through seeking her reaction in the validation interview. I posed the question in the form of the dilemma for an action researcher between following a methodological rule and exercising freedom to follow personal preference.

The course had offered Elliott's model, and requested teachers to justify action steps in evidence from the previous cycle. Lesley unambiguously expressed her position on this during the validation interview, saying: 'I found that very, very difficult to do.' She was dissatisfied not only in failing to meet one of Elliott's criteria of action research, but also in feeling a sense of lacking tight intellectual progression in her study. However, she was also equivocal about the solution to this problem.

On one hand she said: 'I didn't feel I was stepping through this study progressively. It just became blurred. I felt we could have had more preparation to do with this particular model.' Lesley had said that she did not find the Elliott model of action research difficult to understand, so I interpret her statement that she had needed 'more preparation' to refer to closer direction as to how to put it into practice, and an argument for the imposition of methodology.

But on the other hand, she rejected imposition, and defended the individual's right to control their research:

> If you're going to apply strictures to the model then you've got problems. You'll have problems with *me* sticking to that because I found myself going off at a tangent and becoming interested in what I was getting out of it rather than applying the model more rigorously.

In Lesley's view, the course should be *either* about doing action research, in which case stricter adherence to 'the' model is justified, *or* it should be about science, in which case there is freedom to adapt the model. Lesley felt torn between the two, reflecting the ambivalence she saw in the course.

> I think that was what was missing. I didn't really know whether it was the model that was important, doing a bit of action research and never mind about your content. And yet you were obviously quite keen on doing this work on observation with the children, and so if the model is restricting you a bit, you slightly adapt it.

This made me reflect more deeply about the questions: Is this course essentially about primary science or action research? Is the central aim to promote science teaching and learning by the use of an action research approach, or is it to encourage an action research approach to personal professional development which happens to have the teaching of science as its context?

Lesley was clear about the nature of the *lack* of progression in her study:

> Even though I evaluated each action step, each one could have been taken separately, and not in any order. I was trying different things in each action step. Instead of making one major objective and sticking to that, I've brought in added objectives later on.

What was the relationship of the added objectives to the main one, and to

Lesley's action steps? The most conspicuous example of discontinuity for Lesley was in the fourth cycle of her action research, when she felt: 'Yes, it was a fresh topic, and I was looking at it as something where I would have to start again. I just seem to be starting over again at this point.' But shortly after criticizing her study for discontinuity, Lesley restated her uncompromising view of the rigidity of the model:

> I mean I would have thrown John Elliott out of the window [laughs] if I thought it was going to prevent me from following these lines that I'd decided were important to me. As long as I can show within my own model that I'm progressing, then I don't see any problem.

Lesley's classroom-based study was about children's scientific observation. It is summarized in 'Lesley's Participation in the Course' (pp. 63–5). It is worth emphasizing that Lesley's 'vision' of good observation was broadly conceived as part of a child's whole scientific learning. It was not a separable skill to be developed by repetitive practice, but something to be integrated with other processes of scientific investigation, the child's knowledge and understanding, and his/her purposes for learning. I regard the whole of Lesley's classroom-based study as being consistent with the gradual development of her understanding and practice regarding the fuller realization of this vision, and shall attempt to demonstrate this. I shall characterize each of the stages of the classroom-based study to show how they form complementary facets of the evolution of this vision, and to show that they are sensibly related to one another even though they may not strictly conform to Elliott's criteria of action steps (see Figure 3.2).

A Closer Consideration of Lesley's Action Steps

Lesley's action step in stage 2, to structure her participation in the discussion with pupils to support the determination of the tasks, was not logically derived from specific observations during the monitoring of stage 1. However, it can be seen as a sensible experiment in her teaching which could easily have been stimulated by the insights into pupils' capacities to be scientific, which the stage 1 monitoring contained. For example, the favourable impression she had of the pupils' interest in one another's observational comments, as compared with their usual tendency to be argumentative, could inspire confidence in a joint discussion about the planning of the next piece of work. The action step can also be seen as another facet of the adaptation of her theory-in-use away from the use of pre-planned work cards.

The next action step, to use an investigative opportunity which would not have the disadvantageous aspects of the paper planes, did follow logically, and yielded confirmation of the improvements in the teacher's involvement with the pupils in the planning stage.

116

Figure 3.2 Summary of the main stages of Lesley's classroom-based study to suggest their interrelationship

Lesley's account of the action steps taken (*italicized*)	Lesley's monitoring and analysis	My notes on the other relevant aspects of Lesley's development
1 AIR BALLOONS Lesley's *interventions were made as open as possible*, intending to create an encouraging atmosphere for pupils' contributions and dialogue about observations.	Transcript shows Lesley questioning the pupils' observations and seeking their explanations. Lesley was impressed by the interest they showed in each other's comments.	Getting used to setting pupils' work without the use of work cards. Helping pupils use concepts of weight, flying (as opposed to being blown by the wind), air resistance to moving objects creating buoyancy, etc.
2 PAPER AEROPLANES Lesley *posed pupils the question*: 'How to make the best flier?' They decided on criteria, then generated ideas for model making. Lesley *wrote their ideas down* with the intention of helping them explicitly question, predict and hypothesize so as to assist their observations.	Relevant variables were identified by the pupils, mainly the boys, during a good initial discussion. But the practical exploration was disappointing. The girls saw themselves as unable to make paper planes, and 'switched off'. The boys were enthusiastic and 'played' – they did not follow systematic lines of investigation. Lesley blamed the activity for having too many variables.	Trying out an open-ended, problem-solving type of teaching in the context of a familiar experience for young children – making paper planes. Transferring more responsibility to the pupils for deciding aspects of their learning allowed them to display a natural response related to gender self-image. This showed how the subject of the experience affects the pupils' free responses.
3 MAKING HOT AIR BALLOONS Retaining the teaching approach of assisting pupils to be explicit about their ideas, this time *choosing an investigation* with 'a more orderly and progressive series of actions and observations'.	Stages of problem solving were successfully achieved by the pupils. Lesley saw one stage as a cause for concern – the instability and consequent toppling behaviour of the balloon seemed not to have been explicitly noticed or acted on without Lesley's intervention.	Confirmation that the advantages (of a more specific focus of experience) anticipated by the action step could be realized. No consciously held basis for the next action step is apparent, but tacitly, perhaps the valuing of pupil independent inquiry was growing.

Lesley's account of the action steps taken (*italicized*)	Lesley's monitoring and analysis	My notes on the other relevant aspects of Lesley's development
4 STUDYING THE SCHOOL ENVIRONMENT With specific interest in *giving more time* for pupils to carry out their observations, they were encouraged to collect for a nature table and derive investigations from the collection. Lesley observed them and their discussions, making her notes under two headings: description and analysis.	Lesley resisted the wish to impose her categories for sorting the collection, and these emerged from the pupils, with much discussion among them and the labelling of sets of items. Communication of findings was well developed. Interrelationships between observation and other aspects of the whole learning process were revealed.	Unlike the more closely defined tasks that preceded it, this was a different kind of teaching – using a subject focus which provided rich and varied opportunities for individual interests. This suggests it had been motivated by greater confidence in pupils' scientific abilities when released to pursue investigations they have chosen for themselves.
5 CONTINUING THE ENVIRONMENTAL WORK Lesley introduced the *making of models* of objects in the nature collection with the intention of stimulating observation.	The learning of a group of girls studying daisies is described to show the quality of the additional observations which they made as part of making the models as accurately as possible.	Again, an action step without conscious justification in evidence about pupils' observation, but a tacitly selected additional strategy to complement the others, which proved successful in an appropriate context.
6 FOCUSING THE ENVIRONMENTAL WORK The task for all pupils was narrowed to the *study of one tree* in the school grounds.	Much valuable science was done – discovery of clues to the ecological relationships between organisms, including food chains, etc.	The teacher's attention to enhancing the learning process (particularly observation) leads to enhancement in the pupils' gains of knowledge and understanding.

Then came the break between themes, moving from air to the environment. Lesley began with the action step to give more time to the activities of collecting and displaying objects from the school environment to begin the topic. She did not give any logical connections with the preceding work, and subjectively reports in the validation interview her dissatisfaction with the feeling that she was 'starting all over again at this point'. But major factors in the situation were different. A much more open range of possibilities for pupil interest existed within the school grounds, and a different way of working was being tried out accordingly. From a distinctly unprepossessing inner-city location, the children had collected a wide range of things which fascinated them, including pieces of rotting fence, branches, twigs, roots, pebbles, stone chippings, live wood lice, a dead honey bee, worms, an insect pupa, and so on. I believed that it had been Lesley's monitoring of the three previous stages of her study that enabled her to feel sufficiently confident in the children's abilities to resist the wish to impose her categories for sorting, and be determined to give the pupils more time to develop their own.

> By the end of the second week, the sorting and classifying of items far outstretched my expectations. Groupings of objects were reorganized, and labels changed and grew in number as the children's observations and knowledge increased.
>
> (Lesley's classroom-based study, p. 17)

I accepted that Lesley felt she was starting again in that she had to rethink some parts of her developing theory-in-use for improving observation to a significantly different set of practical demands. But she was not starting again in the sense that she tacitly transferred to the topic on environment the insights and practical approaches she saw as positive gains from the preceding work within the theme of air. Despite the absence of a linear, logical progression in the different action steps, I did not agree with Lesley's statement in the validation interview that the action steps could have been made in any order. If she had taught the environment topic before the others, and therefore was at the earlier stage of getting used to not using work cards, without as much experience of the pupils' successful independent learning, then the action step 'to give them more time to observe' would have been something quite different both in its full meaning to her and in its practical expression. My hypothesis was that, being at the earlier stage, Lesley would have assumed a greater need by the pupils for her direction, and consequently would not have elicited the response from them that she did. Understood in this way, the full meaning of an action step is not adequately described by the propositional form in which it is expressed, but needs to be seen within the full context of a teacher's longer-term and immediate purposes, experiences and professional opportunities. The short statement of an action step represents only one facet of a multifaceted kind of development.

Would it have been reasonable to refuse to 'allow' Lesley (or for Lesley not to allow herself) to take an action step in her teaching without having a full, logical justification for the proposed action based on immediately preceding observations of it? I think not. What is quite properly an ideal for the more systematic and controllable situations or phases of action research to aspire to should not also be an inviolate rule for all situations and phases. To count as action research, in the absence of logical justifications for all action steps, the learning process in the research should, I believe, manifest such qualities as empathic observation, testing of ideas, openness of mind to unexpected or unwanted findings or interpretations offered by others, and the substance of the inquiry should show developmental features of professional insight and skill. With these broader criteria in mind, albeit in a partially developed form, it is interesting to reconsider Lesley's claim for her action research.

> Throughout the whole of the study, I have been aware of my own input and interventions. I like to think that the level of awareness I have reached through the process of carrying out this study has enabled me to take a more critical and observant view of my own role in the children's learning. For me, the most significant point to come from this study is the value I place on the importance of listening to, and being interested in, what the children have to say, and giving children time to speak.
>
> (Lesley's classroom-based study, p. 24)

This experience enabled me to see this aspect of action research differently from the dilemma described earlier – between giving greater or lesser specificity to this methodological procedure of action research. I now think that the relationship between the preceding research stage or cycle of action and monitoring and the next can be one of the following:

1   The logical development of an explicit theory in the researcher's mind, such as: 'X seemed to prevent Y from happening last time, so I shall attempt Y again, taking care to eliminate X this time, as far as possible' (the 'classical' logical link).
2   A pressing practical concern in the teaching context, such as: 'P has unexpectedly happened, and without knowing exactly why it is stopping me from achieving Q, I shall have to do something to prevent it from recurring, so I shall try R to remedy P.'
3   An intuitive judgement about a sensible thing to try, such as: 'Having tried A, and seen its effects, although there is no *explicit* reason to try out B next, possibly in preference to C, nevertheless B seems to be consistent with my overall progress towards the improvements to which I aspire, and I feel this is an appropriate time to try it out.'

If theory-in-use is a tacit intertwining of understanding and practice, then any of these alternative forms of progress are of equal potential value in the development of the whole inquiry. In alternatives 2 and 3 (which are more likely to be spur-of-the-moment changes) the retrospective reflection-on-action can lead to improvement in insight and practice. Also, the intuitive grasp of the possible improvements which might accrue could be either one of two alternatives:

- improved means to achieve the same ends-in-view, or
- tacit shifts in the understanding of the ends-in-view which suggest a change in the means of achieving them.

The first alternative corresponds to changing the part of the Elliott model called 'the general idea', but tacitly at first. If this had been true for Lesley, it reconciles her action steps, which apparently lacked a logical basis in achieving a fixed end-in-view, with the Elliott model, which might accept them as tacit shifts in understanding of Lesley's ends-in-view.

Steve's Use of Zigzagging in his Action Research

Steve used to amuse the group because from one week to the next he had often suddenly changed the direction or focus of his monitoring and reflection. It became known in the group as zigzagging. The range of practical issues he tackled is hinted at in the 'map' of substantive issues included in his progress through the course, which is at the end of his case study (pp. 78–9). As an inexperienced teacher, Steve was building up his repertoire of cases to draw on in assessing new science teaching and learning situations. Having completed the course, he found, as science co-ordinator, that similar issues cropped up when he was supporting the science teaching of his colleagues.

Peter: I think your study contains more teaching experiments than …

Steve: Yes, but it's fitted in superbly with going round to other staff because things have come up and I've known what kind of thing might work. Instead of going in blind, I've got an insight from something that I did with my children.

The benefits of zigzagging clearly extended to new contexts, but *was it action research*? At the time, I challenged Steve to justify his changes in direction or focus by making explicit the things in the previous phase which were logically related to the following phase. As part of the course, there had been whole group discussion about working definitions of an action step, during which emphasis was placed on trying to derive sufficiently penetrating thought about a practical problem in one context to gain some new insight about it, which would hopefully form the basis for consciously adapting one's practice in the next appropriate context. It was apparently difficult for Steve to comply with this request with several of his focuses. When I probed into this during the validation interview, Steve related his explanation to the situation on the course where teachers were coming to terms with the meaning of action research.

Steve: Everyone was worrying about: 'Am I doing all right?', and saw your role as saying yes or no, and you must do this, you must do the other. But with the action research, the way I was zigzagging around [*see 'My Visit to Steve's Classroom'*, pp. 71–4] I thought that *was* action research. Finding your own pathways and finding your own ideals. [*Steve then quickly read aloud this section of the case study.*] My reply to that is that I was looking for a magic formula. I wanted the elusive answer to how to teach science. Lack of experience. Having problems with no prior experience to fall back on. So for me action research was trying things out and evaluating them to be useful for your practice in the future. ... But then to sit down and *think* about it.

(validation interview transcript lines 163–78)

Steve's interpretation of action research was one that he was prepared to take responsibility for, rather than one which had to conform to an external formula. From the point of view of a tutor like myself who values evidence of the learner taking control of their own learning, this was encouraging. On the other hand, it creates feelings of vulnerability to criticisms of inadequate tutoring if there are signs of poor understanding by the learner about aspects of the required work which are centrally important to the educational justification for the course. So here was another manifestation of the educator's dilemma: In drawing 'authentic' learning out from the learner, what to do if it doesn't match up to the preconceived qualities of a 'good' learning process?

There is clear evidence of the authenticity of Steve's learning. Given the professional needs of his particular context, he wanted to make as much progress as rapidly as possible with the kinds of practical professional problems which were relevant to a young and inexperienced science co-ordinator who had to be able to hold his own within a school staff where he had been a student. At the time of the validation interview, I was beginning to think about the possibility of intuitive choices being made about changes in practice. No doubt it is desirable for lines of development in reasoning that is detached from practice to closely follow the rules of logic. But for lines of development in reasoning about practice, the question is: Can or should allowance be made for the teacher-researcher making an intuitive response to factors which s/he cannot control, which are perceived to have an influential role in determining the path of development? After all, reflection about practice needs to take account of the wholeness of the situation, and cannot insulate itself from unexpected events in order to maintain the logical purity of a line of detached contemplation. Steve was not aiming to produce propositional knowledge, but to develop insight and improved practice simultaneously. He was trying to advance his thinking and acting interdependently. This was his rationalization for his policy for action research:

Peter: [Using Steve's example of a change in the direction of his action research] Why did you turn to look at the group dynamics problem at that point rather than continue with the previous thing you were working on?

Steve: It's down to personalities.

Peter: So if you were in my position, working with a teacher who couldn't give a tight logical argument for stopping one focus and switching to another, but who, on an intuitive basis, said they were really puzzled, intrigued or concerned about changing to the new focus, would that be sufficient and acceptable grounds for changing?

Steve: That comes down to you as an outsider looking in. You could perhaps help them out … um … I'm not saying I didn't need any help, but you can't strait-jacket everybody into thinking the same. It would make teaching a very boring profession to be in if everyone took the same tack, and I would have felt stunted. Instead of getting knocked over to learn how to cross the road, you can go and ask someone's advice and then take it or leave it. I was concerned to use the time to try out as many different ways, sometimes of doing the same thing, as I possibly could. I had that many things going on in my mind I wanted to have a go at this and a crack at that. I didn't need anyone to say to me: 'Why don't you try this or do that?' I found it much easier to do things and then say: 'I've done this and made a right mess of it so can you help me out?' I'm that kind of person, so the tutor's role is to deal with each kind of personality. I find it all the time now. I'm a bit robust in the things I say and so sometimes I'll say things out of place and jump in feet first and upset people. Some people take it and some don't. I've got to try and curb the way I deal with people. Likewise, your interpretation of what that person needs is the hard part for you as the tutor.

(validation interview, lines 179–206)

This confirms the strength of the self-direction which characterized Steve's action research. Taken in conjunction with his ardent stress upon the value of critical friendship discussion, his preferred style was clearly one that matched his outgoing and spirited personality. Teachers doing action research quite often need encouragement to be more adventurous in their teaching, and to take advantage of critical friendship discussion, but not Steve. My view of his need – to be more contemplative and logical in the lines of progress taken by the research – could be a reflection of my idealization of the action research process as burnished by latent rationalism. Doesn't action research involve more about the whole person than theoretical research? Surely it is not so much a question of being essentially a sound and logical thinker, but being a thinker *and* an actor? And if this entails personal qualities in a broader sense, then should there not be greater latitude in the judgement of the quality of action research to reflect individual differences, particularly personality? If one important personal quality is a well-developed sense of professional autonomy, then Steve demonstrated this well.

Peter: So possibly this zigzagging is a criterion of success – of teacher autonomy?

Steve: 'Go and find out yourself' would be my message to anybody. If they're confident enough to say, 'I've done something wrong', and you can tick and cross yourself as your own critical friend, when there's nobody like yourself [nodding to Peter] to come back to.

(validation interview, lines 224– 9)

The case of Steve's zigzagging again forced me to reconsider my beliefs about action steps needing to be logically grounded in previous monitoring. However, another aspect of the quality of Steve's action research was still slightly shrouded in doubt. It is the extent to which the zigzagging yielded progress in Steve's professional insight and practice interdependently. Can it be said that this was at the level of a 'practical ethic', or was it piecemeal and purely pragmatic craft knowledge, at the level of mere 'kerbstone practicality' (Schwab, 1969)?

Retrospectively, it is possible to construe that a central 'core' of a 'perspective transformation' took place in the way that Steve began to believe in his pupils' capacity to initiate and sustain their own investigations. The associated changes in his practice were to reduce the directiveness of his role, to increase his awareness of the pupils' intentions, questions and ideas about methods, and to respond differentially by giving guidance. A significant shift in his understanding of science also took place, away from 'showing and telling', or 'proving Newton all over again!' as he put it, and seeing the importance of the children's scientific thought processes. After making this paradigm shift in theory and practice, Steve pursued a range of practical problems which did not seem to be coherent in terms of following a linear or additive sequence of theory or practice development. They were not prompted by a single progressive line of inquiry, but by the chance events within his teaching that caught his attention. However, looking back, I think they constituted a consolidation of the paradigm shift by dealing with examples of common problems and applying the newly found principles and perspectives to them. This was undoubtedly with an eye on the need for him, as science co-ordinator, to be able to support colleagues with any kind of problem, and Steve's desire to do so in a way that was consistent with his new beliefs and practices.

Here are some of the focuses which received Steve's attention. They are described briefly with an indication of how I came to see their relevance to the consolidation of Steve's new paradigm. The focuses were:

1 pupil group dynamics,
2 pupils' recording of their science, and
3 using teacher made work cards.

1   Steve noticed that two strong personalities tended to dominate their respective groups to the detriment of the participation of the other members, the 'sleeping partners', as Steve saw them. He tried several practical steps, with limited success, until he eventually accepted the advice of his critical friends during seminar work on the course and put the two individuals together. There was not the explosion that Steve had expected! On the contrary, they co-operated well with one another, and the more subdued members of the groups that they had left, began to blossom. At the time it had appeared to be an arbitrary action step which Steve could not explicitly justify by reference to evidence from his preceding phase of monitoring, but simply seemed to be something that Steve was attracted to, and, in his typically bustling way, wanted to 'go over and sort out'. I began to consider that this was a *subsidiary* line of development to do with trying to foster pupil–pupil co-operation, which was consistent with the *main* line of development – the increase in pupil-centred investigation. Steve's tacit justification for experimenting with the compositions of groups was his growing awareness of the contribution of pupil co-operation to successful science investigation.

2   Similarly, the introduction of a pupil notebook to teach the 'importance of collecting evidence in a logical form over an extended period' had not been grounded explicitly in a need that was evident in preceding classroom monitoring. At the time it seemed to be more in the nature of 'a good idea to try out'. However, he developed the notebooks from a somewhat teacher-controlled form of record keeping to a more pupil-centred aid to investigation, and they assisted in the process of negotiating a version of the science curriculum appropriate for Steve's school.

3   Steve had initially abandoned the closed, knowledge-based work cards he had been using at the start of the course, and relied upon a looser framework of teacher guidance to group investigation. As this appeared to me to be working well in encouraging the growth of investigative skills and attitudes in many of the pupils, it seemed surprising that Steve suddenly reintroduced work cards. His reasons for doing so at the time were unclear, but now they can be rationalized as partly to regain some control over the areas of investigation, and partly to assist the pupils who appeared to Steve to need guidance in initiating inquiry. Again, these were subsidiary aspects of the main developments of his action research, but, with the wisdom of hindsight, and a fuller recognition of the influence of Steve's professional context on his thought, they were supportive of his overall development.

Steve's Use of a Diary for Reflective Learning

During the course, Steve had become a successful user of a reflective diary, and became committed to its use after initial misunderstandings about its nature were overcome. During the validation interview, Steve recalled the expectation among course members that the course would be:

> like going back to university – that it will be pass and fail with a big gold star. I thought the diary had to be some kind of Lindisfarne Priory book that would be put in the British Museum as an exhibit. With my diary, no one bar me would be able to read it. Originally I thought, 'blimey, it's got to be pristine, this', so I started it off all nice. But as you get further and further to the back you can hardly read it. You might as well throw it on the fire, until I realized that it was mine, and for my purposes.
>
> (validation interview transcript, lines 214–23)

This had been one of my first attempts to encourage course members to keep a reflective diary and, despite my best efforts, I had not fully succeeded in separating its nature and purpose, in the minds of many, from that of an assessed piece of written work 'for the tutor'. However, Steve made his diary work for him, and he continued his use of it after the end of the course, adding to its functions the making of jottings about his role as co-ordinator.

> I'm using my diary to think about the problems that come up in my work. I write things down now without hesitation. Whilst on the course, I wouldn't say it was a chore, but you had to think about doing it. Now it's more like a diary in my back pocket. There's so much going on ... [*gives several examples*] ... that the only way you can get your thoughts chewed over is when you've got the time to think back and think over: 'What was there? What did become of that?' The only way you can do that is to make a note of it, however briefly, so you can take yourself back by reading previous thoughts.
>
> (validation interview transcript, lines 82–92)

This description matches the accounts often given by authors on reflective learning about the value of being able to reconstruct one's experiences during reflective times and gain more insight than otherwise. The habit of thinking and acting quickly and with energetic enthusiasm typified Steve. Thinking tended to translate into action more rapidly than for many people. In his own words: 'I never was a very reflective person, I did things by intuition really. Now it's making me sit down and think why I'm actually doing things' (validation interview transcript, lines 103–5).

Steve was emphatic about the nature of the personal professional developments he thought he had made.

Peter: Do you feel that there was anything you developed on the course last year that's been a resource for you?

Steve: Yes. This being able to change ideas. Being able to come back to university and say: 'I've come up against this brick wall', and be able to talk to other people like yourself and critical friends who could look from the outside and look in.

(validation interview transcript, lines 52–7)

He was equally clear about the conditions which had enabled the developments to take place. A major condition for Steve was honesty and openness in discussion.

Steve: I'm a very honest person with myself, and I wouldn't want anything that didn't truly show my feelings. There was no pass or fail on whether you gave a glowing or not-so-glowing report on what you thought you'd achieved. I thought I worked hard on myself, trying out so many different things.

(validation interview transcript, lines 107–11)

Steve had adapted quickly to the opportunities to discuss his own thoughts and his classroom practice, having set aside feelings of accountability to others as an inhibition on his freedom of self-expression. The value of such discussions had been somewhat limited in the early stages of the course because other course members took longer to adapt and give the kind of feedback Steve wanted.

Peter: Did you want to recommend something about the importance of the critical friend discussion on the course?

Steve: This only started to work when people got more at ease with one another and became more honest. Certain people had certain preset ideas of themselves, and weren't very open about the way that they thought or the way they communicated in the early stages. So more time is needed to be given to critical friend discussion in shorter bursts, in small groups and earlier in the course. Some people did more listening than talking and weren't being honest with what they were thinking, in a way. I know I'm one to run off at the mouth anyway. But as time went on, people became more open, and it was great to talk to people like-minded who had gone through the mill and made mistakes, and were willing then to partake. It's difficult to say you've made mistakes, but as the course went on it became quite easy.

(validation interview transcript, lines 117–31)

Summary

This research very clearly points to the importance, in situations such as this, of recognizing the *individual differences* between teachers and their paths of development. Of course, there are trends and commonalities to be found, which can assist in anticipating future work of this kind, and these are considered in the next chapter. However, there may be a strong temptation, arising from deeply held rationalist assumptions about knowledge, to feel that the sooner the analysis moves on to general patterns and the closer it gets to predictive generalizations, the better it will be as a piece of research. If this were so, the inclusion of Chapters 2 and 3 would be justified only in terms of providing the evidence for the subsequent and separate 'findings'. But this research is different. To find generalized mechanisms of professional development, which could confer on 'developers' the knowledge to control teachers' development, is not the intention of this kind of research, even though I admit I had held something of this kind of tacit intention at the outset. Much of the knowledge (or 'findings') about development is contained in the individual stories and the deeper recognition and appreciation of their differences. So the correct justification for Chapters 2 and 3 is to convey, at least through six examples, something of the richness and diversity of the phenomenon of development, arising as it does from the differences in professional situation and (mainly) the human differences in teachers' professional lives. Understood in this way, the value of studying cases is to learn through vicarious experience which, like direct experience, contains ambiguities, complexities and contradictions that defy neat, simple generalization, but nevertheless enable tacit knowledge or *know-how* to be gained about what development is like and how it can be supported. Therefore, the messages for future work are contained as much in these accounts of individuality as in attempts to draw out thoughts of generality near the end of the book. If the term 'findings' has any meaning in this work, they are to be located in the book as a whole. Understanding of the cases and understanding of the attempts to draw out generalities from them need to be seen as interdependent.

4   Common Characteristics of Development

Introduction

The purpose here is to reflect on the evidence about the six teachers depicted in the case studies, and illuminate common features of the practice of using action research for personal professional development. Some beliefs about the teaching and learning of science in the primary school are tested, developed and refined through consideration of classroom events, and possible thoughts and actions to do with encouraging teachers' personal professional development are developed through consideration of events during the course sessions. The analysis is essentially comparative and exploratory – to examine some issues which are commonalities across cases, and other issues which represent the individuality of development shown by a particular person, drawing upon:

1   The evidence base (further extracts from which are used to illuminate certain issues).
2   The case studies, which are in Chapter 2.
3   The individual 'Map of Progress in Substantive Aspects of Personal Professional Development', which was given, with the case study, to the teacher at the time of my interview with her/him to seek validation of both documents.
4   Course members' replies to the questions that they were asked at the validation interview about their case study.
5   The individual 'Diagrams of Practice/Theory Interactions during Action Research for Professional Development', which were prepared later. (Each map and each diagram is placed at the end of each teacher's case study.)

A note of caution is necessary at this point. It is desirable to retain an awareness of the individuality of each teacher's development, and to resist the tendency to regard any generalizations as the only important kind of knowledge, or the only way in which the experience analysed here can or should be transferred to inform future contexts for professional development. Both individualities and commonalities taken together constitute knowledge which could be transferable.

> Education enhances the freedom of man [sic] by inducting him into the knowledge of his culture as a thinking system. The most important characteristic of the knowledge mode is that one can think with it. This is in the nature of knowledge – as distinct from information – that it is a structure to sustain creative thought and provide frameworks for judgement. Education as induction into knowledge is successful to the extent that it makes the behavioural outcomes of the students unpredictable.
>
> (Stenhouse, 1975: 82)

Searching for Commonalities

A significant part of a teacher's participation in the course is to engage in a professional inquiry. The starting point, direction and pace of development, and significant content of the inquiry are all determined developmentally by the teacher her/himself in negotiation with the tutor and with the support of critical friendship relationships with the tutor and a group of other participants. Therefore, evidence was collected to create an overview of these aspects of the teacher's participation. Largely in the language used by each teacher, at each stage of the course, various self-expressions of development, often in the form of questions about professional practice, were recorded. These were placed in chronological order, and, where possible, linked together to form consistent lines of development, including starting points, early stages, the tutor's visit and later stages.

Starting Points for Personal Professional Development

These were expressed at the interview stage. They characterize several kinds of concern which motivate a teacher to enter such a course, and which can be the *overt* starting points for professional development through action inquiry. I am using words and phrases like *expression of concern, question, statement of need* to refer to the same kind of thing: a declaration within the context of a semi-formal interview, which was not for selective purposes, of one's reasons for entering the course.

First, a comparison can be drawn between the kinds of questions raised by teachers which they wanted the course to answer and/or needs they wanted the course to meet. Some of these were in the form of an expert's set of rules to apply to practice. These are in Set 1.

Set 1

- How do I fit it into the day? (A)
- The need for 'valuable resource ideas, knowledge and practical learning activities'. (S)
- How do I put it over? (A)
- How do I write an outline science curriculum for the school? (A)

Then there are questions which can be answered by gaining support for the process of creating answers for oneself, as in Set 2.

Set 2

- What is meaningful science for young children? (A)
- I am concerned about the similarity of pupils' responses to the small group science activities assigned to them. (B)
- I am concerned about the need for progression in pupils' science learning through the school, rather than being piecemeal or haphazard. (B)
- I wish to become more knowledgeable about my science teaching and the children's learning to increase my effectiveness in the class-room. (L)

A second comparison, which can be made from the perspective of action research, is whether the teacher's concerns are explicitly to do with prag-matic or principled kinds of change. Set 1 and Set 2 also show something of this contrast. Set 2 seems to suggest a commitment to an educational ideal, an intrinsic good, which remains unfulfilled in the teacher's present practice. Set 1, on the other hand, suggests that a more technical kind of deficiency is being expressed in response to extrinsic standards or norms.

Third, the degree of conceptual complexity, which might be attributed to the questions, varies in a similarly overlapping way. The first set of concerns could represent an assumption that the nature of a concern and its resolu-tion are relatively straightforward, whereas the second set includes concepts of education that are abstract, complex and problematic.

For a summary, see Table 4.1.

Most of the expressed needs were technical, including all of Steve's and all but one of Angela's (she raised the question of the meaningfulness of science for her Key Stage One pupils). My records of Lesley's responses are

Table 4.1   *The three dimensions of teachers' overt expressions of professional need*

	TECHNICAL		PROFESSIONAL
1	*Imposition of rules* of good practice and robotic skills by an external expert.	*versus*	Support to the *process* of attaining one's own standards of good practice as the 'expert within' (Dadds, 1997).
2	*Pragmatic* change to respond to extrinsic pressures and expectations with mechanical behaviour.	*versus*	*Principled* change to match or to develop one's own educational ideals, beliefs and values, or 'practical ethic' Schwab (1969).
3	Conceptual *simplicity* including recipes and 'tips for teachers'.	*versus*	Use of *abstract, complex* and *problematic* concepts requiring the development of judgement in their use.

enigmatic, and Chris gave little away at this stage. Brenda was an intriguing departure from this trend in the clarity, foresight and autonomy of her responses, all of which are in the professional dimension. This suggests that she already possessed an approach to reflecting about her practice which the course valued.

The course encouraged its members to adopt expressions of need, characterized here as professional, through the development of their professional autonomy, including their reflection on the extent to which their practice matched their own aims and those of primary science educationists.

'Look and Tell' Science

Some primary teachers use a pedagogy of science teaching which I call 'look and tell'. This slightly pejorative tag means that the teacher contrives an opportunity for pupils to *look* at set things, then expects the pupils to accept the teacher's set explanation of the observations and be able to *tell* it back to the teacher, including in the form of 'writing it up'. These teachers' intuitive understanding of science is probably an inductive one that involves making observations on which theories are built. When she looked back on her own version of this kind of teaching, Brenda called it 'party tricks and prompts'. Therefore, this kind of science teaching consists of knowing the science theories, and also the best versions of setting up observational opportunities for the pupils, and then making sure that these two fit together in the pupils' minds, or rather their notebooks, as neatly as they do in the science textbooks. The use by the teacher of pedagogical tricks, such as the use of prepared models and analogies, is sometimes emphasized as part of good teaching of this kind. The purpose of these is to shape and reinforce learners' thinking towards the set version of the science knowledge in the teacher's mind. The use of behaviouristic language, like shape and reinforce, is deliberate. 'How do I put it over?' was one of the questions that Angela hoped the course would answer for her. The teacher's assumed aim of science education is knowledge acquisition, and the pupils' learning process pays lip-service to constructivist kinds of learning processes in scientific inquiry by including tasks which are claimed to involve the so-called 'process skills'. This in effect can mean that pupils are required to make passive kinds of observation, measuring and recording, devoid of active, inquiring scientific thought, such as questioning, hypothesizing or predicting, which they could use to construct scientific theorization of the phenomena that interest them. The process is a convergent one which leads to the 'official' ideas of science.

All of the teachers moved away from their version of 'look and tell' and 'activitymania' (Moscovici and Nelson, 1998), and broke through into investigative science over the period of the course. They did so at different speeds and in different ways, but several features of the changes were common. One of the most significant inhibitions to this change was teachers' perception that the national curriculum, together with associated testing and inspection demands, all aim for the transmission of scientific factual content and such concepts as the 'big' ideas of science (Harlen, 1997). Many teachers find it easier to relate to the subject knowledge aspect of science education aims, and harder to integrate them with inquiry aims in their pedagogy. Consequently, there is commonly a serious distortion of science in much teaching of the science national curriculum in the form of the transmission of content separately from the 'training' of scientific inquiry skills or processes. The breakthrough achieved by these teachers depends on realignments of several interconnected aspects of their professional knowledge, which takes a considerable time.

Early Stages of Personal Professional Development

Sessions in the early stages of the course were intended to stimulate the course members to take an inquiry approach to their thinking and their practice of teaching science, and to encourage their perceptions of their professional needs to shift from the technical to the professional kinds described on p. 132.

Some of the teachers' responses were recorded in my observational notes, some were noted from tapes of course discussion, and others were written responses to my requests for course members to note down their thoughts about their professional needs in the light of the first few sessions.

The increases in number and complexity of the significant professional issues raised by the teachers indicate the generally positive reaction to the beginning of the course. There are fewer questions which suggest a search for the imposition of rules for good teaching, or seeking pragmatic change, or expecting conceptually simple answers. Instead, there were many examples of the search for an understanding of being scientific for young children, whereas there were none before. This is the first category of teacher questions for closer examination.

Reconceptualizing Science

- Can the science go beyond observational work? (A)
- How do I organize *investigational* science? (B)
- I need to pick out and define the science which I feel intuitively is going on in my classroom. (K)
- My pupils tend to give the same measurements (i.e. 'cheat') out of a sense of competition to get the right answer. (S)

These comments indicate that teachers were asking questions or expressing needs to examine classroom events more closely in order to take up the challenge that science learning could be different from 'look and tell'. In one case the teacher's personal inquiry was to check if young children *can* hypothesize, when to date they had only appeared to show the ability to observe, whilst in another it was trying to use conceptual frames from tutor talks at university to test out intuitive assessments that good science learning had been happening. In yet another case, the pupils' assumptions of the teacher expectations (for right answers) were in need of reshaping in order to release the truly investigative capacities and qualities of these pupils' learning.

Reconsidering Assumptions About Teaching and Learning

- Is it necessary for all the children to have the same experience? (A)
- An internal debate: on one hand wondering if my own scientific knowledge is an inadequate background for effective teaching, whereas, on the other hand, wondering if it could be an advantage. (C)
- I was sensitive to my own tendency to lead the children towards my expected outcomes. (K)
- I am learning to acknowledge the value of the teacher taking the role of observer of pupils' learning. (L)

Having been offered modern images of science, it was up to teachers to explore differently, according to their own preferences and circumstances, the implications in their teaching and learning of these images. The climate of the course was intended to be one of encouraging the critical testing out in one's own practice of such images on the understanding that each context requires it afresh. A test of this claim lies in seeking expressions of teachers' independent viewpoints. These are easily found.

- I regard the idea of pupils deciding their own path of inquiry is not the answer to my problems. (B)
- Do we *never* give facts to children? (K)
- I give work cards to pupils because I do not consider that they are ready to make decisions to determine the path of an investigation. (S)

In the first and third of these points a major tenet of an investigative pedagogy is being rejected. It is no coincidence that the first of these statements was made by Brenda, whose independence of mind had been evident earlier. The third extract was from Steve, who had adapted very quickly to the style of the course, and shifted his expectations away from being told by an expert towards using the course as a resource. In the second extract, a misconstrued implication of science as a way of learning – that pupils must discover all facts for themselves and not be told any by the teacher – is being challenged.

Tackling Practical Professional Problems Across a Broad Front

- How best do I ask pupils the right questions – those which will develop their thinking? (B)
- I am thinking more critically about the tasks I set and the questions I pose to the pupils. (C)
- I am sensitive to my own tendency to lead the children towards my expected outcomes. (K)
- I feel dissatisfied with the amount of science that children gain from my science-based topic work. (L)
- I am concerned about the practical problems of open-plan organization and my professional sensitivity towards colleagues in the team-teaching situation. (S)
- I must solve these problems, to do with 'the bay', before 'working on the children'. (i.e. 'How can I fit active discovery learning into my open-plan situation?') (S)

The range and significance of these concerns is evidence of their authenticity as expressions of serious and incisive reflection about the practical problems of enabling pupils to achieve better scientific learning. They represent a strong commitment to improvement allied to a spirit of inquiry and an open-mindedness about how best to achieve both. I believe that this kind of breadth of inquiry is an indicator of the interconnected nature of the various facets of teachers' practical knowledge.

Breaking Away From 'Look and Tell' Science

The course included early opportunities for teachers firstly to carry out scientific investigative learning at their own conceptual level, investigating ice balloons (Ovens, 1987), and then to interpret their learning with modern conceptual frameworks of the nature of science. The examination of science philosophy took place with the assistance of a colleague whose ability to present important ideas in a relevant, entertaining and vivid way had produced several published articles (see, for example, Hewitt, 1986).

It is an essential first step to realize that one can be scientific oneself. To achieve this, it is only necessary to take what may seem to be little more than an ordinary, 'sensible' approach to finding out about an everyday phenomenon, which has aroused one's interest, to find that many of the qualities of scientific learning can be noticed in what a curious person does naturally to answer many questions. This should assist an appreciation that many natural and straightforward kinds of thought and action are at the heart of science, and that we all possess the beginnings, at least, of the ability to be scientific. Having regained confidence, enjoyment and interest in being scientific oneself, at least to some degree, it is easier to identify with pupils' attempts to do the same at their own conceptual level. Close and empathic observation of pupils' learning is needed for the teacher to gain some freedom from the distorting effects on perception of the assumptions about science described as 'look and tell'. Opportunities for this were orga-nized within the course, and teachers were asked to perform observation tasks in their classrooms. Once a teacher comes to believe that pupils *are* able to be scientific in a full and holistic sense, and s/he has gained some successful experience of enabling the pupils to show such ability, or signs of it, then her/his professional inquiry can really get under way. The purposes of the inquiry are not only to learn how to 'make it happen', but also to refine one's personal understanding of the nature of good science learning. Aims and means develop interdependently.

For Lesley, the 'break away' was initiated quickly. She offered to bring her 9–10 year old pupils in to university for one of the observational sessions, as detailed on pp. 110–12, and it proved to be very fruitful indeed to discover their hitherto unsuspected scientific talents, which had not been visible to her. This had been partly because of her subsequent discovery that she tended to 'put them down a bit'. For Brenda, there was rapid acceptance of the idea of pupils' investigation, but her observations of her 5–7 year olds' exploration were interpreted as 'frippering around', until I suggested that this was after all how a young child's early scientific investigations might appear (see p. 138). A similar pattern of the tutor's visit helping to deepen awareness of pupils' scientific capacities can be seen in the cases of Steve, Kay and Angela. For Steve the main barrier had been his overwhelming enthusiasm, for Kay it was simply making her implicit assessments more explicit, and for Angela it was 'letting go' of the close control she felt necessary to maintain. I am not claiming that a simple cause-and-effect relationship existed in these instances between events of a visit and subsequent 'breaking away', but the other factors in each teacher's situation, which probably contributed a great deal to developments, have not been the subject of such close inquiry. Among these factors, peer discussion of classroom experience was very important.

'They're Only Playing'

This is the title of an article (Whittaker, 1980) which raised the same problem as Brenda when she interpreted her pupils' behaviour as 'frippering around' or 'just skimming'. If the teacher relinquishes the tight control needed to ensure that pupils get to see what they're supposed to see (in order to be able to tell), then this is how the pupils may appear to behave. Not only Key Stage One children, but also Key Stage Two children will show this playful type of apparently aimless behaviour in which they rapidly switch from one object to another, or from one way of manipulating materials to another without any apparent aim, control or developmental sequence. Pupils in this situation are sometimes so excited about being given a decent range of resources and the chance for direct experience that it would take a cast iron will to remain single-minded and controlled! Teachers in this situation are faced with the feeling of losing control both behaviourally and intellectually; they can no longer feel secure in their predictions about what the pupils will do or ask next. The cost–benefit ratio (Doyle and Ponder, 1976) looks disastrous! This is surely a Catch-22 situation for teachers.

Temporarily standing back to consider curriculum development at national level during the pre-national curriculum era, it seems unsurprising that the curriculum development projects in primary science (as in other subjects) successively claimed that teachers' failure to develop the investigative pedagogy was due to inadequate support in the classroom. Nuffield Junior Science had presented a philosophy through case studies of teachers' investigative teaching, and would have liked to expand the personal support to teachers through continuing professional development courses (Wastnedge, 1968). But the Schools Council initially interpreted the problem rationally, and set up successive projects to give increased support mainly as technological innovations rather than support to the process of reflective self-development by teachers. There were teachers' books of investigative ideas (*Science 5–13*, 1972–5), a standard checklist for assessing pupils' development of investigative skills, attitudes and concepts, albeit through the medium of a course rather than only through published material (Match and

Mismatch, 1977), as well as a plan for policy development and pupils' work cards (*Learning through Science*, 1980). Whilst the publishers' work card factories boomed, perhaps the real teacher development, which was achieved in the 1980s, came from the patience of the enabling types of science advisory teachers who supported classroom teachers through their personal struggle with the Catch-22 of investigative teaching.

To return to Brenda, two important questions remained for me about my interpretation of 'frippering and skimming' as science. Is there a danger that a course tutor is merely selling a new dogma in place of the teacher's old one? Is it a course tutor's task to help Brenda to accept it, or to put faith in her intellectual independence and ask her to treat anyone's interpretation as a hypothesis for testing? As Brenda's case study describes in more detail (see p. 33), the session I observed turned out to have inspired pupil inquiry for several weeks afterwards during which the pupils continued to find new things they could make, do and talk about with shiny things. The richness of their knowledge base at the end, derived from the growth of confidence in their inquisitiveness, was convincing enough for Brenda to believe in a constructivist interpretation of 'frippering and skimming', and to make the breakthrough to an investigative pedagogy. This was *an* ending, but not *the* ending because new questions and problems were thrown up, in Brenda's case, how to organize it for sixty pupils!

The Impact of the Tutor's Visit to the Course Member's Classroom

The classroom sessions tended to fall into one of two kinds according to the relationship between the teacher's practice on the day and her/his usual practice.

In Type A situations there was no *significant* departure from the usual practice reported by the teacher, and, in this situation, the visit tended to produce a clear focus for the development of practice in the form of the recognition of a specific problem and exploration of ways to meet it. For Chris the session followed the same 'circus' pattern of organization she had established for the half-term programme of science, and the problem for her was the organization. The visit led to a recognition of the disadvantages of a circus in encouraging boredom and discouraging investigative science, causing a limited pupil response.

In Type B situations a significant, unplanned departure from routine teaching did take place, and usually took the form of the teacher relaxing their control in some way. It tended to have the effect of stimulating the pupils to show abilities that had not been so apparent before, and therefore suggested that a factor in the teacher's role, which had been exerting a constraining effect on the children's learning, had been identified. For Angela the session began as planned with an activity she had structured to meet prescribed knowledge aims. But then she was faced with a dilemma between ending the session prematurely, as she would normally have done, because things were apparently going out of her control (and getting rather messy) or allowing it to continue because I was present. She chose the latter, and the pupils' investigations really 'took off' in an exciting, free-wheeling way with a rich mixture of fresh ideas and purposeful investigation. Angela had seen the pupils show 'higher skills of scientific thinking' in a new way, and recognized an enabling quality in the more relaxed role she had taken, albeit unintentionally. This experience caused her to re-prioritize her aims for the pupils' science learning. A fuller account of this is in 'Angela's Step in the Dark – Reconsidering Science Conceptual Knowledge Aims' (pp. 92–4).

From the point of view of personal professional development, the teacher's experience of the classroom visit is like a walker making contact with a guide during the long walk along an unmarked kind of Pennine Way. One kind of outcome is a shared examination of both the terrain and the map to yield an agreement about where the best path forward is to be found, in an *evolutionary* kind of way, as in Type A. But another outcome, Type B, is when the guide encourages the walker temporarily to suspend a preoccupation with following the map and to do a little relaxed roaming, and finds that a surprise view can be seen just a short distance away, opening up much more desirable ways forward, and enabling a refreshed view of the significance of the map. This leads to something of a minor *revolutionary* change. In both cases, the aim of the guide is only partly to assist this particular part of the walk, but mainly to encourage the improvement of the walker's capacity to find their own way.

The other visits to this cohort of teachers exemplified this typology. For Kay the visit was Type A in that the outcomes were a joint assessment of the events which took place, and to which Kay contributed much of the thinking. So, too, for Lesley there was an evolutionary kind of progress made. For Brenda there was a 'letting go' which did not occur very much in the session of the visit, but did so in the subsequent one because of the reassessment that took place during the visit. There had been very many examples of pupil behaviour that Brenda had not previously regarded as scientific learning, but as 'skimming' or 'frippering' and in need of teacher intervention to divert attention to the 'real' science. It was something of a revolutionary change for Brenda to let go, firstly of the idea that pupils were not being sufficiently scientific and secondly of the practice of diverting them away from their own rich exploration. Finally, Steve's discovery that his interventions were seriously inhibiting the pupils' investigations had a revolutionary kind of impact on his desire to monitor the pupils and himself to reassess his role as teacher.

In every case, the invitation to pursue progress along individually determined lines of inquiry, which develop the teachers' thinking about their teaching and their teaching practice interdependently, has been responded to positively, and, in every case, the process was furthered by the tutor's visit.

'Do We Never Give Facts to Children?'

Kay asked this question near the beginning of the course, voicing a frequently held misconception of an investigative pedagogy. It is an example of the part-by-part dismantling of the interrelated ideas of 'look and say' science. One of the first changes that teachers expect to have to make is to stop telling the pupils the answer, because investigation is supposed to be about the pupils constructing it (the answer) for themselves. This is an important move towards pupils asking their own questions or raising their own problems, which are the essential starting points for investigation. But when it becomes clear that the pupils do not then automatically construe *the* answer, the one that the teacher thought to be the necessary learning outcome, and the one that is the 'official' science idea endorsed by the curriculum, then the approach seems to be failing. Brenda encountered this problem in September and said, 'Pupils deciding their own path of inquiry is *not* the answer to my problems', and again in November, when I visited her, when the pupils exploring shiny things had not come up with the definition of a good reflective surface as she had wanted. Trapped by the dogma that pupils mustn't be told anything (hence Kay's question), and observing pupils' seemingly disorganized and apparently aimless play, teachers may rightly reject it. Without support to persevere, they may also reject an investigative approach and may not go on to develop either a different epistemology or a constructivist view of children's learning. Consequently, they may not begin to appreciate the different kinds of information-giving strategies which the teacher needs to introduce and the more subtle ways in which subject conceptual knowledge can be used to advance pupils' science learning.

Developments During the Later Stages of the Course

The evidence for this material consists of the written report on the piece of action research carried out by each course member, along with extracts of the tapes of some course sessions and my observational notes, both derived from the discussions within critical friendship study groups which took place during the conduct of the action research work. The major audience for the teacher in expressing these views was therefore that of professional peers.

It is striking how the style of these statements appears to signify a stance of independent professional inquiry. Having become accustomed to the expectations of the course, teachers might have adopted this style of self-expression as the result of simple conformity to perceived demands. But this seems unlikely since the burden of a set *medium* would surely be accompanied by a banality of *message* as learners use 'producer strategies' rather than learning strategies. This does not seem to me to be so. The content of these statements does not exhibit platitude or trite and cliché-ridden conformity. Bearing in mind that the audience for many of these statements was a group of peers who functioned as critical friends to one another's development, it seems less likely that this would have been either desirable or sustainable. Where the statements express a growth of commitment to an ideal or particular course of action, it is likely that this was not primarily derived from (for example) published ideas about good primary science teaching and learning, in isolation from practice, but was dominated by reflection in and on practice, as illuminated by ideas and ideals from many sources. The critical community of course members held on-going discourse which made available to its members vicarious experience and debate about theory – practice interactions. The course members' evaluations of the course process placed a very high emphasis on the importance of this discourse. Many statements dealt with issues of central importance to the teacher's role, and many exhibit a considerable sensitivity to pupils' learning. Therefore, leaving aside at this point the content of the statements, and focusing on the commonalities of the professional development processes they represent, I shall attempt to identify some of the characteristics.

Developments in Dominant Professional Concerns

Newly expressed concerns appear in the statements which represent deeper and broader thinking about individual teachers' theory and practice than they showed earlier. For example:

- I am seeing how much they are able to learn without the teachers' intervention. (B)
- I am focusing on pupils' intellectual independence in devising their own investigations, and succeeded in 'letting go' of my control over their work, releasing their investigative ability. (C)
- It is possible that not giving every pupil the same experience may be an advantage. (K)
- I am still concerned with pupils' independent thinking, and I recognize that this may mean accepting some responses from pupils which are unexpected and at first sight disappointing. (K)
- In this sense particularly, I am becoming more analytical about my own teaching. (L)
- If maths understanding can be assessed by pupils getting right answers, how do I assess science understanding? (S)

Recognition of Professionally Significant Dilemmas

These are difficulties in teaching which are of the kind Berlak and Berlak (1981) refer to in their analysis of observations of primary schools in the UK. The first example is the dilemma between professional solidarity with colleagues versus individual professional judgement, or the societal dilemma between equal allocation of resources versus differential allocation:

• I am wrestling with the general constraint I perceive to be imposed by the school's organization of the curriculum, which prevents me from allocating additional time to expand science teaching in the way indicated. (A)

The second example is the control dilemma between teacher versus pupil control of standards, combined with the curriculum dilemma between personal knowledge versus public knowledge:

• I feel dissatisfied by not feeling in control of the pupils' learning, and feel the desire to ensure more concept development by pupils. (S)

Empowerment

Expressions of growth in individuals' self-confidence and capacity to control their own development may take the form of feeling liberated from what had unknowingly been a restricting or limiting idea that was no longer believed to be reliable. For example:

• I feel *more confident* about science and my own ability to evaluate children's scientific learning. (A)
• I am less anxious about the need to 'feed' the children information. (B)
• I am abandoning my desire to direct their planning and am adopting pupil-centred, investigative work in which there is not the same experience for all. (C)
• I see this now as 'an obsession' and 'so structured it could be inflexible'. (C)

'Do All of the Children Need to Have the Same Experience?'

This question was regularly asked during the course, usually by a teacher who had taken for granted that the answer was yes, but was no longer so certain. The question may presuppose a simple concept of 'experience', as something 'out there' which happens to the learner with predictable, standardized effects. There is also the assumption that a simple relationship exists between the experience and the learning, in which the latter is directly caused by the former. This is reminiscent of the naive empiricist view that *truth is manifest* to the keen observer – those who cannot 'see' the truth should just look harder! Another possible reason for raising this question may be an educational ideal of equality of opportunity – it is every pupil's right to have equal access to the good ideas and learning processes of science.

The question was raised by Angela early in the course, and it took some time of patient study for her to satisfy herself that a simple 'yes' is not appropriate. Her teaching had tended to have a standardization of both provision and expectation of outcome. But when pupils were given 'intellectual elbow room' to influence their investigations, it became clearer that an apparent similarity of experience was (legitimately) leading to different ideas being formed and used by different pupils, according to their differences as learners. Given such chances to be expressed, the infinite variability of pupils' existing ideas, past experiences, present interests, skills, etc. totally engulf and overwhelm the apparent similarity of experience as variables in the situation, and mean that each pupil's learning has properly to be viewed uniquely. As an illustration of this, a detailed comparison between more constrained and less constrained situations, and the consequent increases of individuality and scientific quality of learning, has been extracted from the evidence about Chris's teaching, and is presented on pp. 96–101.

People's immense capacity to 'misconstrue', or rather to think differently, exists because we are creative, not merely impressionable. It is this creativity in construing understanding in our learning of science which is the most under-understood aspect, as well as the most neglected. It casts doubt on the common assumption that all pupils should come to know the same things as one another, and in the same way as one another, which is implied by the setting of national curriculum attainment targets. The insidious message is that children are to have the national curriculum for science transmitted or delivered to them. In order to 'train' student teachers to do this, they now:

> must be taught ... how to recognise and address common pupil errors and misconceptions in science ... and how to challenge them in order to ensure that pupils develop a more scientific understanding of the idea in question.
>
> (DfEE, 1998: 8)

As elsewhere in the national curricula for both schools and for teacher education, creativity is not valued compared with conformity. Therefore, the strongly implied teaching method in teacher education and in schools appears to be that of transmission. Alternative conceptions are intolerantly labelled 'misconceptions'. It is the teacher's role to *ensure* the elimination of incorrect ideas by substitution with correct ones through *challenge*. It is clearly implied that the necessary method of challenge is: 'effective exposition to promote pupils' scientific understanding and to address misconceptions' (DfEE, 1998: 9).

This signifies a return to the discredited kinds of science teaching which have caused so many people to switch off from science. The conceptual context of this study (see pp. 14–17) gives some reasons for rejecting much of the incoming change of this kind. Further objections arise from socio-cultural theories of learning which are rapidly gaining interest. According to Lave (1988), learning is situated in its own context and, according to Cole and Cole (1989), context is the interconnected whole that gives meaning to the parts. Learners should be engaged in activities that are *authentic*, and which model the practices of scientists so as to engage in the thinking, knowledge and tools related to the practices of scientists. A critical characteristic of authenticity is that the activities should be personally meaningful to the learners (Murphy, 1996). These theoretical perspectives are in harmony with the kinds of developments in teaching in which these teachers were involved during their participation on the course.

Teachers often worked out their own answers to this question about the similarity of children's experience through giving closer attention to the children's thinking about their experiences and deciding how best to challenge them *in situ*. Characteristically, there was development of a teacher's practical theory interactively with experimental changes in practice.

Teachers' Science Knowledge

The 'look and say' science pedagogy stems from the perpetuation of an over-simplified and outdated image of science which still tends to characterize some science education in secondary schools and higher education, as well as textbooks, and the media. It is also becoming more common in those primary school classrooms in which the teacher regards the requirements of the national curriculum as a coercive force for the 'coverage' of conceptual knowledge content. The use of this pedagogy may also be more commonly used by a teacher whose science background is 'above average', by the possession, for example, of a first degree in science. Because this kind of science education is likely to have been acquired by being a learner in a 'look and say' pedagogy, it may itself be a barrier to gaining a broader and more modern image of science, and hence the use of a more enlightened pedagogy as a teacher. In the cohort studied here, the teacher who had the 'best' science background (as indicated by formal qualifications) was Angela, who acknowledged that being in this situation had indeed been a source of difficulty for her. She had been accustomed to thinking of science as an edifice of certain, fixed theoretical knowledge which had been erected inductively from the 'facts' of practical science. The tacit theory about learning science, which is consistent with this authoritarian, positivist image of science, is for the learner to accept and adapt to the existing structure of the subject. There seems little room for the learner's own theorization since this would probably not lead to the desired knowledge acquisition. Therefore, giving the learner some practical experience has the merely instrumental value of confirming and demonstrating the manifest truth of science knowledge to the learner.

A central feature of recent research into primary teachers' teaching of science (see, for example, Osborn and Simon, 1996, Summers, 1994, and Summers, et al., 1997) is the emphasis on the importance of an adequate level of subject knowledge. This 'level' is not defined and yet it is asserted to be associated with ineffective teaching of science in schools. But no evidence is provided that ineffectiveness exists in the teaching of primary science, nor is there a proven link between ineffectiveness and a teacher's lack of subject knowledge. These authors may pay lip-service to other relevant factors, such as the investigative aspects of science, but the kinds of teaching which their work depicts have heavy overtones of transmission aimed at narrow conceptual knowledge objectives that do not involve the pupils in thinking scientifically. This kind of work is increasing rather than reducing the obstacles to the improvement of science teaching in primary schools.

Teachers who are steeped in inductive science feel they need to possess the subject knowledge which enables them to teach science, that is, the facts that explain the phenomena in the set observational tasks which constitute a 'look and say' pedagogy. Learning more science was commonly a significant aim for teachers at the beginning of the course. This was mainly because when they contemplated open-ended situations in which there are no clearly predictable answers, they felt vulnerable to the criticism that teachers don't know what they're supposed to be teaching, and agonize about the 'bright' pupils who might ask the awkward knowledge questions which they, as teachers, can't answer. But no teacher can know all that might be needed to answer every question which might be asked by learners who are engaged in authentic investigative learning.

One of Chris's statements near the beginning of the course suggested she was at this turning point in her view. She said: 'I wonder if my own science knowledge is an inadequate background for effective teaching, but on the other hand, I'm wondering if it could be an advantage.' The battle cry of many a science advisory teacher in the 1980s was that teachers can teach science well in the primary school without knowing a lot of science. This is another step, of partial understanding, in many teachers' development of an investigative pedagogy. (It is a more helpful over-simplification than the idea that you never give facts to the children.) A teacher who is beginning to value pupils' own scientific ideas and inquiries can give a great deal of valuable support by being a co-investigator, provoking further inquiry, getting the learners to check back on progress thus far, or whatever best supports an intelligent route to answering the learners' own question. This role is one that a less scientifically knowledgeable teacher can adopt. In which case, the professional development need is not simply for more science conceptual knowledge, but how to recognize these virtues in pupils' science, and also how to see such inquiry as a challenge and an opportunity to the extension of one's own scientific learning, not only to increase one's personal knowledge, but also to enhance investigative abilities. In this situation, increasing a teacher's science conceptual knowledge alone suggests that better decisions may be possible with regard to planning, recognizing better and more investigable questions, and making wiser challenges to children's thinking. But such components of teaching are as much to do with the *know-how* of *applying* the subject knowledge in creative ways to unique investigative situations as the possession of the subject knowledge in isolation from its professional use. Teachers on this course were encouraged to increase their science knowledge mainly in such contexts – to meet specific planning and pedagogical situations in which the children's learning would be enhanced by the teachers' use *and development* of their science knowledge through the teaching. In this way, knowledge retains the vital quality of being held as problematic and dynamic rather than fixed and certain in the minds of both teacher and learner.

The 1980s and 1990s have seen a growing emphasis upon the teacher's possession of specialist subject knowledge in order to teach more of it to children. In primary schools prior to this period, the amount and the quality of science being taught were both low, so this was certainly a desirable development. However, this trend has been expressed, in science at least, by developments having epistemological assumptions which are overwhelmingly rationalist in character. There is a strong reductionist temptation for science educators and researchers to try to work out a formulaic method of ensuring pupils' science concept knowledge acquisition. Constructivist theories of learning have been presented as the basis for the promotion of constructivist pedagogies which advocate a fixed sequence of phases of teaching, such as orientation, elicitation, etc. (see, for example, Driver, 1988). Emerging from a secondary school perspective, and with rationalist overtones, there is a new theoretical orthodoxy in the separation of teachers' subject knowledge from pedagogical content knowledge and general pedagogical knowledge. It originated in selective and distorted interpretations of Shulman's influential work (see for example Grossman, *et al.*, 1988). But the logical neatness of this analytical separation should not lead us to conclude that there really are these distinct aspects of a teacher's knowledge with a separate existence in the process of teaching. This has been assumed and not tested. Furthermore, much of the research, which claims to show that the possession of science knowledge is the key variable in causing pupils' science learning, is not only unconvincing, but is also inappropriate to the development of investigative science in the primary school. Using pre-test and post-test methods, the research is characteristically concerned with knowledge products and not learning processes. A critique provided by Michael Golby, Anthony Martin and Martin Porter (1995) gives their views on the defects in the conceptualization of the relationship between know-ledge and teaching raised here, and goes on to consider more generally the epistemological and ethical problems of this kind of research.

Those determined to redress what they see as a *deficit* in teachers' science knowledge have taken the current trend as a justification for them to engage in transmitting 'correct' knowledge to teachers in ways that shift the image of science back to the authoritative one of an edifice of certain, fixed knowledge. Curiously, subscribers to the deficit model often claim to be constructivist in their beliefs about how learning takes place! In apparent unawareness of the contradiction, it is as if a body of objective knowledge exists independently of scientists and teachers (and that there is complete agreement about it among them all), and then learners can have it trans-mitted to them so that they construct (or rather replicate) it for themselves. In 1992 the editorial board of *Primary Science Review* took a different view. Faced with the submission of articles for publication from science know-ledge 'experts' a policy was made which assumed that teachers best learn science knowledge *interdependently* with developing their understanding of how to use that knowledge for teaching (see Ovens, 1992: 2). To meet the needs of primary teachers, authors were encouraged to treat science knowl-edge, particularly its counter-intuitive concepts, as tentative, and to address the problems of using the science knowledge being discussed in an article to relate to specific teaching and learning contexts, including some information about examples of teachers' actual work and children's responses. Knowing how to use subject knowledge occurs in a variety of important ways, for example, to *know how* to answer children's unexpected questions, to *know how* to discuss with them the unpredictable outcomes of their genuine inves-tigations, and to *know how* to help them to construct meaning for themselves. It depends on a far more significant and more complex kind of knowledge than the mere possession of the subject knowledge alone. It depends on being able to integrate knowledge from different sources so as to match the significant characteristics which the teacher perceives about the situation in which s/he finds her/himself. Each unique occasion on which this integration takes place is an experiential case, and teachers' *know-how* grows by the building of a 'repertoire of cases' (Schön, 1983). Such cases are likely to include, from time to time, ones in which a teacher's understanding of the science conceptual component is developed by the unusual ways in which the children's perspective gives a new slant or a fresh problem. This approach was endorsed by Her Majesty's Inspectorate (HMI) in their claim that: 'Students' use of certain science concepts and skills can be advanced through working with children as well as through learning science at their own level' (DES, 1988: 4). They went on to say that: 'Methods used in teacher education constitute part of the message about teaching that students will receive' (ibid.: 9), and 'For students fully to understand the meaning of this kind of learning, [constructivism] it is important for them to have experienced it for themselves' (ibid.: 10).

In this course, teachers were encouraged to deepen and extend their science knowledge within the context of its professional use. The first way in which this occurred was during the planning of schemes and sessions, and the anticipation of task setting and questioning of children. These tasks were discussed in groups of critical friends during course sessions. The second way was in reflecting during and after the teaching upon the integration of conceptual science knowledge with procedural science knowledge, and all of the other significant components in the whole professional context. Each case that threw up problems or questions was shared across the group, making constructively critical feedback possible and also making cases available for vicarious learning about (among other things) the professionally contextualized aspects of subject knowledge applied to teaching.

The Concluding Stage of the Course

What follows is a summary of the statements of personal professional development written by each course member and brought to the final course session for sharing and discussion. The statements were intended to be a retrospective summarization of the progress achieved, not only in a celebratory and congratulatory way, but also in a reflective way, to encourage course members to be more aware of their own powers of autonomous development, using the capacities they had exercised during the course. With the task having been set in this way, the statements do not tend to convey a sense of the potential for further growth, unresolved questions and problems, or new ones, or commitments to persist with present things or to try new things. All of these elements were present to varying degrees in the discussion rather than in the statements.

Commonalities in Course Outcomes – Teaching Primary Science

1   The teaching of science by every course member changed from a version of the formal/structured/directed type (Elliott, 1975) to a more informal/unstructured/guided or open-ended type.
2   All course members increased their understanding of, and skill in, enabling pupils' scientific investigative learning, and developed an increased appreciation of pupils' scientific learning.
3   Most course members gained a clear grasp of the *holism* of scientific investigation, that is a *gestalt* recognition of the integration of the dimensions of personal and social purpose, knowledge, skill, ethics, attitudes, techniques, resources, values and critical communication within each investigation appropriately.

4   Some course members showed an appreciation of the intrinsic value of pupils' scientific learning as opposed to its instrumental value (to, for example, educational or life prospects).

5   All course members were able to enter at some level into debates within science education of issues such as the knowledge and process inter-relationships.

Other Commonalities in Course Outcomes – Personal Professional Development

6   All of the course members showed development of an appreciation of the norms and values of action research.

7   All grew increasingly able to learn from classroom experience through discussion and reflection on evidence, exposing their ideas to the risk of testing both against practice and also in debate.

8   All became more self-confident, not only in their science teaching, but more generally, as professionally autonomous people, able to discuss their own practice with colleagues openly.

9   All showed increasing awareness of their own development as an unending process of growth which is, to a reasonable extent, under their own control rather than in the hands of 'experts'.

5 Describing, Enabling and Assessing Development

One of the distinctive characteristics of the work described here is that, as the course tutor, I attempted to be reflexive about the development that the teachers were being encouraged to achieve. My own professional development was interwoven with theirs, and I wanted to learn about both. Wherever possible, my reflection about one area of development has been informed by reflection about the other. Therefore, it seems appropriate to begin this chapter by presenting aspects of my own action research in a similar way to how the work of the teachers has been presented.

My Personal Professional Development

During the conduct of my own action research, it became increasingly important for me to question its epistemological basis. What might be my justifications to claim that I know certain things about action research for personal professional development? To be consistent with the action research approach itself, any answer could not be one derived from theory which is based on thought separated from practical contexts. It would have to be one emerging from and feeding back into the practical professional context of being able to understand my practice of action research. Its potential value could be as a resource to teachers conducting action research, who, like myself, become concerned about these kinds of questions. Anyone carrying assumptions such as scientific notions as objectivity, about how to justify a claim to knowledge, is likely to want to find some kind of convincing, or ideally irrefutable, basis for making their claim. Assumptions that all rigorous research should be 'scientific' are widespread, with meanings of rigour commonly being bound up with the exclusion of personal and intuitive dimensions from the research process. The rationality of science is thought to lie in the authority of reason and its application to empirical data. Imbued with this view as tacit knowledge, I felt repeatedly driven to search for a way in which a quasi-scientific method could be found to provide an authoritative basis for my claims to knowledge.

Gradually, I overcame this difficulty, mainly by recognizing and accepting the ways in which I was learning from doing action research, including the part played by the personal and intuitive elements, and also by examining more closely some views about the nature of scientific knowledge.

> Kant challenges us to use our intelligence instead of relying upon a leader or an authority. This should be taken as a challenge to reject even the scientific expert as a leader, or even *science itself*. Science has no authority. It is not the magical product of the given, the evidence, the observations. It is not a gospel of truth. It is the result of our own endeavours and mistakes. It is you and I who make science as well as we can. It is you and I who are responsible for it. Science, one might be tempted to say at times, is nothing but enlightened and responsible common sense – common sense broadened by imaginative critical thinking. But it is more. It represents our wish to know, our hope of emancipating ourselves from ignorance and narrow-mindedness, from fear and superstition. And this includes the ignorance of the expert, the narrow-mindedness of the specialist, the fear of being proved wrong, or of being proved 'inexact', or of having failed to prove or justify our case. It also includes the superstitious belief in the authority of science itself, or in the authority of 'inductive procedures' or 'skills'.
>
> (Popper, 1983: 259–60)

To accept that an answer to the epistemological question does not lie within a quasi-scientific research method is to deny the dream of establishing a higher, or preferably ultimate, ground on which findings could stand. This, in turn, seems to lead me to reject the possibility of an objective method, and accept that methods and findings must consequently be purely relativistic and subjective. *Relativism* and *subjectivity* are such pejorative terms in our scientific society that, especially for a person with a growing appreciation of science, it is difficult to contemplate an alternative. Is it possible to go *beyond objectivism and relativism*? In the book by Richard Bernstein with this title,*Beyond Objectivism and Relativism*, a situation like mine is described as being in the grip of the 'Cartesian Anxiety' – the dread of there not being a fixed point on which to base all thought. His advice is to regard relativism not as the dialectical antithesis of objectivism, but as parasitic upon it.

> Reason is not a faculty or capacity that can free itself from historical context and horizons. Reason is historical or situated reason which gives its distinctive power always within a living tradition.
>
> (Bernstein, 1983: 57)

Bernstein asks for a method to be used to give breathing space for a new theory to develop that would overcome the otherwise plausible opposition of objectivism and relativism. He introduces the views of Gadamer as affirming that practical wisdom comes from the on-going interpretation of our own tradition of thought through dialogue, questioning and conversation. There is a dominant role to be played by judgement in the interpretation and application of rules and criteria. He cites Alasdair MacIntyre (1977) on the practical character of rationality: 'Objective rationality is therefore to be found not in rule-following, but in rule-transcending, in knowing how and when to put rules and principles to work and when not to' (quoted by Bernstein 1983: 57).

A Gadamerian view is that understanding is always in the process of coming into being. It is not achieved by abstracting ourselves from our historical context and securing the objective meaning, but is always subject to the pre-judgements that constitute our being. A Gadamerian hermeneutical interpretation of the writing of the case studies of the teachers would be as follows. Meaning does not exist objectively in the case record, waiting to be understood independently of me as the interpreter, but the meaning is nevertheless possessed by my written records and the tapes. A happening called 'meaning coming into being' took place in which I used my pre-judgements to try to reach out to the subjective meaning of the author (for example, when reading course members' writing about their teaching) or the meaning of the speaker (when listening to course members' speech on tape). My pre-judgements are the outcome of my personal and cultural history and tradition. Therefore, in making information about these available to others, it is possible for the interpretations to be checked by them for expressions of biases which have this origin. This is a justification for the inclusion of autobiographical material, such as that in 'The Personal Context' of Chapter 1 (pp. 7–10), in reporting this kind of inquiry. My *enabling* pre-judgements were those which I was prepared to risk and test through dialogue, and my *blind* pre-judgements were those which I did not risk testing in creating an interpretation. My formulation of meanings was not a 'final' understanding, since it inevitably contains some pre-judgements, neither can it claim to be objective, that is free from 'contamination' of interpretation, but it can be counted as rigorous provided that it is open to risking it by test through dialogue. The test is not through appeal to 'brute evidence' (as in a final test of empirical verification), but through the test of a person's interpretation of evidence. The original meaning of dialogue in hermeneutical philosophy refers to the reflective dialogue in the interpreter's mind between existing understanding and the text. Here, dialogue includes the presentation of my evidence and my interpretation to the teachers on the course, to open a dialogue with them about the extent to which, despite my biases, the case studies and other analyses represent their own interpretations of their professional development. Although my understanding is limited by the presence of pre-judgements, it is not closed but is essentially open to understanding what is alien to it. The basis of a critique of my interpretation is my willingness to ask questions of the object of study which might challenge my pre-judgements. As a person, insofar as I am never simply an individual, neither are my horizons closed or utterly bound to one standpoint.

We are always understanding and interpreting in light of our anticipatory pre-judgements and prejudices, which are themselves changing in the course of history. This is why Gadamer tells us to understand is always to understand *differently*. But this does not mean that our interpretations are arbitrary or distortive. We should always aim (if informed by an 'authentic hermeneutical attitude') at a correct understanding of what the 'things themselves' say. But what the 'things themselves' say will be different in the light of our changing horizons and the different questions that we learn to ask. Such an analysis of the ongoing and open character of all understanding and interpretation can be construed as distortive only if we assume that a text possesses some meaning in itself that can be isolated from our pre-judgements. But this is precisely what Gadamer is denying, and this play between the 'things in themselves' and our pre-judgements helps us comprehend why 'understanding must be conceived as part of the process of the coming into being of meaning' (Bernstein, 1983: 139). Meaning is always *coming into being* through the 'happening' of understanding.

Gadamer links philosophical hermeneutics with the Aristotelian distinction between *phronesis* (a form of ethical know-how in which what is universal and what is particular are co-determined), *episteme* (knowledge of universal certainties) and *techne* (technical know-how by the application of rules). For Gadamer, understanding is *phronesis*. '*Phronesis*, unlike *techne*, requires an understanding of other human beings' (Bernstein, 1983: 147). This understanding has moral qualities, specifying knowledge at a particular moment.

> The person with understanding does not know and judge as one who stands apart and unaffected; but rather, as one united by a specific bond with the other, he thinks with the other and undergoes the situation with him.
>
> (Gadamer in Bernstein, 1983: 147)

Quoting Clifford Geertz, Bernstein says that understanding is deepened by dialogue such as in the

> continuous dialectical tacking between the most local of local detail and the most global of global structure in such a way as to bring both into view simultaneously. ... Hopping back and forth between the whole conceived through the parts which actualise it and the parts conceived through the whole which motivates them, we seek to turn them, by a sort of intellectual perpetual motion, into explications of one another.
>
> (Geertz, 1976: 239, cited in Bernstein, 1983: 95)

So dialogue takes on additional meanings, which are to link the reflective process of understanding texts with reflection on people and actions, including one's own, and in both cases, reflection of particularities and generalities interdependently. Understanding is not about thought or action separately, but interdependently. There is no specific technique or set method with a linear sequence of development in which the authority for claims to knowledge is vested. Inquiry is fragmentary yet holistic, dependent for its progress on the skill, knowledge and judgement of the inquirer.

Although there are no general or extrinsic standards of rationality, this does not necessarily mean that there are no ways of creating standards of rationality to critique a person's interpretation of something. The standards come from :

1   The interpreter's attitude to the subject – a willingness to acknowledge and work out one's own pre-judgements, which are operating within the interpretation;
2   The critique of the interpretation offered by others from their own vantage point, whose standards are therefore inevitably limited by their own preconceptions.

On this basis, my understanding (for example) of the teachers' professional development derived from the case studies is not detached from me as a universal certainty, but linked with me by my past, present and future active participation in the events, and the pursuit of realizing moral values to do with the improvement of education, in an unending process of becoming.

Gadamer's philosophy offers encouragement to a belief in various components of an action research approach to personal professional development. For example, critical community discussion of the progress of a teacher's research is justifiably rooted in a non-subjectivist understanding of the process of knowledge creation.

In Gadamerian terms, the general strength of my claim that I have learned is assessed by the extent to which I have been risking and testing my enabling pre-judgements. The risking and testing is through reflective dialogues with firstly, physical evidence of events, secondly, the accounts of the co-participants in the course (with whom I have a bond of commitment) and thirdly, the understanding of others with relevant experience in trying to grasp their subjective meanings of the universal and particular ideas about the practice under study. Since understanding and practice are interdependent, my learning is only fully demonstrable in both forms, *know-how* and *knowledge that*. In other words, descriptions of improved practice as well as expressions of improved understanding are necessary, each to help explain the other, and, in both instances, by reference to the values underpinning the purposes pursued. Finally, all of this is part of a continuing process of becoming.

The ideas of Donald Schön (1987) also try to bridge the objective–subjective divide in the following way.

He produces knowledge that is objective in the sense that he can discover error – for example, that he has not produced the change he intended. But his knowledge is also personal; its validity is relative to his commitments to a particular appreciative system and overarching theory. His results will be compelling only for those who share his commitments.

(Schön 1987: 79)

This approach transforms the problem of eliminating sources of bias into the methodological strength of dealing with biases 'humanly' and positively through the maximization of openness, awareness and honesty. There are no obsessions with certitude because understanding is always in a state of becoming. When the pressure of accountability to others is perceived as a potentially positive stimulus rather than as a personal threat, an autonomous professional is able, in collaboration with others, to reflect on how to develop her/his own rationality as something more than subjectivity.

Insofar as the personal submits to the requirements acknowledged by itself as independent of itself, it is not subjective; but insofar as it is an action guided by individual passions, it is not objective. It transcends the disjunction between the subjective and objective.

(Polanyi, 1962: 330)

Using intuitive judgement, tacit knowledge and individual passions, people can develop the capacity to manage the complexity of professional practice and its improvement, given the necessary enabling conditions. Margaret Donaldson's research (1978) on young children's reasoning showed that the level of complexity of the problems they can solve is increased considerably when the problem is one that makes 'human sense' to them. Likewise, research into posing logical problems to adults has found that solutions that would require lengthy, time-consuming and complex logical reasoning to work out and justify formally can be solved much more rapidly by imagination and justified by intuitive judgement. In connection with this, one of the contributors to the Alpbach symposium, Koestler (1969) postulated a mechanism for the involvement in the mental processing of potentially overwhelming richness of sensory inputs to the mind. He questioned the hierarchy of importance of different mental events, and proposed that conscious thought should not be regarded as the highest level since it is affected by abstract rules of thought which reside in what he termed the 'super-conscious'.

A new abstraction seems *never* to be the outcome of a conscious process, not something at which the mind can deliberately aim, but always a discovery of something which *already* guides its operation. This is closely connected with the fact that the capacity for abstraction manifests itself already in the actions of organisms to which we surely have no reason to attribute anything like consciousness, and that our own actions certainly provide ample evidence of being governed by abstract rules of which we are not aware.

(Hayek cited in Koestler, 1969: 320)

The rational character of this approach lies in the improvement of rational choice as part of the professional development of persons who want to improve their practice in the educational system. This rejects an approach which attempts to coerce persons to adhere to the supposed rationality of an imposed version of the system. Improvements come about through the modification of present practices rather than the imposition of the rationalist myth described by Paul Hirst.

Rational choice can only be the development of the more adequate coherent satisfaction of important wants overall. It is necessarily a modification of present practices, which, even if aided by practical and implicit theoretical considerations, must necessarily be assessed in practice itself. There can be no detached clean slate position from which all possibilities can be assessed ...

To pretend otherwise is simply to be deceived by at least part of the 'rationalist' myth.

(Hirst, 1993: 193)

Regrettably, the rationalist myth has successfully colonized the regulation of much of professional life with its siren promise of certain knowledge and full control.

According to Schön (1983), the crisis in public confidence in the professions in the 1970s had been caused by the technical–rationalist practice of the 'infallible expert' kinds of professional people. Taking heed of this analysis, there had been a growing influence of the 'reflective practitioner' model of practice upon teacher education. So it is deeply ironic to find that a new version of the 'infallible expert' model of professionalism now seems to be the one implicitly wished upon us by the current policies for education in the United Kingdom. The infallibility is now derived from the precise and rigid formulae of standards, set plans and teaching procedures (such as in the literacy hour). However, rather than imposing an 'infallible expert' kind of professionalism, perhaps it would be more accurate to say that the technical rationalism of present policy is simply destroying teaching as a profession. Some characteristics of current policy are summarized here in juxtaposition with a 'reflective practitioner' model of professionalism which underpins this book.

Table 5.1   Contrasting technical and humanistic forms of rationalism

Technical rationalism and the 'infallible expert'	Humanist rationalism and the 'reflective practitioner'
A low tolerance of ambiguity, error or uncertainty, since what has been 'put in place' as the correct system or procedure must be known and adhered to by all in a static situation which regards error and uncertainty as failure, yet, paradoxically,	There is tolerance of ambiguity and doubt about important aspects as a desirable basis for continuing to learn and to improve practice (error is seen as a stimulus to learning) in a dynamic situation.
there is also an urgent emphasis on getting things done as quickly as possible.	Reflection on problematic aspects is preferred to hasty, premature and ill-considered action.
For surveillance and accountability purposes, there is a demand for extracting decontextualized information and passing it upwards through the hierarchy to the relevant controlling person.	Most knowledge is gathered in the context of its use, and can therefore retain the full complexity of a practical and tacit grasp of the whole situation, and it is immediately available to those people to whom the teacher is accountable.
An overwhelming mechanistic reliance upon static, simplified, but explicit, knowledge and information that is recorded in ways which fix it and make its originators accountable in a system of distrust.	A trust in this mainly tacit knowledge which is held in dynamic complexity by the professional understanding of the practitioner, who also uses it directly to guide improvement in action.
The complexity of teaching, learning and assessment activities must be reduced in order to create systematic and deterministic mechanisms for monitoring and controlling events and people.	The complexity of learning and assessment activities is accepted as being too great for a centralized system to control in detail, so that much more effort is directed towards supporting the practitioner's own capacities to manage it.

My Changing Vision of the Aims of the Course and of the Research

Early in the life of this course, I believed the ideal kind of primary science education is that which is inherent in the quotation by Ron Wastnedge (1968) on p. 14, and the ideal teacher could be described as a Nuffield Junior Science type of teacher. I also believed that it was possible to operate a continuing professional development course with the dual aims of imparting this ideal and simultaneously of facilitating teachers' autonomous action research. Then I began to recognize a contradiction in that position. Although I have found that the same kind of philosophy underpinning investigative primary science could also apply to investigative professional development, I also wanted, tacitly, to get teachers to conform to my primary science ideals in a covert way, not explaining and justifying my position or in other ways making it open to criticism. This is not to say that there were no criticisms of investigative science pedagogy, but teachers made them in spite of, rather than because of, the conditions of the course. So I came to appreciate that a desire for all teachers uniformly to confirm the correctness of investigative science was a personal bias which I should have used explicitly as a resource to the course, a position for teachers to react to and criticise constructively. This enabled me to see that there should be a single aim of the course, which is for the personal professional development of teachers whose practical professional problems, for the purpose of this award, happened to be within the sphere of science education. Similarly, the conscious aim of my research evolved away from trying to improve the effectiveness of the course in producing 'clones' of Nuffield Junior Science type teachers towards improvements in the realization of the practical ethic of autonomous professional development of teachers as reflective practitioners. Perhaps the process of professional development should always be of greater importance than the content of the development. Figure 5.1 summarizes the changing ideas about the aim of the course.

Figure 5.1 Diagram of practice/theory interactions in the development of the aim of the course

Professional practices and experiences	*Professional assessments, reflections and analysis*
The explicit aim at the beginning of the research was: 'To enable each teacher to make significant professional progress in the ability to promote scientific learning by the pupils, present and future.'	
	Although I was unaware of this, I had as a *tacit* course aim to convert course members into clones of the Nuffield Junior Science ideal of the primary science teacher (as I saw it). The method was for teachers to use action research instrumentally to change their practice.
Some course members were closer to this ideal in their thought and practice at the beginning of the course than others were at the end, even though all had developed professionally, that is, they made progress in their under-standing and practice of teaching towards an investigative pedagogy.	

(continued over)

In the following year, at revalidation, the course aim was re-analysed into five principles of procedure of professional inquiry specifying the course process through which the aim was to be achieved. The panel questioned the 'dichotomy' between the specification of content of science education and the process approach which appeared to be content-free.

Rather than conforming to pre-determined steps on the one path to my ideal of primary science, more teachers appeared to develop their own aims and practice of teaching science which took account of modern understandings of science and pupils' learning, which the course offered, and were integrated with the experiences of teaching in the classroom, but which were more individualistic and independent of my narrower view.

I became more aware of the strength of my assumptions about my ideals for primary science, and how they had tended to remain covert in my conscious practice, as if I could pretend to be neutral about 'good practice', whilst secretly having a clear ideal in mind. Perhaps I had wanted to be able to prove the superiority of my ideals.

I saw that course members still tended to be inhibited from criticizing my ideal because of my not making it explicit to them as my professional preference.

I realized the contradiction between having a fixed view of primary science and claiming to promote autonomous teacher professional inquiry.

(continued over)

I began to be more open about my preferences, declaring them as a bias for comparison with the course members' biases, and which I expected course members to argue against on the basis of evidence where appropriate.

This is a preferable state of affairs, but necessitates a change in the main aim of the course to become the professional development of teachers through action research with primary science as its content.

Action Research Methodology

Experience of my own action research led me to doubt the notion of there being a fixed method of action research, finding support for this in the cases of several teachers. Lesley's progression was tacit, unrelated to taking conscious action steps and Steve's zigzagging rapidly enlarged his repertoire of cases in a tacitly coherent way. Like Lesley and Steve, and also Clem Adelman (1989), I now consider that the purpose of an inquiry – a practical ethic – must take priority over methodology for the action researcher. Similarly, the critical friends to the action researcher, including a course tutor, should accept this priority. Teachers conducting action research, attempting both the greater actualization of their ethic and deeper under-standing about it, should feel free to begin to create their own methodology and interpretations, initially on the basis of their existing ideas, and then to subject both to development through critical friendship 'discussion' with people and texts. Developments in my understanding and my ability to foster action research can be seen in the following summary (Figure 5.2) of the development of the first of the two assessed assignments on the course.

Figure 5.2 Diagram of practice/theory interactions in the development of the curriculum assignments

Professional practices and experiences	*Professional assessments, reflections and analysis*
In the early days of the national curriculum even the teachers on this course were reluctant to 'take the plunge' in the classroom and have a go at teaching science, preferring to discuss it purely at the levels of theory about primary science.	
	I decided that 'extrinsic motivation' was needed to stimulate teachers to overcome the instrumentality of their approach. It was applied by requiring a written report of an assignment based on teaching science.
The assignment required them to plan, teach and evaluate at least one session of science. Their reports tended to be 'product oriented', lacking self-criticism and a questioning or developmental attitude to the teaching.	
	Why did this occur? Were the desired attitudes absent, or were they evident in any other aspect of the teachers' involvement with the course?
In most cases, teachers' small group discussions showed greater openness and self-criticism, and a less frequent tendency to try to *prove* the achievement of 'good standards'.	
	The accountability pressure of the assignment was slanting the teachers' approach away from giving open self-accounts of needs and aspirations. Could the course member peer group be a more appropriate context for the review of the experience of doing the assignment and learning from it?

(continued over)

I tried out the idea of passing the assignments, together with some tutor comments, around to be read by the members of the peer group. The assignments stimulated discussion about both the teaching and the nature of the assessments of it. The teachers gave strong approval to the exercise

The discussion was successful in raising valuable points about important professional issues, and moderating the tendency for tutor comment to be biased towards the 'desirability ethic'[1] or theory detached from practice. Would the peer group be a better context for the whole assignment, that is working from preparation through reporting back to final critique? Would the tutor involvement be better concentrated on the *process* of the assignment rather than its product?

In the following year of the course the assignment was no longer formally assessed. The teachers prepared for the task by clarifying a professional need with the peer group beforehand. The tutor's visit to the classroom was changed to increase the emphasis on giving assistance with evidence collection and discussion of teacher reflections on the session immediately after. Written and photographically illustrated reports were then presented to the group for critique. The response was highly enthusiastic.

(continued over)

1   An approach to practical decision-making which emphasizes the merits of the underlying aims and principles rather than the feasibility of the methods (Doyle and Ponder, 1976).

Reports were shorter with critical incidents described to illuminate the professional need in action. They were used in the teachers' discussions in school as well as at the university. Discussions were more purposeful, critical and supportive of progress, either to take new action to meet the need or to redefine it and modify the direction of development.

In my own action research, a central practical problem caused mainly by my tacitly rationalist thinking was that of how to analyse my evidence. This is summarized in Figure 5.3.

Figure 5.3 Diagram of practice/theory interactions in the development of methods of analysis in my own action research

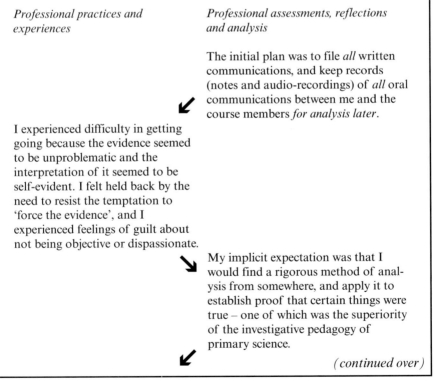

Professional practices and experiences

Professional assessments, reflections and analysis

The initial plan was to file *all* written communications, and keep records (notes and audio-recordings) of *all* oral communications between me and the course members *for analysis later*.

I experienced difficulty in getting going because the evidence seemed to be unproblematic and the interpretation of it seemed to be self-evident. I felt held back by the need to resist the temptation to 'force the evidence', and I experienced feelings of guilt about not being objective or dispassionate.

My implicit expectation was that I would find a rigorous method of analysis from somewhere, and apply it to establish proof that certain things were true – one of which was the superiority of the investigative pedagogy of primary science.

(continued over)

I tried to use the constant comparative method (Glaser and Strauss, 1967) with my records of teachers' responses to the course and found huge amounts of time were dissipated by seeking connections between information which had become meaningless and abstract by separation from the context in which it originated.

I chose to abandon what would otherwise have become an arid intellectual puzzle-solving exercise of following a methodology which held out no prospect of speaking to my practical professional needs. I looked for guidance on the conduct of case study in preparation for the analysis of my monitoring of course members.

The literature was confusingly vague and contradictory about the methods and procedures of case study, and also on the kinds of purposes and outcomes which are appropriate.

Guided by my wish to be able to understand more closely the nature of the course members' professional learning, and specifically to be able to trace the cause–effect relationships at crucial moments in their developments, I decided to go ahead with a common-sense approach to the collection of evidence and writing of the studies.

I made naturalistic interpretations of the evidence to produce portrayals that, as far as possible, were accurately conveying the teachers' own perspectives and perceptions about events. Each was given validation as a fair account by the teacher portrayed, and several significant issues arose from the discussion of the account with the teacher(s) concerned, which led to further study.

(continued over)

The studies were rarely able to obtain evidence of any crucial moments of the kind anticipated, that is, when key stimuli caused defined changes which counted as important learning steps in professional development. But, overall, a quite different set of characteristics emerged, many of which are unlike the tacit model I had held.

During this period the issue of the pedagogic style (see Figure 5.4 for details of the substance of the inquiry) came to the fore – a teacher evaluation session prompted a review of evidence. Fortunately, the evidence base was sufficiently detailed and well organized to permit easy interrogation.

It was relatively easy to check the accuracy of the claims made by course members about my communications with them, and propose a hypothesis about the cause of the perceptions they had provoked. The simple and obvious method of testing the hypothesis was to provide evidence of instances of the kind of action which was held to be problematic, and to analyse them jointly with course members.

Each course member received the evidence of the communications I had with her/him and was able to describe their perceptions at the time. We were able to arrive at the shared view that the hypothesis was supported by the evidence.

The evidence has been simply analysed by the use of a crude system of classification which was intended to distinguish the different intentions of my various utterances and writings.

(continued over)

Course members had little difficulty in using the classification and, ignoring its logical deficiencies, were able to respond.

It was thus possible to construct a valid account of the nature of the misunderstandings.

Professional Autonomy

There is something of a contradiction within a course which fosters teacher autonomy and which takes a single approach – that of action research. Although there is coherence between the version of autonomy meant here and the action research philosophy, a teacher is entitled to reject the approach on offer, believing in a different kind of method of promoting autonomy. The criticism by some course members of the lack of assessment feedback from the tutor is an example of their difficulty in accepting the reflective practitioner approach, although it could be said that they were unwittingly expressing a wish for greater dependence on the tutor. This is described shortly. All course members are always asked to trust a course and surrender some autonomy in the short term to gain a basis for understanding it and influencing it in the longer term, although these course members did not necessarily expect this course to include support for the strengthening of their autonomy. This position is neatly expressed by Donald Schön in the form of a proem by a tutor to course members:

> I can tell you that there is something you need to know, and with my help you may be able to learn it. But I cannot tell you what it is in a way you can now understand. I can only arrange for you to have the right sort of experiences for yourself. You must be willing, therefore, to have these experiences. Then you will be able to make an informed choice about whether you wish to continue. If you are unwilling to step into this new experience without knowing ahead of time what it will be like, I cannot help you. You must trust me.
>
> (Schön, 1987: 93)

In an earlier book, Schön encourages the client's attitude to the professional to take the following form:

- judge the man [sic] rather than his knowledge,
- confront claims to expertise without hostility,

- look for the limits of the expert's confidence,
- confront the expert when you don't understand, etc.

(1983: 301)

These sorts of characteristics are ones I would regard as healthy indicators of course members' confidence in their ability to take a partnership role in their own development. As regards the authority of the expert, a Gadamerian view is a useful one: An authority is not someone to be obeyed, but someone whose knowledge can be recognized and accepted to be superior to one's own, and therefore whose judgement can be trusted. The expert may be allowed to implant her/his biases, legitimized by the person her/himself, into one's thought. There they should not be treated as fixed understandings, but should be open to risking and testing. This is how I would wish course members to regard my authority as a course tutor.

All of the statements of personal professional development in this book reflect several important qualities of mind which characterize professional development, not least of which is that of autonomy. According to Dearden, autonomy is: 'Independent judgement using criteria (which could be general rules, goals, principles, standards and values)' (1975: 7). Therefore, evidence of professional autonomy would presumably lie in signs of a person's ability to make independent judgements using criteria. The independence of the judgements, in Dearden's view, is not equivalent to originality in the sense of novelty, but independence does imply *origination*, that is, how it came to be that the judgement is his/hers, independent of compulsions (constraints or obligations) of either external or internal origin. Dearden also requires that any education aimed at developing autonomy should specify at the start the kinds of things it expects people to exercise independent judgement of, and what kinds of criteria it expects them to use.

Using this approach, a claim that these teachers developed their professional autonomy during this course should therefore rest on evidence that their expressions of judgement have originated not in external or internal compulsions, but by an independent use of those criteria which the course cultivated. Such criteria would be the 'general rules, goals, principles, standards and values' of progressive primary science education and of action research for personal professional development.

It would seem that any course which aims to develop a person's autonomy, as Dearden sees it, should have an inquiry or research dimension to it if a further quality of autonomy is to be found. This is that the person must have reflected in *doubtful* terms, questioned the criteria of judgement and, in turn, doubted their reflection as a secure basis for proceeding, and so on. Therefore, autonomy is a process which it is impossible to complete. Autonomy is therefore judged as a matter of degree. Autonomy has 'its own inner logic of development, as it were, implying as an ideal its own growth towards completeness and integrity. It represents one out of many forms of the perfectibility of man' (Dearden, 1975: 10). Also, the pedagogy of the course would have to be aligned to the process of the development of autonomy throughout, rather than inserting it as an extra.

This analysis is consistent with the philosophy of the course and this research in that they all share a process perspective. Developing autonomy is the same as exercising it since this implies internal growth which cannot be measured against an absolute, external standard. Indeed, one of the qualifying characteristics of an autonomous judgement is its doubtfulness. However, if autonomy is not entirely 'out there' for all to see, neither is it entirely subjective and arbitrary. Exercising, and therefore developing, autonomy is something a course member might claim to do (or the tutor might claim on her/his behalf) by virtue of the subjective experience of making certain judgements which s/he claims to be her/his own. But, for this claim to be accepted by Dearden, the judgement would have to be a doubtful one, that is a reflective and tentative one, and the judgement would have to be demonstrated to others to have originated not in external or internal compulsions, but in a choice made by reference to criteria related to progressive primary education and action research. This constitutes a public test of autonomy which is not absolute since it relies on the (autonomous) judgements of others. Such judgements, in turn, should of course attempt to meet another public test that they too are doubtful, and have originated not in external or internal compulsions, but in choices made by reference to criteria related, in this case, to the professional autonomy of primary teachers on science courses that use an action research approach. The rationalist critic of this stance will no doubt point out the infinite regress in this position, but would not, I think, be able to offer as substitute any objective or absolute criteria.

A possible difficulty with the use of the word 'judgement' here is its associations with the finality of legal judgements or the infallibility of 'The Judgement'! So it is important to bear in mind the sense of *becoming* autonomous, which implies that autonomous judgements are *the most justifiable ones for here and for now*. It is the very long-term, dynamic nature of education which makes this concept so appropriate to situations where, in order to act, spot judgements have to be made, but which are often immediately rendered obsolete as fixed rules for action by changing events. However, the difficulty of applying the concept to teachers is the holistic complexity of the judgements they make. This is not an argument against trying to do so, and I have taken extracts from teachers' own statements to try to give examples of the kinds of discussions of how this concept of autonomy might apply to the teachers' developments on this course.

Example 1

Angela: I acknowledge that my own attitudes towards 'the system' had worsened my view of the constraints it had imposed.

Angela experienced external compulsion to adhere to certain principles in planning her teaching. Her own professional judgements grew more and more at odds with these principles. The judgements used criteria such as the constraining effects they had upon the pupils' expression of their capacities to engage in exploratory and investigative scientific learning. This criterion is itself based upon published accounts of the nature of science and science education, and her observations and assessments of classroom events as discussed with and validated by critical friends of both the course members and tutors. Eventually, Angela was able to overcome the *compulsion* to adhere to the principles, and enter into negotiations. This yielded a compromise that allowed Angela an increased expression of her own judgements in her teaching. To the extent that her judgements were recognized, she was able to feel that she had gained an increased measure of control, through the compromise that was reached, over her own practice, and therefore the greater expression of her own judgements. Therefore, she was better able to justify her actions to herself, the pupils, the parents, etc.

This is a clear case of autonomy which is *not* the unfettered, unjustified and self-indulgent action of a professional person whose professional autonomy is vested exclusively in her/his unself-critical and unaccounted judgements. This undesirable and disreputable meaning of autonomy has no place in teaching. The autonomy Angela exercised here was first of all doubtful in that the judgements she subsequently acted on were consciously open to doubt about:

- the nature of the compromise arrived at (bearing in mind the policy of the school),
- Angela's understanding of the published ideas used in her criteria,
- the ideas themselves,
- the accuracy or the validity of the observations of the classroom used in her criteria,
- the efficacy or the validity of the critique of her judgements offered by her critical friends, and
- the appropriateness of re-negotiating the compromise at some future time.

Following Dearden, Angela's autonomy was, secondly, independent and, thirdly, originated by her to the degree to which she contributed to the compromise reached and acted upon.

Example 2

Steve: I anticipated the discovery of a 'magic formula', but have experimented with many alternatives and I now understand their advantages and disadvantages.

As explained in detail on pp. 121–7, Steve learned to tolerate uncertainty and live with the idea that there is not a single best way of teaching. He became much more able to learn reflectively from his experience. This led him to justify an approach to the school's science curriculum which was different from that of the course. Other examples of teacher autonomy can easily be seen elsewhere in the book.

Changes in Teachers' Professional Autonomy, and its Links with Research and Professional Change

About thirty years ago, before central intervention in education began, primary teachers, who were rarely graduates, were perceived to sustain a restricted and individualistic kind of professional autonomy which could be equated with Schön's (1983) infallible expert. But, today, a virtually all-graduate profession is increasingly embracing a reflective practitioner version of professionalism with the possibility of a kind of professional autonomy which is appropriate to the currently held expectations of accountability.

With the aim of a 'world-class education system' in mind, the questions for the new millennium are: How are we best influencing a teacher's choices and processes of making choices, and how are we harnessing her/his capacities for creativity and criticism? The recent trend has been for a very rapid and far-reaching centralization of control with a simultaneous decentralization of blame. If this trend continues, there will be more directives, inspectors, auditors and other accountability mechanisms to ensure that they are followed, and ever closer definitions of standards and norms. The teacher will be expected to adopt (not adapt) more prespecified techniques and procedures, which are regarded as 'effective' by 'educational scientists' far distant from and with no contextual knowledge of her/his classroom of children. There will be little need for the teacher to reflect on educational aims interactively with the means of achieving them because both will have been laid down. So what will teachers do with their capacities to decide, create and criticize? Those who are willing to do so may put them all on one side, irrespective of what they believe to be the best for their class of children. Others face increasing difficulties, and many have already left the profession. Some of these may have been 'weak' teachers, but many will have been teachers whose individuality of choice, criticism and creation was central to their professionalism. It enabled them to create constructive responses to the unpredictability of the classroom, and the uniqueness of their own professional development, which the 'effective teaching' movement seems to be trying to eradicate. The values underlying the current trend are to minimize trust in people and to maximize control, coercion and standardization.

In his analysis of the political roots of recent educational policy, Jim Graham (1998) claims that the educational reforms of the New Right were based on an economic–rationalist paradigm which aims for a low wage and low skill economy. By contrast, the New Labour government has claimed that it aims for a high wage, high skill magnet economy so that the United Kingdom can be successful in the competitive international knowledge market. However, there have been no changes to educational policies which would be consistent with this change of aim. Graham points out that: 'Flexible, highly skilled workers are not produced by a rigid education system delivered by teachers whose professionalism is dysfunctionally over-regulated by prescriptive national qualification structures.' (Graham, 1998: 9). He goes on to say that the New Labour focus on 'Education, education, education' is:

> far from being a radical transformation to recognise the importance of teachers as professionals in the premier division of international economic and social activity, the current policies are locked in the Tory legacy of blinkered bureaucratic myopia essentially committed to maintaining the traditional patterns of power and control at the expense of precisely the social and economic objectives they purport to achieve.
>
> (Graham, 1998: 12)

Leaving aside the puzzle about the origin of this contradiction between the government's economic aims and educational policy, the article indicates the kind of teacher professionalism which *would* be consistent with the creation of the flexible worker of the twenty-first century and hence a confident, thriving economy fit for globalization and the interdependence of world markets. Referring to the work of the Organization for Economic Co-operation and Development (OECD) and the United Nations Educational, Scientific, and Cultural Organization (UNESCO), Graham argues that there has to be a rejection of the 'educational "command economy"' and its 'outmoded culture of:

- predominance of systematic knowledge (facts rather than controversy),
- specialisation (compartmentalised subject knowledge),
- traditional transmission mode of teaching (discouraging personalised active learning and reflection), and
- top-down communication and control.'

> (Graham: 1998:15)

The following extract of an OECD report is used to show why this technical rationality version of professionalism should give way to one of reflective rationality with a redefined relationship between individual professional autonomy and collaborative professional action.

> The more complex a professional activity becomes, the more policy interventions have to take into account the views of the practitioners and leave space for local adaptations. This assumption is based on the understanding that in complex modern societies many local practical

problems cannot be solved for the institutions by central regulations. Instead, the problem-solving capacity of these institutions and of the persons working in them has to be improved. ... Innovations in complex situations cannot be cloned. ... The principle implies that any substantial innovation must be 'acquired' by teachers in a very personal sense. This means that they must be able to transform it ...

(OECD, 1996: 11, cited in Graham, 1998: 15)

This echoes the viewpoint of John Elliott (1991a) about the relationship between changes in society and the radical professional approach needed in our teachers. His argument can be summarized as follows:

1   The occupational context of the practice of the professional person in a liberal democracy is not static and predetermined, as befits a stable and unchanging state, but fluid, complex, ambiguous and learner-centred.
2   The nature of the professional role is not that of the 'infallible expert' who imposes predetermined images of clarity, but that of the reflective practitioner, one who seeks clarity in professionally problematic contexts through reflective interaction with the context and with colleagues.
3   The characteristics of professional competence are related to the ability 'to act intelligently in situations which are sufficiently novel and unique to require what constitutes as appropriate response to be learned *in situ*' (Elliott, 1991).
4   The professional knowledge is not in propositional form, but a personal synthesis of reflectively processed situational understandings derived from experiential learning.
5   The nature of the professional learning is the study of real practical problems in genuine contexts to enable the interaction of theory and practice in the learning process throughout.

Such an approach contains a particular view of change, and how to manage change, which is highly appropriate to situations where rapid renewal is taking place. It also implies an approach to professional research which advocates insider, practice-based, qualitative approaches such as action research. It is within this context that the teacher's autonomy could be redefined for the new millennium.

The Tutor's Visit to the Course Member's Classroom

One of the most important ways in which the course enabled teachers' personal professional development was for the tutor to make two visits to each teacher's classroom. The first visit was to assist the teacher with the preparation of the curriculum assignment and the second visit, a term later, was to assist with the conduct of action research for the preparation of the classroom-based study. It was possible to justify the retention of these visits, in the face of pressure for economy, on the grounds that they play a distinctive and potent part in assisting teachers' professional development.

Observational visits are a pivotal course experience because each one can bring together any or all of the other aspects of the teacher's course experience and learning to date, and relate it to the task of teaching science, bearing in mind that the main aim of the course is for the teacher's teaching to progress so as to improve the science learning of the pupils. The valuable features of a visit include:

1   The teacher has an opportunity to work with the tutor on 'home' territory.
2   The teacher may assess the tutor's competence and credibility as a teacher of young children, and also the tutor's awareness of, and empathy with, practical teaching concerns, such as the characteristics of the children or the school's physical resource constraints.
3   The teacher has exclusive access to the tutor to discuss anything, including matters requiring privacy or simply to articulate personal thoughts more freely.
4   The tutor can see several aspects of the teacher's working situation, helping to obtain a deeper understanding of the teacher as a professional person, and having been obtained, the understanding can subsequently feed back into course sessions in many ways.
5   The tutor can use observations to check and to change the image previously formed about the teacher's teaching from her/his own accounts up to that point.
6   The tutor can use the discussion of the meanings of events they have both witnessed, firstly as fixed reference points for future discussion during the course, and secondly to learn about the teacher's professional perspectives, beliefs, values and professional needs in a much more reliable way than in course sessions.
7   The tutor can try to identify with the teacher's expressed professional concerns.

The teacher is invariably and naturally apprehensive about the visit in the following ways:

1   Feeling vulnerable to being judged and found wanting in some way.
2   Apprehension derived from aspects of the practices described or shown during course sessions which have appeared to the teacher to be superior to ones s/he usually uses.
3   Fears that the pupils will not behave well or show what they can do, or in some other way do something to suggest incompetence on the part of the teacher.
    The teacher may be suffering from 'conscious incompetence' or feeling 'de-skilled', or both if s/he has been attempting innovations.
    Unless the teacher is completely immune to the 'perfect teacher syndrome' (Ovens, 1986) s/he may have suspicions firstly that there is only one right

way to teach science to everyone, everywhere, all the time, and secondly that the tutor knows what the right way is whilst s/he, the teacher does not.

The stresses for the tutor include the limited time in which to attune to a new situation and make many significant decisions to stimulate the teacher's self-evaluation, and leave the teacher more positively inclined to take greater control over her/his own professional development. If the teacher does not appear to have begun to question her/his own practice, which was uncommon, then the tutor needs to challenge the teacher about matters relevant to the teaching observed. If the teacher is questioning her/his own practice, then the tutor needs to sustain an appropriate degree of uncertainty to protect the emergent professional inquiry. This can be done, for example, by asking the teacher to offer alternative interpretations and courses of action, using evidence about the teacher's and pupils' actions for the tutor to offer alternative interpretations and courses of action, and seeking pupils' interpretations and suggestions. If the teacher appears to be using an inquiry approach to professional development, but expresses dissatisfaction with the uncertainty being experienced because there does not seem to be clear progress, then the tutor can try to alleviate this, without closing off avenues of inquiry, by affirming the changes in the teacher's thought, and possibly the changes in practice also. The tutor should show a calm, accepting manner which is unshakeably positive towards the teacher's development.

During my experience of carrying out these visits, I began to reflect on how best to use them to help teachers to evaluate themselves. I felt that I needed to move away from being an expert to being more like a counsellor in assisting with the clarification of thoughts and feelings. According to Carl Rogers (1951), this is best achieved by *not* offering advice from one's own expertise, but by giving close assistance to the teacher in working out her/his own solutions instead. This approach seemed to be appropriate to the kind of professional relationship with a teacher which acknowledges their experience of teaching and shows respect to her/his maturity as a person. Also, it accords with a valuing of professional autonomy, which requires that a continuing professional development tutor should leave the teacher in a better position to continue developing her/himself at the conclusion of their association than at the beginning. Finally, this is also consistent with a general belief that people learn best from their experience and the sense they are helped to make of it for themselves. As Huxley put it: 'Experience is not what happens to a man, experience is what a man does with what happens to him.'

Another source of theoretical and practical guidance arose from the concept of a neutral chair to learners' discussion which was a prominent feature of the Humanities Curriculum Project (Stenhouse, 1972).

My espoused theory of the pedagogy of visiting a teacher's classroom could be summarized as follows:

1   Acknowledge the authority of the teacher in her/his own classroom by asking for instructions about organizational matters, such as where I should sit, and professional matters, such as what s/he wants me to observe, and whether I should have specific questions in mind when I monitor events and talk to pupils.

2   Make many descriptive notes in order to be able to reconstruct events in discussion afterwards, giving close attention to the pupils' thoughts and feelings, unobtrusively asking them questions where necessary.

3   Respond to the teacher's questions about their teaching by referring back to her/his aims, values, beliefs and assumptions whilst making non-judgemental utterances as far as possible. Seek the teacher's evaluations of things by asking questions like: 'Is that what you wanted/expected/hoped for?' and avoiding giving my own explanations of things to seek the teacher's understandings, including expressions of surprise and puzzlement.

4   Try to draw out deeper reasons for the teacher's conduct of the session in relation to assumptions and understandings about aims of science education, how pupils learn science, and the associated teaching dilemmas such as content and process, instruction and inquiry, and so on.

5   Try to arrive at a summary of points to guide the teacher's continued personal reflection and classroom monitoring, and also to identify issues for exploration in discussion with critical friends and through reading and writing.

For my own action research, as well as to support the teacher, I made audiotape recordings of:

- the brief talk between myself and the teacher before the lesson,
- significant parts of teacher talk during the lesson (such as task setting and summarizing),
- samples of pupils' talk with one another,
- my conversations with pupils, and
- my talk with the teacher after the lesson.

Also, I made notes of my observations during the lesson and of the discussion afterwards. At the end of the visit, I left the notes and the tape with the teacher. At the next course session, the teacher usually returned the notes and the tape for me to study, and subsequently we gave a joint report of the lesson to the rest of the group, drawing them into discussion about issues raised. After the visits had been completed, at the end of the first term, I invited course members' evaluation. About half of the group expressed strong criticism about the generally non-directive stance I had been taking, saying it was their main criticism of the course. There were other criticisms of a minor kind, and there was much positive feedback also, but I was galvanized to search for a better understanding of what was happening.

I responded in two stages: first, by reflecting on the criticisms using my recollections of the visits, and second, by examining the evidence of each visit to try to analyse my theory-in-use. At the next course session, which was the first one in the following term, I fed back to the course members individually my analysis of the evidence about my visit to each of them, and we discussed the pedagogy of the tutor visit again as a group. As stage one of the evaluation, I identified nine points from the course members' views. They are listed below. About half of the course members were the main critics of my role.

Summary of teachers' views

The tutor should give more:

- general assessment that the teacher is 'on the right lines' (Steve),
- help to the teacher to be more critical about their own class teaching – 'it's hard to stand back' (Judith), 'can't see the wood for the trees' (Chris) and 'I've nothing to judge it by yet' (Brenda),
- support to the development of arguments within professional debate by giving definite answers to questions, that is, by taking a clearer stand (Brenda and also Steve),
- ideas about how to develop the science work with the children (Chris),
- guidance to teachers in a parallel way to the guidance that (good) teachers give to pupils (Judith),
- more detailed information about the course commitments at an earlier stage (Chris, *et al.*),
- coherence to different strands of the course (Judith),
- guidance about how to present an analytic memo (Lesley), and
- encouragement to regard anecdotal material as relevant to the reflective diary and not to expect deep or profound analysis or philosophy (Brenda).

The perception of several of the course members seemed to be that development is enhanced by more transmission of tutor expertise, and constrained by insufficient transmission of tutor expertise. The kind of expertise which I found most problematic to transmit was:

- Assessment of the teacher's science teaching, either to affirm that it is 'on the right lines', or to criticize it in a pass/fail sense (with the tutor's role here being that of judge).
- 'Tips for teachers' about what to teach next, how to teach it or how to comply with a course requirement (with the tutor being in authority).
- Saying where I, as an expert, stood on controversial issues.

Both a neutral chair approach and a Rogerian counselling theory would rule out all of these kinds of transmission as inhibiting influences on the development of teacher autonomy. I began to wonder if my tacit justification for adhering closely to a counselling role was that any theory of the tutor's role should be a complete theory of how I ought to act, and it simply needed to be applied purely and consistently. A deeper reason for this could be that my general understanding of a good theory, as in science, is as a literal and comprehensive representation of the truth. If so, the correct use of a theory would be to follow it submissively in all its implications, and apply it without criticism. Perhaps a habit of thought had transferred itself from my tacit belief about science to my search for a way of thinking and acting as a visiting tutor. At conscious levels of thought, I would have denied that a scientific theory is necessarily like that, and I would claim to have a more sophisticated view. But, despite my possession of more recently acquired and better informed, conscious ideas about science, maybe my tacit beliefs about theory as certain truth were acting as a 'hidden influence' on my actions and my justifications for them.

Faced with this challenge, I wrote an exaggerated contrast between two models (see Figure 5.4). In adopting a counselling theory, I had rejected a transmission theory which it seemed that the course members preferred.

Figure 5.4 A juxtaposition of transmission and counselling models of the tutor role for classroom visits

	A *transmission* model	A *counselling* model
1	The tutor is in possession of expert subject and professional knowledge and transmits it as generalized truth to teachers.	The tutor is a co-learner with the teacher, who is regarded as in possession of expert knowledge of her/his learning and her/his own professional context.
2	The tutor makes the assessments of the teachers' learning in some sense on behalf of the authority of the course.	The tutor encourages each teacher to assess his/her own learning in relation to their *own* professional learning context and aims.
3	Assessments of teachers are based either on absolute performance criteria or the tutor's hidden preferences, which teachers either meet (and pass) or not (and fail).	Assessments of present teaching are judged in comparison to earlier teaching in order to assess the progress of each individual teacher's professional insight and practice 'ipsatively'*(English and English, 1958).
4	The course process is not deliberately open to conscious critical analysis by teachers.	The course process has explicit criteria which teachers can use to assess it. *(continued over)*

177

A *transmission* model	A *counselling* model
5 The tutor makes all of the significant decisions about the course operation.	The tutor negotiates with teachers about significant parts of the operation of the course.
6 The tutor role is that of 'specialist' or 'expert' who can diagnose problems and prescribe solutions, like an external broker or custodian of knowledge about what good primary science is.	The tutor role is neutral chairperson and counsellor, providing a sounding board for teachers' ideas and acting as a stimulus to teachers to think through their ideas and practices for themselves.
7 The teacher has an intellectual and professional dependency relationship with the tutor.	The teacher has intellectual and professional independence from the tutor.
8 The tutor minimizes uncertainty for the teachers and gives answers to teachers' questions (sometimes whether they ask them or not!).	The tutor arouses or affirms teachers' uncertainties by asking them questions and reflecting teachers' questions back to them.
9 The emphasis of the course is upon products – final, polished, conclusive work as proof of the teachers' achievement of the desired level of performance. These are produced at the end of the course, for the tutor only, and for summative assessment.	The emphasis is upon the process of development – rough, interim, tentative inquiring work as a vital (living) part of the experience itself – produced during and throughout the course for peers, as well as for the tutor, for formative assessment.
10 Insofar as the course affects practice, such influences are dependent upon the teacher as an individual, mostly in isolation, working out her/his own connections and implications, trying them out and reflecting on the outcomes. The course influence on practice may be an attempted adoption of the tutor's idealization of good practice.	As a central principle, the teachers' existing practice is taken as the starting point for development. Teachers' assumptions and implicit understandings are made more explicit through discussion, and the course encourages each teacher to develop her/his practice by drawing upon the critical friend seminar group and tutors as resources.
11 The implicit values are to do with authoritarian control, standardization of procedure, conformity to generalized standards of assessment, and the certainty and mechanistic uniformity of the product.	The implicit values are to do with democratic control, creativity of procedure, context dependency of procedure, developmental basis for the personal judgement of standards and humanistic diversity of product.

* 'Ipsative scaling is a method of assigning scale values that take the individual's own characteristic behaviour as the standard of comparison, for example, rating a response as better or worse than is usual for the given individual is simple ipsative scaling.' (English, H. and English, A. (1958: 278)

Reflexive, critical commentary on the numbered points of this juxtaposition to raise further questions

1   The tutor cannot escape from being an 'expert', having studied texts and worked in science education, and it is probably inevitable that the tutor will transmit her/his knowledge. This could be done either explicitly or implicitly (by the ways in which knowledge shapes actions, decisions, procedures and language). Therefore, some kind of transmission is bound to be a *component* of the overall pedagogy. However, an item of a tutor's knowledge may not need to be perceived as generalized truth, but as a problematic yet potentially valuable alternative way of thinking. Such a perception may not negate the expertise of the teacher which is assumed by the counselling model. Could practice be guided by more than one theory if there were some kind of meta-theory to guide the choice of which theory to apply in different contexts? *How is the tutor wishing to use a hybrid model to know which contextual features to look for in order to exercise judgement about which forms of action are appropriate?* This seems to be an example of some kind of *dilemma analysis* (Winter, 1989).

2   Although a counselling theory of the classroom visit should inhibit the tutor from giving assessments of the teacher, closer examination of the records of my utterances showed something different. At the beginning of a discussion with a teacher immediately after the classroom observation, I almost always made a positive comment about the session so as to reassure the teacher and try to create a confident foundation for her/him to discuss the more problematic aspects. Nevertheless, some teachers considered that yet more tutor assessment would have been desirable. *Why was this so for some, and not others?*

3   Since the course carried an award, a pass/fail distinction is ultimately inescapable. However, the assessment criteria are intended to relate to the quality of the learning process rather than absolute standards of achievement. Is it realistic to expect teachers to tolerate the uncertainty of the *relative* assessment which a developmental model of a course requires? And anyway, *what is progress in professional development?*

4   There had been no criticisms of the operation of the explicit criteria for the course process, indeed, they had been used effectively by course members to mount constructive criticisms during the meeting. See also the next point.

5   Some parts of the course were justifiably criticized for insufficient negotiation having taken place. This is a matter for technical improvement rather than reflection on aims and means.

6   This point of juxtaposition relates back to the first point, and hits a central tension in the course. There are inevitably some situations in which the tutor's role as counsellor either cannot operate sensibly, or if

it did so on all occasions, it would be a barrier to teachers' participation in primary science education debates, and therefore entry into this intellectual community. *How can an expert give specialist knowledge without diminishing the value of the learner's personal knowledge or weakening the learner's autonomous control over her/his learning?*

7   The teachers were demonstrably exercising independence of thought and action.

8   The protection of teachers' autonomy was not criticized, yet this is logically dependent on the tutor *not* acting routinely to remove teachers' doubt by giving an expert view. So teacher uncertainty is an essential fact of life on a course that deals with knowledge as open to question and to practical test. This was a contentious point for the teachers who wanted more transmission of knowledge by the tutor. Would they lose their autonomy if the tutor acted as they wanted?

9   The two forms of assessment sit uneasily side by side in the course. This is another example of a practical dilemma in which there are virtues in both alternative courses of action, and judgement about when and why to act in one or other way is necessary.

10   The operation of the course seemed to be dominated by the counsellor model.

11   My own values had led me to espouse the counsellor model, however, some teachers' values may have been more like those which would underpin expectations of a tutor to function in transmission mode.

Further development of the theory of the tutor's role – stage two of the inquiry

After the final session of the autumn term at which the criticisms were made, I looked through my records of my interactions with course members as evidence of my theory-in-use. Three categories of tutor statement were chosen, each consistent with a contrasting tutor role. Instead of the simple contrast between transmission and counselling, the transmission role was split according to whether the tutor's comment was mainly an assessment, as if an inspector, or was mainly an evaluatively neutral idea, as if a non-judgemental specialist advisor. So there were three categories of comment: *inspectorial, counselling* and *specialist advisory*. The records of the statements I'd made to each teacher, during and after the classroom observation, were marked using highlighter pens. Three different colours were used to indicate statements according to the three kinds of roles. The marked records were then returned to each teacher at the first session of the following term. Course members were asked to comment on whether they thought the statements highlighted were matched to the correct kinds of roles named, and which specific *assessments* they thought I should have given to them at any stage.

My comments usually included positive evaluations (especially during the discussion after the classroom visit), which included clear examples of what *I* would have regarded as 'telling someone they are on the right lines'. Most of my comments were counselling types of utterance but many were specialist advisory and some were inspectorial.

The self-reflection prompted by this task made me more aware of the adjustments I had tacitly made in my responses to match different teachers' individuality. There are obvious difficulties in the logical clarity of the distinctions drawn between the three categories. But I did not need to know the precise truth about these events, I needed knowledge of sufficient clarity to reorganize my understanding in order to reshape my practice, and put them both to the test. This is a situation in which Carl Rogers (1951) would say that it is better to get a first approximation of the significant than to seek precision about the irrelevant. In this spirit, I asked the course members to give me their reactions.

The teachers were surprised by how much I had said and written that was outside the non-judgemental stance they (and I) had cast my role in. Brenda said it was 'amazing' how much evaluation I had given. Her comment that: 'It didn't feel like that at the time' is a revealing one. The hypothesis I offered to them was that they had expected a much more emphatic kind of evaluation from me. This was endorsed by all. Steve had expected a teaching practice 'crit.'. There were no disagreements with my categorization, but there was a clear split in opinion about the possibility that a tutor's specialist advice was easily interpretable as evaluation. The main protagonists of tutor specialist advice, Steve, Judith and Chris, were certain that it would not be taken as criticism, the most robust expression of this view being Steve's remark at the end – that if the teacher didn't agree with what seemed to be criticism, s/he would simply ignore it. On the other hand, Kay, Kath and Angela were in favour of the tutor minimizing evaluative comment, and offering mostly counselling with some carefully limited specialist advice. They placed priority on the avoidance of threats to the teacher's self-confidence and positive self-image. Brenda seemed to see value in both points of view. From my opinions of their personalities, I would relate the different views broadly to the apparent degree of personal assuredness and fearlessness. Steve, Judith and Chris showed a lot of self-confidence, whereas Kay, Kath and Angela had quieter, more shy kinds of personalities. The group made no specific suggestions for ways in which I should have given a course member evaluative comment.

The Value of the Tutor's Visits to the Classroom

At the end of the course, the following evaluation came from the course members partly from their statements of personal professional development and partly through concluding discussion. Lesley chose to emphasize the visit most, and gave three gains which she attributed to it. Combining her points with those made by the others, their evaluation is broadly as follows:

1   The visit often forces the teacher to do something positive. If there is a reluctance to 'take the plunge' (either to do science in a more practical way, or with a more investigative approach), then this reluctance is often overcome, and the teacher may even take a 'step in the dark'. The current pressures on primary teachers are such that science is likely to be taught with too little direct practical experience of objects and phenomena for the pupils, and with such experience being used in confirmatory rather than investigative ways.

2   The rapport between tutor and course member is strengthened by the one-to-one contact during which more intimate and individual matters can be discussed than is usually possible at the university. By giving support in a constructive, non-threatening way, the teacher can be encouraged to feel confident about being successful on the course.

3   The tutor has an opportunity to win professional respect for competently performing the tutorial role on the teacher's 'home ground'. The role may take several forms, and not necessarily include showing competence as a teacher of young children, although this undoubtedly helps, but even if it is only at the level of interacting productively with children to assist their learning. It certainly includes being able to empathize with and discuss practical problems relating to any aspect of classroom life with as much awareness of the perspective of classroom practitioners as possible.

4   The tutor has an opportunity to assist the teacher in integrating theoretical ideas (from course discussion or from the literature) with practice *as it occurs*, and also to act as a role model in trying to grasp situations, and propose action steps through the use of close observation of events and discussion with pupils.

5   The shared experiences form the basis for interchanges in discussion over an extended period during which it is helpful to refer back to certain events as clear reference points for understanding. The interchanges can occur across the group, increasing mutual awareness and openness, and enriching the content and quality of discussion.

This inquiry led to several changes to the course for the next cohort. One change was the closer integration of the tutor visit into the course structure. There were seminar presentations of the visit followed by discussion. Increasing amounts of course session time were allocated to these seminars in recognition of the professional educational value of the evidence collected, the issues raised and the quality of critical discussion based upon them.

Looking back over this inquiry, my initial espoused theory seemed simplistic in its adherence to a non-judgemental stance. However, Rogerian counselling does remain as a fairly good basis for a tutor's role in supporting a teacher's personal professional development. It may be particularly appropriate to take the role of a counsellor:

1   To people whose personality appears to include characteristics such as shyness, vulnerability to criticism, and a strongly developed (or over-developed) capacity for self-criticism.
2   During the early stages of the professional relationship during which the tutor is learning about the teachers' personalities, and is also trying to establish the extrinsic conditions for an inquiry approach to professional learning.
3   Under circumstances in which the teacher is more likely to feel sensitive to comment that could be perceived to be critical, such as during the tutor's visit to the classroom and at certain times during course session discussion when the teacher feels that s/he is 'put on the spot' (by the tutor or another course member) and appears to be being assessed.

But it may be less appropriate to take the role of a counsellor:

1   To people who appear to be self-confident and accustomed to relating to others in direct and forthright ways, speaking plainly, possibly with a less well developed self-critical attitude.
2   During the later stages of a professional relationship when the tutor has learned about the teacher's preferences and mutual trust has developed so that an unintended lapse in understanding is likely to be corrected without damaging the relationship.
3   Under circumstances where the teacher is more likely to feel secure in their self-image.

A revised theory of a tutor's role for supporting teachers' personal professional development is as follows:

1   In many situations, the tutor will take the role of a *counsellor* – someone who seeks to support the teacher in pursuing her/his own independent line of thought or action within her/his own autonomous professional development. Being a counsellor means being non-judgemental, but speaking and acting in ways that enable the teacher's learning to draw upon *internal* resources for inquiry, such as making tacit knowledge more explicit, discussing ways of reflecting on past experience, and so on. When the tutor is being a counsellor, the teacher may sometimes feel a little frustrated by the apparent absence of direction or certainty which comes from the difficulty of controlling one's own learning rather than giving control to the tutor, or expecting the tutor to assume control. The teacher can ask the tutor to suspend the role of counsellor, or the tutor may wish to do this in certain circumstances. The best kinds of counselling are those that assist the teacher to develop their ability to learn.
2   In some situations, the tutor may take the role of an *advisor* – someone who supports the teacher by offering specialist or expert ideas or advice

about either the science aspects or the professional development aspects. Being an advisor means describing what is hoped to be the most useful item of information, knowledge, skill or understanding that a teacher seems to need for her/his immediate development, and helping teachers to learn from such *external* resources for inquiry. The tutor's experience of advising may lead to certain items being chosen by the tutor and presented to all the teachers together. Otherwise, the best items are chosen jointly between tutor and teacher(s), and are most successful in the long-term when they lead to the teacher improving her/his skills of getting advice.

3   In other situations, the tutor may take the role of an *evaluator* – someone who supports the teacher by offering judgements, assessments or criticisms about either the science aspects or the professional development aspects. Being an evaluator means making available what are hoped to be the most supportive and constructive evaluations that the teacher needs for her/his development, and helping teachers to learn from such *external* resources for inquiry. The tutor's experience of evaluating may lead to certain evaluations being chosen by the tutor and presented with great care to all the teachers together. Otherwise, the best evaluations are chosen jointly between tutor and teacher(s), and lead to the development of the teacher's ability to evaluate independently, mainly through the joint evaluation of shared experiences.

4   When the tutor is in either situations 2 or 3, s/he should try to make explicit the reasons for making the offering (of knowledge, skill, understanding or evaluation). When the tutor and teacher are jointly defining the nature of the teacher's needs (for either knowledge, skill, understanding or evaluation), they should try to make it clear to one another how the need is identified and the reasons for the choice of offering.

5   In yet other situations, the tutor may take the role of *co-inquirer* – someone who gets so interested and curious about the teacher's inquiry that they start to regard it almost as if it were their own. Being a co-inquirer may cause the enthusiasm to jumble up the roles of being a counsellor, adviser and evaluator, and not keep them in balance with one another. This may lead to overplaying the adviser and evaluator roles, and not ensuring that it is the teacher's own learning which is always in mind as *the* aim. The teacher *may* benefit from the tutor adopting this role, but probably only for very short periods.

6   In all situations, the tutor's personal and ethical stance is that of identification with and supportive commitment to the teacher's own inquiry. The qualities of openness, honesty and trust, which Erich Fromm (1957) argues is a *sine qua non* of education, need to be shown and discussed as essential values.

The developments described above are summarized in Figure 5.5.

Figure 5.5 Diagram of practice/theory interactions in the development of a tutor's pedagogy to enable action research

Professional practices and experiences	*Professional assessments, reflections and analysis*
	The norm for tutor visits to student teachers was to *supervise* them and act as the 'infallible expert' in teaching, dispensing universally applicable models of good practice.
Whilst observing student teachers, I found the application of such a model to be problematic. However, my shortcomings as an 'infallible expert' were more than compensated in certain cases when an autonomous approach by a student was more successfully leading to her/his own development as a teacher.	
	Anticipating visits to qualified teachers on the continuing professional development course, I needed to adopt a different model. Carl Rogers' theory of client-centred therapy was attractive as a means of encouraging teachers' professional autonomy and was consistent with enabling them to take an action research stance to the development of their teaching.
Conscious adoption of the principles of a client-centred counselling approach led to the development of techniques of avoiding making judgemental statements and drawing out teachers' tacit knowledge	
	This assisted in the achievement of the kinds of aims I had in mind, and client-centred counselling became well established in my mind as the basis for my conduct of many interactions with the course members, not only during the visit.
During a course evaluation task, somemembers of the group expressed criticism of my non-directive stance. They wanted me to tell them if they were 'going along the right lines' and to give other forms of more explicit assessment.	*(continued over)*

Examination of the records I had made of the classroom visits to the course members showed that my theory-in-use included tacit differentiation in individual differences. I found that I did make judgemental statements that negated the espoused theory in practice. I began to reflect critically on the over-simplifications of counselling as an adequate basis for the tutor role. I asked individual course members to examine records of my communications with them, which had been classified into three types: counselling, advising and assessing.

The course members largely accepted the classification and agreed that I *had* made statements which gave advice and assessment as well as counselling, but for some, their subjective experience of this had been that the assessment was not of the emphatic kind they had expected or wanted. For others, a strong preference against tutor assessment was felt to be more supportive of their development.

I began more consciously and deliberately to differentiate between the course members in assessing their individual needs for an appropriate balance between varied kinds of support based on, but not restricted to, client-centred counselling.

During a course evaluation at the conclusion of the course and in the validation interviews eight months afterwards, I sought further opinions about my role and found that the criticisms had disappeared in all cases but one (Chris) where they were much less strongly expressed.

With the next cohort, I maintained the use of the revised version of the theory and monitored course member reaction, which did not regard it as a problematic issue.

Implications for Course Design

In John Elliott's autobiographical writing (Elliott, 1991b) he refers to the development of the humanities curriculum of the enlightened secondary modern school where he taught. Here, the pupils were meeting the same sort of life issue repeatedly within the guise of the different disciplines of study rather than bringing all relevant disciplines to bear on the same issue together. Improvement came from the integration of the disciplines.

Developments in this course have been similar in that there has been the move away from dealing with central issues of teaching and learning in decontextualized tutor-structured presentations to a more open structure in which teachers meet them afresh in each context of study of the evidence from someone's classroom. The notion of course structure came to apply more to the efficient organization of the collaborative action research process than to the organization of the transmission of content. As in Philip Boxer's conjectural paradigm (Boxer, 1985), which is described below, each action research seminar provided repeated opportunities to consider holistically the course members' immediate problems within the contexts of specific practical manifestations in classroom practice. Group members helped one another to find analytical frames through their attempts to interpret events. Since the immediate problems were often an expression of the deeper problems and dilemmas of teaching and learning, a course member could encounter the same difficulty, for example, 'the Catch-22 of investigative teaching', in several guises, and have experience of working out the ends and means interdependently and differently in each context.

The development of the pedagogy of the course moved from a hybrid of the two models shown in Figure 5.6 on p. 188 to a closer approximation with the process model on the right.

The Conjectural Paradigm of Course Design

Another way of conceptualizing the character of the course and its pedagogy is by using the analysis of four paradigms of course design derived by Philip Boxer (1985) from his study of the teaching of management courses. He identifies three ways in which he found that managers had become 'stuck' in their development: fragmentation, alienation or impotence.

> Fragmentation was a kind of all-consuming 'busyness' in which the manager seemed to have vast numbers of things to get done by yesterday, with none of them leading anywhere. Alienation took the form of having lots of things to be done with good reasons for doing every one of them, but with no feeling that any of them mattered at all. Finally, the impotent manager was unable to connect events as they were unfolding with his desires or the form in which they were taking.
>
> (Boxer, 1985: 122)

187

*Figure 5.6 Rationalist versus process models of continuing professional
development curriculum planning*

The set of knowledge items and understandings selected by the tutor before the session as intended learning outcomes.	*Knowledge objectives*	Determined loosely beforehand by the tutor's choice of learning opportunity, and specifically by the teacher (tacitly) during the session as s/he responds to it autonomously.
The tutor's conception of the most rational sequence and form of activities and ideas for teachers to follow, to achieve the objectives. Processes have instrumental value to the tutor – as a means to achieve the chosen objectives.	*Learning processes*	Within the frame set by the tutor, the teacher selects her/his own version of a rational sequence, and chooses or creates learning activities as an expression of the teacher's personal capacity to be professional. This is of intrinsic value to the tutor.
Selected beforehand by the tutor in defining teacher needs and learning objectives.	*Learning resources*	Broadly anticipated by the tutor, but chosen specifically by the teacher during the session.
Tasks are specified to establish the predetermined learning process, and the session must not be allowed to deviate from this or unwanted 'results' may appear and incorrect learning may take place.	*Tutoring strategies*	By close observation of the teacher's responses during the session, the tutor discovers at specific levels what are the teachers' needs and their own objectives, and then creates an appropriate teaching response.
This is assumed to be essentially the public knowledge of the 'subject'.	*Nature of professional development*	Not only the public knowledge but also the learning capacities and attitudes involved in being professional.
This is used prior to the session to assist the tutor in determining the knowledge objectives.	*Public professional knowledge*	It is used during the session to assist the tutor in disciplining the teacher's thinking *if* this is judged to be the appropriate teaching response.
By testing for the achievement of the pre-set learning objectives.	*Assessment of the teacher's learning*	By judging qualities of mind inferred from the teacher's response, and taking into account the manifestations of his/her needs and objectives.
By testing for the achievement of the pre-set learning objectives.	*Assessment of the tutoring*	By judging the extent to which the whole session constituted an enabling rather than a constraining context for learning.

Philip Boxer distinguishes between the *picture* and the *frame* of a professional problem as it is used in teaching. He suggests that either a course session or a whole course can be categorized as belonging to one of four paradigms according to whether the picture of the problem (the particular way of seeing it in which sense is made of what is seen) is either given by the course or left open to the course members, and whether the frame of a problem (the point of view from which to examine it) is again, either given by the course or left open. The matrix of possibilities is shown in Table 5.2.

In the *emancipatory* paradigm the teacher gives a tool, such as an algorithm of particular behavioural skill, to apply to a range of freely chosen problems, but this carries with it the assumptions of the point of view from which problems can be examined. It leads the learner to hold bits from someone else's picture, which could never properly fit with her/his own frame, and hence to *fragmentation*.

In the *revelatory* paradigm the teacher gives a picture and certain things that are known about a problem so as to encourage learners to develop their own points of view towards it. The freedom of response is limited by what has been made known about the problem. This approach could provide, for example, case studies and simulations. My interpretation of the kind of case study referred to here is that of a teaching method rather than a learning method; that is, a contrived account intended to be a stimulus for the discussion of a particular issue or to illustrate the application of a generalization to a particular instance, rather than a holistic inquiry intended to be a resource to learning from vicarious experience. A similar distinction is made by John Elliott (1989b) who calls the latter kind of case study 'educative'. In order to be educative, the case needs to be written about real situations, which are described with as much of the real complexity and ambiguity as possible, to create an authentic picture. This paradigm, according to Boxer, has some success in developing learners' skills, but there was always the problem of defining relevance and transferring learning back into the 'real'

Table 5.2   *Four paradigms of teaching and course design (after Boxer, 1985)*

		The *picture* of the professional problem – the way of seeing in which sense is made of what is seen	
		Given	Free
The *frame* of the professional problem, the point of view from which to examine it	Given	**Instructional**	**Emancipatory**
	Free	**Revelatory**	**Conjectural**

world where, paradoxically, there were enough problems already. This rein-forces the abdication of authority and leads to an increase in *impotence*.

In the *instructional* paradigm the primary concern is the learning of particular ways of making sense of particular problems. Acting in tradi-tional ways, the teacher gives both the problem and the tool with which to analyse it so that certain knowledge is specified and transmitted. This rein-forces the sense of *alienation*.

In the *conjectural* paradigm the teacher gives neither, leaving learners free to choose what to try to make sense of and how to make sense of it. The teacher encourages the learners not to accept, but to question the taken-as-given bases of meaning, and reflectively to analyse both the picture of their own problems, and the ways in which they frame them. Learners are likely to use strategies to avoid such choices, feeling more comfortable in other paradigms, and 'to avoid learning by adopting the teacher's solutions rather than applying himself [sic] to developing his own' (Boxer, 1985: 123).

Using this analysis, I would recognize elements of the inferior paradigms and their pathology, particularly the emancipatory paradigm as one that tended to dominate earlier stages of the development of my course. For example, whilst in the instructional paradigm, the course used tape-slide mate-rial as both the picture and the frame for teachers' study. Later, in revelatory mode, similar material was used as pictures, and I invited teachers' own anal-yses of them by replaying the parts of the tapes with the authoritative explanatory commentary switched off. Other material was used which contained ways of analysing material in an emancipatory way. Later still, in conjectural mode, all of these resources continued to be available to teachers, and were chosen by them either for their own use in small groups or within a tutor-led session, which they commissioned, to serve the needs of their own inquiries at the times and for the specific purposes which they determined. In ways that resonate with the developments of my own course, Philip Boxer came to realize that at the beginning of the study he had thought of the aim of his course to be concerned with enabling the manager *to have a strategy* in order to make strategic choices, defining 'strategic' in terms of the ambiguous nature of the problems in the situation being faced. He came to see the aim as enabling the manager *to be strategic*, defining 'strategic' in relation to the manager's self. 'Hence judging the quality of development is something for the manager to do and not me.' (Boxer, 1985: 117).

To achieve this he became self-employed to remove the institutional or training context, and work directly with the manager's reality. This mirrors the part I played in supporting teachers' action research by making visits to their classrooms.

Course Members' Views on Resources for Personal Professional Development

At the final session of my course the course members read to one another the individual statements of personal professional development they had written about their participation in the course, and discussed them comparatively. The following points were made and approved by the group as a fair reflection of their shared views about the main resources for their professional development, not necessarily in order of importance, followed by comments on the shared characteristics of professional development. Recommendations for changes to the course are given in bold, and illustrative quotations in italics.

1   One's critical friends, both course members and tutors, are first and foremost a sounding board for one's own ideas, and secondly as a resource of ideas and experience. **It was recommended that the time allocation for this should be increased yet further.**
2   Visiting schools led generally to gains in confidence.
3   Reflection on the course members' original statements written at the beginning of the course about their thoughts and practices at the time were important to look back on to see their development. *Lesley: 'Good grief! Did I actually do that to the children?'*
4   The classroom-based study had been useful. **It was recommended that it should be written up in stages with additional tutor support.**
5   Their reflective diaries had helped them clarify their minds.
6   The published resources, the course reader, recommended books and previous course members' classroom-based studies had been helpful.
7   Their photographs of classroom events had helped to prompt self-reflection similarly to the use of the diary.
8   Taping themselves during their teaching was valuable, and particularly recommended by some.
9   The tutor as a role model (in two respects): first, the pedagogy of the course in which the learners' own ideas had been valued by the tutor (*K: 'The way you were positive about things then, encouraging us.'*), and second, the classroom visit when gathering close observations for reflection.
10 Having access to the 'map' of professional development, which I had prepared part way through the course, and given to the course members (as a forerunner of the final version of the 'Map of progress in substantive aspects' presented after each case study.)
11 Accumulating the portfolio of professional development, which included any item of professional significance to the course member's reflection about her/his development, was valuable.

These were changes to a course that received generally enthusiastic praise from course members. It had been usual for many teachers to arrive well before a session and leave some time after its formal ending, wanting to talk about inquiry work, the latest experiences from the classroom and the best ideas for improvement. One unsolicited comment was that teachers looked forward to a course session as an important and exciting part of each week. It seemed that the course gained its own momentum and vibrancy as a social unit.

Assessing Personal Professional Development

Before asking how it can be assessed, the prior question is: What *is* personal professional development? It is not asked with the intention of obtaining a definitive understanding for its own sake, but as a step to action to use the understanding to improve the practice of assessment. Initially, a distinction is made between the process and the content of professional development, the latter being, in this course, the area of primary science education.

The Content of Development

A description of the content of the development achieved by each teacher is given by a 'Map of progress in substantive aspects of development', which is provided at the end of each case study. An attempt to produce a summary of the whole *group's* substantive achievements showed how meaningless such a document is due to the inevitable oversimplification. For example, at a superficial level it could be claimed that all course members learned that *young children can inquire scientifically, using thinking skills such as questioning, hypothesizing and problem-solving, given appropriate opportunities.* However, the real meaning and significance of this for each teacher was strongly individual in character. For Brenda, a major component was her reassessment of children's 'skimming' and 'frippering' behaviour as an early stage of inquiry. The organizational pressures on Brenda had probably made it difficult for her to observe pupils enough to perceive this earlier for herself. When she reassessed the pupils, this led her to modify her organization. Lesley had been concerned about the apparent unresponsiveness of her pupils, but had tended to attribute this to the inner-city situation of her school, in contrast with Brenda who taught in an affluent suburban area. However, after a critical event at the university, Lesley became more flexible in her teaching, and she elicited much more pupil initiative and perseverance than before. At the heart of this development was the growth within Lesley of an awareness of the rigidity of her own views and a greater confidence to be critical of her own teaching. Such characteristics were already well developed in Brenda's approach. In Steve's case, there was also a gradual release of children's scientific autonomy from teacher constraint, which, he discovered, was not his rigidity so much as his own enthusiasm which tended to swamp the pupils' thinking.

Further examples could be cited that are consistent with the view that the meaning of any substantive course outcome, which appears to be common to all course members, can only be properly understood separately for each by knowing how s/he thinks about it in relation to his/her own personal beliefs, experiences and context. It is much more accurate to regard the substantive professional knowledge as a personal construction than as impersonal objective truth statements which are 'out there'. Such statements suffer from what Joseph Schwab calls the 'simplicity of meaninglessness which comes from being out of context' (Schwab, 1978: 4). Each teacher's thinking about a particular aspect of professional knowledge varies according to how s/he has constructed personal meaning out of experience, discussion and reflection, and, furthermore, continuing professional development means that reconstruction will take place differently in response to fresh experience, further discussion and continued reflection. Assessment of each teacher's thinking by comparing it with a fixed specification therefore seems rather absurd. 'Education as induction into knowledge is successful to the extent that it makes the behavioural outcomes of the students unpredictable.' (Stenhouse, 1975: 82).

Teachers are sometimes implored to avoid 're-inventing the wheel' in their practice, that is, to be better at applying others' knowledge about practice to their own practice. This technical metaphor is inapplicable to professional development except for the simplest technical items of practice which would be better called 'tips for teachers'. Michael Bassey has claimed that: 'Rediscovery of the wheel isn't bad – there is a sense in which *you don't discover it until you've done it!*' (emphasis added) (1985: own notes from a talk).

An appropriate practice of assessment needs to embrace both a person-centred component, which takes account of individual, contextual and developmental aspects of each unique course member, and also a component that reflects the course member's use of knowledge from the community of science educators to discipline her/his thinking.

At the final session of the course (referred to on p. 191) the group produced the following list, in no order of importance, of the main characteristics of their professional development achievements:

1   Opening up their teaching to pupils' influences on their work improved not only the science, but other areas of the curriculum as well, through having greater confidence to stand back from one's own practice and question it. *Angela: 'I felt defensive to start with, thinking everybody else was doing it and maybe I wasn't.' Peter: 'Did anyone else feel like that?' Chorus from others: 'Oh yes!' Angela: 'Coming to terms with it was quite hard really – a few sleepless nights!'*

2   Personal involvement in the progressive changes. *Angela: 'Like the phrase "innovation without change", you can't do that. You've got to change yourself somewhere along the line.'*

3   Recognition of developments can neither be anticipated, nor appreci-
     ated fully (if at all) at the time, but retrospectively, and considerably
     aided by critical friends. *Kay: 'You find your changes when you look
     backwards.' Steve, Brenda and Angela agree. Brenda: 'Other people were
     more helpful in identifying developments.' Steve: 'They're so small to you
     because you're wrapped up in your own environment.' Kay: 'You need
     other people to help assess what you've done.'*
4   Development is not a pre-set linear path. *Steve: 'I was looking for a
     straight line, and not finding it, I thought I was going wrong.'*
5   Development is gradual. *Brenda: 'Things take time.' Steve: 'I was
     expecting things to go bang – straight away.' Angela: 'With John Elliott's
     view, you expect it all the time. He gives the impression it's all clear cut,
     but in real life it's much fuzzier.'* Teachers recommended that the reflec-
     tive self-evaluation and action research should not start with the
     classroom-based study, but at the beginning of the course, and should
     incorporate the curriculum assignment.

Professional Values

Inquiry-oriented development clearly depends upon open-mindedness to
one's own practice and to the comments about it made by others. In order to
achieve such a degree of honesty and courage, several enabling conditions
need to be established. One of the most significant of these is the rapid
creation, from the earliest possible stage of the course, of a climate of trust
in which honesty and openness can flourish. There needs to be trust in the
tutor not to abuse an authority position but be seen to be alongside the
teacher in pursuing their inquiry. There also needs to be trust that other
course members are being equally open and honest in their accounts, and
that everyone's talk and action are motivated by interest in the improvement
of inquiry work to improve practice. The points made in 2 refer to the initial
difficulty in attaining this ethos within the group. In the case study of Steve
more details about this are given from his perspective. Although it is necessary to 'spend' emotional energy to achieve this ethos, once established, it
saves people from any further wasteful, ongoing expenditure of emotional
energy on *pretending*. People are free to reveal that they do not know something that it seems that they ought to know, and are free to criticize or
question something that seems to be generally accepted. Both situations are
ones in which learning is made easier. These are some of the values and
qualities of intellectual inquiry, harnessed by teachers for the purpose of
taking personal responsibility for their own professional development, in the
context of a community of critical friends who value one another's professional autonomy.

   This approach to professional development is negated by the govern-
mentally promulgated values of technical and economic effectiveness and

efficiency. It embodies a version of accountability which destroys professional trust and causes pretence at every level. For example, the wave upon wave of central initiatives increases the need for teachers to pretend to know. The culmination of this vicious circle of pretence is the surrender of independence of thought and action, and also, for many, a sense of humiliation and disaffection.

The dominant approach to teacher development has become one in which the teacher is required to be more accountable for more things to more 'others'. The relationship between the 'developer' and the teacher is one that accentuates the developer's superior knowledge and their right to exert control, and it is also one that minimizes the developer's trust in the teacher to develop her/himself professionally. It is as if trust in teachers is an irrelevant luxury within the determination to 'drive up standards'. Trust is distrusted as an excuse for mediocrity (at best) of 'standards' and a fruitless dissipation of resources. There is too much risk that if they are left to their own construction of meaning and their own improvements of practice, teachers will do these things differently, both from one another and from *the way* which the developer knows is the best way. Accountability and effectiveness movements are ultimately about conformity. The main difficulty perceived by those developers, who are certain that they know best, is how to get the teachers to conform in thought and action. A foolishness of centralization is that in finding ways of ensuring conformity of action in the name of the attainment of 'standards', unthinking use is made of methods that are anti-developmental. Just as development, as defined here, depends on dialogue and drawing on tacit knowledge within face-to-face relationships that are characterized by openness and trust, so we find ourselves required to submit to procedures of audit, such as in the model of inspection used by the Office for Standards in Education (OfSTED), which deny trust, stifle dialogue and destroy openness. Paradoxically, pressures for conformity will drive standards down by stimulating ever more devious ways of pretending to conform to the imposed practice, with neither commitment to it, nor understanding of it, but disdain for those parts of it that harm children's achievement. Such pressures will negate a teacher's reflection on aims and how to achieve them in the face of the very complexity and unpredictability of the classroom which conformity measures seem to deny. Worst of all, such pressures weaken one's capacity to develop oneself.

Michael Power is Professor of Accounting at the London School of Economics and Political Science. In his book, *The Audit Explosion*, he analyses what he calls the flimsy intellectual foundations of auditing in many sectors, and criticizes claims that audits improve quality and accountability. His alternative is to balance formal quantitative scrutiny with trust-based, localized and face-to-face accountability, with the priority to create quality rather than just to police it. In the 'Summary' of his book he says:

Audit has assumed the status of an all purpose solution to the problems of administrative control. Despite concerns about its costs, the benefits of audit are assumed by its proponents rather than proven. Audits are not simply answers to problems of accountability. They also shape the contexts in which they are demanded in important ways. Submission to audit has become such a benchmark of institutional legitimacy that resistance and complaint look like attempts to preserve abuses of privilege and secrecy.

Audit arrangements can bring an end to dialogue inside and outside organisations, rather than helping it. Concepts of performance and quality are in danger of being defined largely in terms of conformity to auditable processes. Indeed, the construction of auditable environments has necessitated record-keeping demands which only serve the audit process.

In looking beyond audit we shall need to recognise that a certain style of accountability, which values independent scrutiny, is one value among others. Audit displaces trust from first-order to second-order verificatory activities. We may need to rehabilitate trust at the level of first-order performance, change the organisational conditions under which audit appears to emerge naturally and even give up on the ritualistic details in which accountability is discharged by audit. In doing so we need to reposition audit as a local and facilitating practice, rather than one that is remote and disciplinary, so as to enable rather than inhibit public dialogue. This will require a broad shift in control philosophy: from long distance, low trust, quantitative, disciplinary and ex-post forms of verification by private experts to local, high trust, qualitative, enabling, real time forms of dialogue with peers. In this way we may eventually be in a position to devote more resources to creating quality rather than just to policing it.

(Power, 1994: 48–9)

The course members who developed themselves as primary teachers of science did so by engaging in progressive debate about what counts as effectiveness rather than accepting a particular version or norm to which compliance and conformity were demanded. Their debates were about theories and practices, and how they could be used to test each other. They took place as 'local, high trust, qualitative, enabling, real time forms of dialogue with peers' informed by their own 'audit' evidence. This led each teacher to confront the complexities of the relationship which different ideas and ideals have with the kinds of practices which might enact them or confound them. Audits of effectiveness were in the hands of the teachers, who helped one another's capacities to judge wisely, context by context, to grow in an individual way for each teacher as s/he construed different aspects of development as a primary teacher of science. Experience of this approach leads to a view of development which stresses above all else that teachers are people. 'People cannot be developed. They can only develop themselves.' (Nyerere, 1973: 27). They develop themselves best when trusted to do so by those who wish to encourage improvement, and when there is trust by the teacher in the developer. Some teachers *may* be able to develop themselves in spite of the lack of such trust, or even as a reaction to its absence.

This book is about people who developed themselves as primary teachers of science. The diversity of development is to be valued and protected as an indicator of the validity of the development achieved, since people are different. The differences between us are part of our humanity. If teaching is a lot to do with human relationships, then it is to be *expected* that teaching will necessarily vary from teacher to teacher, as will the kind of development necessary to improve learning. However, it is very important to appreciate that although each teacher's teaching and their professional development was distinct, as each selected a different focus of personally crucial issues to be confronted, there were recurrent issues, which emerged from each unique context afresh, which were examined in context by the group. In this way, each individual's development contributed to the development of others in the group, firstly by providing the breadth of evidence from which general principles developed (or as Schön would put it, the repertoire of cases was extended), secondly by keeping a breadth of view of significant issues, and thirdly, by appreciating their interconnectedness.

As a fundamental precondition, teachers developed trust between one another and in the tutor. The trust elicited a responsibility to act to each other as critical friends. Most importantly the growth in the capacity to develop oneself was at the heart of the progress achieved. All this is based on the assumption that teaching is a profession in which intellectual inquiry for action research is more important than the mere adoption of technical skill or the acquisition of craft knowledge. Teachers need to be critical and creative thinkers. If we do not educate teachers as such, but train them as technical operatives or crafts people we shall get robotic practice. If we treat existing teachers as robots rather than critical and creative thinkers, then the thinking teachers will leave the profession and we will be left with robotic practice, and teaching will have ceased to be a profession. Just as teachers are encouraged to be robotic rather than reflective in their teaching, so children will be encouraged to be robotic rather than reflective in their learning.

The Most Significant Characteristics of Personal Professional Development

In every case, it struck me how gradual a teacher's progress seemed from my perspective. My familiarity with the kinds of pupils' responses and teachers' ways of eliciting them had made the development seem 'obvious'. However, having conducted my own action research and experienced the feelings of being in the dark and of needing to proceed cautiously, I can empathize with this gradualness much better. When something seemed to me, as the tutor, to have been successful in a teacher's development, I felt it was appropriate for them to move on to further development, but the teachers needed to repeat and consolidate their grasp and their patterns of action before similarly feeling ready to do so. Angela showed this most strongly, because of her situation and her own difficulties in coming to terms with it, but Brenda also needed some time for her positive redefinition of 'frippering' to be consolidated through further work in other contexts. Lesley felt dissatisfied with her classroom-based study because successive stages in it had seemed like an accumulation of repeated versions of the same kind of teaching. In trying to evolve her pedagogy, she felt at the time it had not progressed from one episode of topic work to the next. But, in discussion with her later, we agreed that there were signs of small gains in early episodes contributing to larger gains towards the end. In some senses, she had to begin again with each new topic because the new teaching understandings and practices had to be applied to the next topic for the first time. However, in other ways, she was progressive, for example in giving more control over their learning to the pupils.

The general image of the process of personal professional development through action research which emerges can be summarized under the following five dimensions.

1 Personal

A strong sense of ownership appears in many teacher statements. There is recognition of the ways in which professional changes involve alterations not only to ideas held dispassionately, but also to parts of the persona such as values, beliefs, attitudes and subtle kinds of knowledge often referred to as 'awareness'. Given the personal nature of teaching as an individualized form of activity with the heavy involvement in total relationships (not just intellectual ones) with many pupils, there is usually considerable person-to-person commitment, if not over-commitment. As a result, changes in routines of practice and their forms of understanding are inevitably far reaching.

2 Social

The establishment of critical friendship relationships was almost always cited as being the most important single factor in promoting development. The dominant role was apparently that of enabler or counsellor rather than expert, but also as an assistant evaluator of critical parts of one's development. The seminar groups became important reference groups for the teachers' re-evaluations of thought and practice. The giving and receiving of support and reassurance about similarities of personal reactions to the course or to classroom events was very common. Also, visits to classrooms helped to reduce the social isolation of classroom teaching, which prevents teachers' assessments of one another, which in turn would support self-assessment and cast doubt on the otherwise certain assumption that every other teacher is better at teaching science than you.

3 Emotional

Most of the teachers gave very clear indications of their feelings of threat to their personal and professional self-image, which they experienced in the early stages, which tended to encourage reactions of defensiveness. This situation was usually short-lived. It was important to overcome this initial reaction in order to enable self-disclosure within critical friendship discourse, and naturally, some teachers adjusted more rapidly than others. The adjustment stage was usually accompanied by expressions of relief of the emotional strain of keeping self-doubts and apprehensions undisclosed. Many teachers found that they had many such feelings in common with one another.

Other powerful feelings were experienced and expressed during seminars, such as excitement at witnessing pupils' responses which constituted significant improvements in the quality of their learning. There was a common experience of frustration at appearing to be 'de-skilled' by attempts to improve one's practice. There were expressions of elation at having made a breakthrough in insight and/or practical achievement. There were moments of humiliation at realizing a contradiction between one's own theory and practice, and guilt about a perceived failure to fulfil real or imagined commitments to the pupils. This was particularly common during the early and middle stages of the teachers' action research when there was deepening awareness of the unintended effects of one's actions on the pupils.

4 Intellectual and practical

The nature of the knowledge gained by the development of practice is initially tacit. From an apparent absence of self-awareness there is a slow process of a gradual emergence of conscious and explicit forms of recognition by the teacher of her/his practical knowledge. This process is mainly achieved through communication with others, and takes place under the general guidance of the teacher's image of the value of the teaching and learning to which s/he aspires. It does not show many, if any, characteristics of an incremental, linear, cumulative or logically controlled form of intellectual progression. Consequently, it is inappropriate to pre-specify intentions or outcomes with precision for more than the immediate future. Similarly, developments in practice do not follow a systematically planned scheme of skill development. Instead, they consist of repeatedly taking actions which are justified by the needs of the situation, some of the actions being creative responses to those needs, which thereby constitute separate, small advances in practical technique which sometimes can be recognized to be progressive only retrospectively. The kinds of changes in thought and action interdependently usually include, at some point, a 'perspective transformation'. This involves change in a large number of inter-related items of belief, knowledge, action, perception, value and awareness which constitute something of a professional paradigm shift. The significance to their development of reading published materials is variable, but can be significant to those who use other's conceptual frames as learning resources. Although at first a teacher may be reluctant to write reflectively, they may come to be able to accredit their appreciation of their own and the children's improvements to being able to refer back to reflections made at earlier stages, particularly at the beginning.

5 *Assessment*

Each course member's process and content of professional development was a unique combination of these dimensions, which can best be known and therefore assessed by the person her/himself. Since s/he was asked to take responsibility for her/his own learning during the course, including:

- the initial identification of professional needs,
- selection of learning opportunities during course sessions,
- choice of focus for the tutor classroom visit and the issue to report on afterwards at university, and
- the focus for the classroom-based study.

S/he was also inevitably asked to take responsibility for the assessments needed to make all these decisions throughout the learning process. The tutor and the course members were of course important resources both of criticism and of fresh ideas for reflecting and making the decisions, but they could not be made for the course member. Therefore, the best person to be able to review the whole process and content aspects of the development is the course member her/himself.

In recognizing the educational value of their development, many teachers have said at the conclusion of the course that their favourable self-assessment of their development was sufficient justification for having taken part, regardless of a formal assessment and an institutional award. But others, for whom public recognition of their achievements is a necessary step to career development, needed something more. Ignoring current practice, the most natural form of public expression of an assessment in this situation would be for a teacher's achievements to be the subject of critique by someone who is sufficiently knowledgeable about both science education and the individual's inquiry work. Someone with experience of making such assessments can develop what Eisner (1985) calls an educational connoisseurship of evaluation. Following Eisner, the criteria of assessment could be ones which are emergent from the development itself, and which the teacher her/himself identifies as of greatest relevance to the realization of the chosen practical ethic in her/his practice. This is similar to, or in advance of the position taken by Stenhouse, who advocates that the tutor's role in examining course work is not that of marker, assessing against a marking scheme of objectives, but that of a critic, one who exercises judgement in reacting critically to it.

> The worthwhile activity in which tutor and students are engaged has standards and criteria immanent in it and the task of appraisal is that of improving students' capacity to work to such criteria by critical reaction to work done. In this sense assessment is about the teaching of self-assessment.
>
> (Stenhouse, 1975: 95)

But Stenhouse himself acknowledges there is variation in assessments from person to person resulting from this approach, and he refers to the conflict between it and formal examining which may have greater reliability, but whose standards override 'the standards immanent in the subject'. His advice is to seek a compromise between the two. This seems to be easier said than done because of the size of the chasm between the humanist and rationalist philosophies upon which they are based.

How Can Professional Development be Formally Assessed?

Four criteria were used by the course to assess in broad terms the teachers' use of an action research process for personal professional development:

1 Justified use of appropriate methods of systematic evidence collection.
2 Warranted drawing of inferences.
3 Selecting action to improve practice which is grounded in reported experience.
4 Conceptual clarity and internal coherence.

In the light of my own action research I came to have reservations about the rationalistic and technicist overtones in the implicit model of professional learning detectable in these criteria. It is as if a predetermined mechanism conveyed by the criteria must be followed, and the techniques mastered to ensure good quality professional development by virtue of the authority of *the method*. I would now prefer to have an expression of the intrinsic values of course members' worthwhile professional learning captured in some assessable way. In addition to this principled objection, there is a pragmatic one that good professional development, as judged intuitively, has not always coincided with the best achievement of the activities and qualities specified in these four criteria. Good classroom-based (action research) studies were ones in which the teacher clearly gained greatly, both in understanding and practice, such as those of Kay, Lesley and Steve. They were not necessarily built upon evidence bases that were models of systematic efficiency, or used closely argued logical inferences from evidence to justify action steps, and so on. Brenda's study did show a relatively more explicitly ordered and rational progression that was in harmony with her personal learning style, but if she had been given the choice, I doubt if she would have expected or wanted her style to be imposed on the others. The teachers did not find the criteria easy to use, although there was improvement in the following year due to the use of multiple copies of past studies by teachers for critical discussion about many aspects, including assessment.

The criteria were based upon assumptions about what is to be assessed, which had been influenced by what I came to regard as a rationalistically biased version of action research. They were then imposed upon the course members regardless of whether this caused distortion of their inquiry or constituted a fair assessment of it. An alternative basis for the choice of assessment criteria could be based empirically on an understanding of the important qualities that teachers use in conducting inquiry for personal professional development. Drawing on his experience of professional education in three professions, John Elliott (1991a) claims that the model of the reflective practitioner best describes the kinds of learning which professionals need to engage in to be able to respond in an intelligent, problem-solving way to complex, dynamic and unpredictable situations in their practice. He defines quality indicators as: 'those qualities of judgement and decision-making which are indicative of capacities to make wise and intelligent responses in novel and unpredictable situations'.

As examples, he cites the following:

Quality indicators or manifestations	The generic capacities or competencies underpinning them
open-mindedness	understanding situations holistically
tactfulness in communicating with others	empathy
reflective and non-defensive responses to criticism	self-monitoring

Elsewhere, Elliott (1991b) has argued for the appraisal of teachers to be related not to superficial, low-inference criteria of observed performance, which presuppose craft or technical models of teaching, but to self-accounts of practice within which quality indicators and generic capacities can be identified on the assumption that teaching is a reflectively theoretical practice. Many similarities exist between this proposal and the requirements of formal course assessment. The assessment of the self-accounts would require high-inference judgements to be cross-checked and challenged by people who work closely with the appraisee over a prolonged period, and the existence of fixed criteria of assessment would give protection against subjective bias in the use of intuitive criteria. There may be reservations about the use of criteria which so closely relate to the personal qualities displayed in the performance of teaching. One of these is that the motivational and emotional elements of the criteria stem from personal characteristics that are a fixture of the personality which cannot be controlled. Elliott denies this, citing Rom Harré's view that they are: 'grounded in the systems of belief developed about oneself and others which are acquired in the social process of personal development' (Elliott, 1987: 82).

The capacities are therefore modifiable by influences upon a person's belief system. Using this approach, McKee (1990) has identified six capacities of teaching that are learned through experience:

1   Accurate empathy: the ability to listen and understand what others think and feel.
2   Evaluative practice: the ability to establish a learning environment which facilitates responsiveness to pupils' learning needs. This involves the ability to subordinate control to responsiveness to pupils' learning needs.
3   Evaluation of pupil learning practice: the ability to evaluate the quality of pupil learning.
4   Self-evaluation: the ability to reflect on the tacit theories that influence practice, which implies the ability to be self-monitoring.
5   Cognitive initiative: the ability to see oneself as determining the processes of learning.
6   Empowerment: the ability to foster feelings of personal effectiveness in others so that they feel more capable of solving their own problems.

A small-scale attempt was made to work in this way with the improvement of the assessment of personal professional development in mind. The approach was similar to that used in research cited by Elliott (1989) in seeking the qualities within people which underpin their capacity to show good practice. Instead of interviewing practitioners about 'critical incidents' in their practice, I used the seminar discussion of small, critical community groups of teachers on the course. Just past the half-way point of the course, I asked the groups to discuss the presentation of one of its members in the usual way, and then turn to the task of trying to identify the capacities that the teacher appeared to have used in achieving any contribution, however small, to her/his professional development. The task was structured by three questions which asked the group to decide firstly if they regarded anything in the presentation could be counted as a development for the presenter, secondly what evidence there was to support such a view, and thirdly, what the powers or capacities were that the teacher had used in order to achieve her/his development. The whole group generated the following list by this method, and discussion went on to include consideration of the difficulties involved.

Teachers' views about the powers or capacities underpinning their personal professional development

1   Willingness to see faults in oneself as a teacher.
2   Not being scared to look at oneself.
3   Being prepared to do something about it when a dissatisfaction is experienced.
4   Getting enjoyment from 'resisting stagnation'.
5   Being brave about checking out your practice.
6   Being analytical in thinking about events.
7   Empathizing with pupils and the effects of one's teaching upon them.
8   Observational powers in the classroom.
9   Insightful/intuitive approach.
10 Sensitivity to children's needs.
11 Awareness of oneself as a teacher interacting with the pupils and judging their reactions to oneself.

Several similarities with McKee's and Elliott's qualities can be recognized, for example, accurate empathy is apparent in points 7, 10 and 11, and self-evaluation in points 1, 2 and 5. The 'intellectual zest' reflected in point 4 is distinctive, and it is encouraging bearing in mind the tendency to view teaching as lacking intellectual stimulation to teachers (Elbaz, 1983). I was unable to clarify the allusiveness of point 9.

Factors which tend to inhibit the process and/or diminish one's confidence in one's powers and capacities for the professional development process were stated by the teachers to be as follows.

1   So many things compete with one another in your thinking, which makes it hard to establish anything like a progressive picture of one's development.
2   So many of the things to think about are intangible and therefore the whole task seems 'airy fairy'.
3   You feel a strong tendency to set yourself impossible goals, and you tacitly expect a 'Eureka!' experience.

4   The difficulty in recognizing present work, or things done in the recent past, as any kind of worthwhile development is because it seems to take so much time to be able to stand back and appreciate them.
5   The assumption (in the classroom-based study) that one is supposed to come up with a large document which will change someone else's teaching!
6   The idea that one must collect evidence to prove things irrefutably to others rather than develop one's own practice.

This experience has reinforced my view of the difficulty of the assessment task for both tutors and course members. In Donald Schön's (1987) work on dealing with clients' fears there is recognition of the importance of overcoming the unconscious inhibitors to both creative and rational thought. He proposed the following model. Non-conscious mechanisms may prevent the conscious expression of certain 'hidden' ideas, and this causes fears which the person believes to be unique to him/herself. But when the fears are confronted, for example, by the realization that other people also fear the same things, then the person experiences a feeling of relief and is enabled to describe the fears and express the 'hidden' ideas. The person is also enabled to reflect on the non-conscious mechanisms, and interrupt their inhibiting effect from occurring automatically. This theory of reflection tacitly underpinned much of the work of this course. The relief which accompanies the expression of hidden ideas, overcoming the associated fears, was largely what prompted the course members to make such strong references to the emotional components of their list of professional reflective capacities shown on p. 199.

Conclusion

Quality indicators appear to offer the most promising frame for creating criteria of assessment from an understanding of professional development in action as opposed to a theoretical version of development which may have rationalist assumptions.

6 Development through Action Research

The outcomes of the work described in this book can not be conveyed fully by the following attempt to summarize them in what are inevitably theoretical terms. This is because the outcome of practical reflection 'is both a theory and a form of action' (Elliott, 1987: 163) or, to put it another way: 'Theorising about the nature and purpose of a practice is not a separate activity, albeit an interacting one, to reflecting about how to proceed competently with it' (Elliott, 1989a: 13).

As 'naturalistic generalisations' (Stake, 1980), the outcomes are embedded in the practices described in Chapter 5 (and in the reflections about what aspects of them are thought to be worthwhile) as much as in the theoretical ideas summarized here. The brevity required to summarize is inevitably distorting.

> Reason can put into propositional form only what is necessarily a limited element in any situation, trading in any given instance in categories that necessarily strip practical realities of all their other aspects, exclude unique particularities, and ignore all tacit considerations. What is more there are no good grounds for believing that any array of such general principles, however extensive, could even in principle capture the full character of practical situations.
>
> (Hirst, 1993: 191)

Nevertheless, the epitome for action research for personal professional development which is represented by this work occupies the rest of this concluding chapter. My meaning of *epitome* is not so much the literal one, 'an abstract of a book', but the figurative one, a 'thing representing another in miniature' (*Oxford Illustrated Dictionary*) (1962). The attempted clarity, as conveyed by the apparent certainty and simplicity of the presentation, disguises the numerous unanswered questions, puzzles and criticisms which attend any such developments. The most important intention, however, is to convey my commitment to the broad approach represented by this work in overwhelming preference to the approaches that seem to dominate teacher education in England at the time of writing. Hopefully, what precedes this chapter has gone some way to explain, justify and validate these commitments in practice. The epitome begins with an epistemological basis for setting out a way in which action research is a desirable paradigm for professionalism and professional development.

Epistemological Considerations

The rationalist paradigm of the development of education, which has been increasingly dominant in the United Kingdom in general and England and Wales in particular, for more than a decade, involves taking centralist control over the aims or ends of education, stating them with operational precision and the setting up of surveillance and control systems to ensure their achievement. This has led to the proclamation and enforcement of clear and certain prescriptions for action.

> But there can be no educational development without teacher development; and the best means of development is not by clarifying ends but by criticising practice. There are criteria by which one can criticise and improve the process of education without reference to an ends–means model which sets an arbitrary horizon to one's efforts. The improvement of practice rests on diagnosis, not prognosis.
>
> (Stenhouse, 1975: 83)

By contrast, the humanistic paradigm represented by the work of Lawrence Stenhouse and many others sees education as being more about people and relationships rather than systems, and consequently accentuates the uniqueness of individuals and contexts. Perhaps Stenhouse is overstating the argument for beginning with a critical attention to practice by implying that a clarification of ends is not also part of development. But he is surely correct in saying that an ends–means model (such as that of the national curricula) sets arbitrary horizons and that prognostication does not improve practice. Criticism of practice and the diagnosis for improvement cannot take place with any depth of meaning at the centre, only in each classroom, since (it is worth repeating): 'No two schools or classrooms are so alike in their circumstances that prescriptions of curricular action can adequately supplant the judgement of the people in them' (MacDonald, 1985).

Central attempts to change teaching have sought to ignore this and to ignore teachers' existing professional knowledge as prejudiced or just wrong. In reply to the rationalistic wish to eliminate all 'hidden influences' on a person's thinking and action as sources of error, Gadamer (see Bernstein, 1983) has defended pre-judgements as constitutive of a person's being, and the necessary condition to learning. Therefore, personal professional development must begin by accepting that a teacher's existing practice and her/his understanding of practice, has been shaped by her/his personal characteristics, ideology, professional biography and current context. The development process is one that enables the teacher to examine her/his personal professional persona in the light of evidence about how it influences practice, and in the light of the views of others, not least pupils, parents, colleagues and policy-makers. This includes the discovery and testing of hidden influences upon one's beliefs and actions. Enabling pre-judgements have to be tested and, perhaps changed, whilst the blind pre-judgements have to be opened and confronted. This Gadamerian view may, however, tend to overlook that in reflection-in-practice, situated reasoning repeatedly *creates* responses to problems, and in reflection-on-action the empathic reaching out to others requires conceptual and emotional powers of *invention* and *discovery*. Creativity is involved also in the task of understanding as a personal construction during the 'dialectical tacking' referred to on p. 153. So recognition is also given to the *positive* contribution being played by the non-conscious aspects of teachers' thinking. Such creative powers are most likely to be expressed and used when external enabling conditions prevail.

An Inquiry Model of Professional Development

A teacher's development is encouraged to take the form of a professional inquiry which has improvement of one's own practice as its aim. Three main components of the inquiry seem to be:

1   Giving reflective attention to how one comes to have one's own *interpretation* of one's actions and the ideas of others with the intention of self-development.
2   Appreciating the ideas of others, to *understand* their perspectives and to use them to test and develop one's own interpretations and actions.
3   An observant and curious *application* of ideas to the improvement of practice and of practices to the development of ideas.

Assuming that others can recognize the distinctions drawn here, and in the hope that it may be helpful to present the dynamic interactions between these components, I have summarized them in Figure 6.1 on p. 209. In doing so, I am apprehensive about the unintended effects of this kind of presentation to those whose understanding is not assisted in this way, and who prefer to resist this kind of approach. The mechanistic tone of this and other summarizations in this chapter are consequences of the way of thinking I am accustomed to using. Its limitations have been pointed out by those teachers depicted here who challenged what they saw to be shackles rather than guidelines to their own thinking and practice of action research. They have found more encouragement in the ways of thinking of people like

Marion Dadds, who herself looked at 'neat models' of action research which were lacking 'affective dimensions' and wrote:

> I had a daily urge to lift the flaps and corners of the action research arrows, spirals and boxes; to take a closer look at the embroiled underworlds below the clean theoretical diagrams. I had the need of additional and different discourses.

(Dadds, 1995: 3)

The dynamics of an inquiry, the interactions between three components, are aided by the activities shown in italics.

There is no fixed starting point within this dynamic because each teacher may find a different point at which to enter the interconnected triangle of components and begin to set up the interactions between the constituents,

Figure 6.1 Three components of an inquiry model of professional development

Personal, reflective interpretations of the particularities and situational understanding which relate to my inquiry aims, values and practice
- *trying to see myself as others see me, professionally, and trying to put myself into their situation*
- *trying to stand back from my inquiry by having a conversation with myself about it*
- *keeping a reflective journal or jotter to record passing thoughts, feelings, puzzles, doubts, fears, insights, worries and excitement to do with my own understanding of both my evidence and also the ideas of others*
- *thinking critically about my practice in the light of my values and aims,* and vice versa
- *looking back over my records to increase my awareness of how my ideas and practices are changing, my development is occurring and I am gaining the capacity to develop myself.*

Understanding of others' ideas from
1 published material about:
- *evaluating the central ideas and values of my inquiry*
- *assessing others' action research*
- *understanding an action research approach*
2 comments of 'critical friends' including:
- *responding openly to their questions, criticisms and new ideas about my inquiry*
- *being open to alternative interpretations of my evidence, their reactions to my interpretations, ideas about possible action steps, and their accounts of their own relevant experiences*
3 feedback from a visitor to my classroom as:
- *observations, instance interviews, reflections.*
- *questions, criticisms and new ideas about my inquiry*
to discipline my thinking.

Application: evidence of the actions and events (in the person's past and present professional practice) in which ideas (action steps) are tried out and monitored for their effects on the situation and the people involved.
Gathering, saving, presenting to others and trying to make meaning of my evidence about the children's learning, my teaching, my talking with them about their ideas, feelings and their work, Evidence in the forms of: *making observational notes myself or by visitors to my classroom, taking photographs, making audio and (possibly) video recordings of classroom work or of instance interviews with the children carried out by me or by a visitor, selecting examples of the children's work, gathering structured or semi-structured forms of evidence such as a tick sheet about events of significance to my practice.*

although *application* may more often be the starting point than the other two components. Nor is there any suggestion that there should be conscious control over an inquiry exerted by this model. It is meant to be a resource for evaluation of the inquiry process in that it suggests that all components need to retain a lively interaction with one another and that they all need to play an appropriate part.

The *internal resources* available to professional inquiry by a teacher are:

1* Past experiences which can be consciously recalled to mind and subjectively described, explained and evaluated verbally.
2* Tacit knowledge (including past experience) which is not immediately or readily brought to conscious thought or verbally expressed, but can be 'activated' (see Altrichter, et al., 1993: 48–9).
3 One part of what I have called 'hidden influences' – the mainly evaluative, emotional and attitudinal factors which constitute a set of non-conscious predispositions to act in certain ways – including Gadamerian pre-judgements of both kinds: enabling and blind.
4 Another part of what I have called 'hidden influences' – the non-conscious capacity to discover, design or create a personally new synthesis, a selection or combination of thoughts and/or actions which influence conscious thought and action.
5 An espoused theory of practice – a set of conscious predispositions to act in certain ways.
6 Perceptions of important aspects of the present situation in which a practical problem is understood to exist.
7 The person's definition of the practical professional question or problem which initiates the inquiry.

The result of interactions between these aspects is the person's action or practice which feeds back into and changes each of the aspects (in Fig. 6.1, p. 209) of the person through reflection.

The *external resources* available to professional inquiry by a teacher could be:

8 Physical records of events and one's actions to aid reflection.
9 Observers' and participants' subjective interpretations of events and one's actions to aid reflection.
10 Dialogue with critical friends regarding aspects 1, 5, 6 and 7, which take the form of conscious explication of one's own understanding and the critical search for understanding of others' expressions of their relevant understandings.

---

*   Perhaps 1 and 2 equate with Schön's (1983) repertoire of cases.

11 Dialogue with critical friends regarding aspects 2, 3 and 4, which take the form of being open to their perspectives to aid the recognition of previously non-conscious aspects of one's own 'hidden influences'.

12 Reading about the events, actions, interpretations and theories about the experience and reflections of others.

13 An ethos of trust, openness and honesty throughout the group of people involved in aspects 9–11.

Within the kind of communication referred to in 10, a problem may arise from what the person regards as being 'de-skilled' (not taking wise action or taking unwise action) and 'de-witted' (not thinking intelligent thoughts and thinking unintelligent thoughts). Critical friends' offerings will include different lines of reasoning and different kinds of evidence, provoking personal choices between them to determine one's present thought and immediate action. *There is no infallible method of making the best choice.* All that can be done is to make the best possible use of the resources available. The choice between different arguments, different methods of inquiry, or the application of different criteria depends on personal knowledge of the alternatives available, personal judgement about which are appropriate, and personal skill in using and interpreting them. Therefore, part of the development includes widening the available knowledge about methods from which to choose. Important resources for this include books by Altrichter, et al. (1993) and McNiff, et al. (1996). There will also be the impact of 'hidden influences' on the choice, either at the time or when the action is taken, in resolving conflicts between alternatives. If time is the limiting factor on the decision-making process, then 'hidden influences' may well be the immediate determinants, and reflection-in-action and, afterwards, reflection-on-action will become more important.

Within the kind of communication referred to in 11, the person also needs to be open, but about matters that are less emotionally neutral and personally detached. This is the most personal aspect of development in that it requires the kinds of capacities and powers which are involved in such a whole-hearted commitment as teaching or action research. The challenge is to tolerate ambiguity or uncertainty, and forbear defensiveness when others find self-contradictions and inconsistencies in one's motives, reasoning and courses of action. Considerable qualities of courage and honesty are needed for such intimate self-knowledge to be the subject of open discussion.

All of this applies to both the substance and the methodology of the inquiry. In both, there are no objective ways of knowing *the* correct way to think and act. One must start with one's present internal resources, and select or invent what is needed in the light of emerging issues and practical problems with the support of external resources.

Combining my reflections on both the experience of conducting this research and these ideas from the literature, the following set of characteristics in Figure 6.2 contains ones which seem justifiable and which I try to use to guide my own professional practice.

Figure 6.2 Desirable characteristics of action research for personal professional development

1   Everything must be consistent with the centrally important principle that the inquiry is ultimately controlled by the inquirer, whose creativity, self-esteem, and capacities of empathy, open-mindedness and processes of self-critical reflection are paramount, albeit in negotiation with others.

2   The inquiry aims to pursue the inquirer's own human purposes in seeking the solution of personal and social problems of practice. The aim is not for *true* knowledge, indeed it is not initially aiming for knowledge at all. Of course, the inquiry will probably very quickly reach a point at which new knowledge is needed, but *instrumentally*. However, questions of accuracy, reliability and validity of the knowledge required and the methods for obtaining it will not be answered by applying standard rules of (for example) scientific rigour, but by critical deliberation on the degree to which any rules are relevant to the purposes of the inquiry, including the fulfilment and questioning of central values.

3   The definition of the inquiry problem includes the relevant subjective components, such as values, statements of beliefs, tacit, pertinent knowledge and the conduct of the inquiry, similarly does not rule out subjective components but deals with them appropriately.

4   Rules of scientific rigour are an important resource, among others, for the criticism of the inquiry methods and findings, particularly for the development of knowledge, but there is no essential requirement to reach for any greater conceptual clarity, precision of evidence or purity of method than are necessary for the solution of the problem. The inquiry does not require findings to be proved, it seeks improvement of practice.

5   The definitions of the inquiry purposes and the problems studied should also be the subject of criticism in order to lead to their refinement in the light of reflection on the moral issues involved.

6   The interpretations contained in the inquiry should be subject to the critique of dialogue in which participants' pre-judgements are made explicit and open to test through 'dialectical tacking'.

7   The meanings of particularities and generalities should be considered interdependently – the growth of understanding of one contributing to the deeper understanding of the other.

> 8 The meanings of theories and practices should be considered interdependently, the growth of understanding of one contributing to the deeper understanding of the other.
> 9 The inquiry is founded on the ethical basis of respect for persons and other democratic values.
> 10 The inquirer conducts the inquiry collaboratively, not only in relation to participants in the context under study, but also with a wider critical community of co-inquirers.

Pedagogy and Course Design for Enabling Personal Professional Development

The enabler makes conscious choices between taking the roles of counsellor, adviser and evaluator according to assessments of each context, the teacher's personality and her/his professional needs, and the issues under discussion (see pp. 183–4). The enabler engages in second order action research into her/his own practice, with the aim of improving it, through carrying out inquiry into the practical professional questions and problems of understanding and supporting the professional inquiry of the teachers with whom s/he is collaborating.

A course should *not* be designed with a systematic, propositional knowledge base (for transmission to teachers) which is conceptualised as a *syllabus* (defined in the *Oxford Illustrated Dictionary* (1962) as 'the concise statement of subjects of lectures in a course of study') that must then be divided up into bite size pieces and arranged according to the course designer's preconceptions about progression and continuity of delivery. This causes the common concerns about 'coverage' of the syllabus and content overload. It invites the transmission of decontextualized answers to a series of questions that teachers may not have asked, and may not wish to ask. It encourages the knowledge base to be seen as definite and non-problematic. It inhibits the teacher's search for personal relevance and meaning through finding links between the different conceptual areas transmitted and between conceptual matters and practical matters. The course time for this task and other aspects of teachers' learning how to learn is limited by the course preoccupation with transmission, as if learners can only learn what has been transmitted to them.

The course design must be based on personal knowledge and its construction by the course members. The knowledge base can be conceptualized as a map. It is as important for the learner to learn how to find their own way around with the map provided (and the modifications to it *en route*), together with other sources of guidance, as to learn about the items that the map represents. Therefore, the learner uses the map to make personal choices and decisions about which content is to be learned, in what sequence, and how much time is needed to learn it, including the task of making links between the different conceptual areas and between conceptual matters and practical matters. The choices are guided by the need to pursue professional inquiry and solve professional problems that are identified as significant for each teacher differently in her/his professional context. The knowledge involved is always in a state of becoming rather than being cut and dried. Knowledge is not an authoritative imposition on a person's thought, but a way of disciplining it. 'This is in the nature of knowledge – as distinct from information – that it is a structure to sustain creative thought and provide frameworks for judgement.' (Stenhouse, 1975: 82). The general map consists of a series of general questions that provide the frame and stimulus for teachers to ask more specific, personally relevant and practical context-related questions. These then become the intellectual focuses and motivational drives for inquiry work through gathering evidence, reading and seminar discussion. Decisions about continuity and progression are therefore shared with course members through discussion about the progress and achievements of the inquiry project work. Those conceptual areas, which are not prominent in one course member's own inquiry, are almost bound to appear on at least one of the other inquiries. All inquiries are shared across the cohort, giving every member the opportunity to learn about concepts, not in isolation, but within ongoing inquiry work. Concepts are developed in the context of their use to further the professional inquiry of a colleague. Since course members already know much about each colleague's professional context, purposes and problems, they can see the significance and relevance of developing and using such concepts. Through all of this, teachers' capacities to develop themselves are being given the fullest opportunity to grow. The teachers have a stake in one another's development.

The general 'Map of personal professional development' for this course is shown in Figure 6.3 on p. 215.

The organization of any course or other organized form of continuing professional development should give careful consideration to the inclusion of:

1　Pre-planned tutor inputs to a group of teachers which are *restricted* to the initial stage and to appropriate points subsequently for the purpose of setting broad conceptual and operational frameworks, establishing, sustaining and formatively evaluating the professional development process of inquiry.

2　Maximization of the use of critical friendship work within a community of practitioners, as a very high priority, for the discussion of substantive and methodological aspects of each teacher's professional inquiry, and the giving and receiving of personal affirmation, constructive criticism and creativity.

Figure 6.3 A general map of personal professional development possibilities in primary science

My ideas about science and science education

How do I understand aims of science education such as *being scientific*? How do I see the relationship between science as a subject and as an investigative way of learning? How does this influence the ways in which I teach science? How can I justify both the science I teach, and how I teach it? (to parents, for example)

Personal professional aspects of myself as a teacher

Why am I doing this course? What do I want to achieve by taking part? What aspects of science conceptual knowledge interest me? What aspects do I know and understand best and which do I need to develop? What aspects of science procedural knowledge and ability are my strengths, and which do I need to develop further?

My science teaching

How do I see my usual ways of teaching science? How do I evaluate its strengths and needs? How can planning, teaching and assessing best enable my pupils to learn science? How can I arouse children's curiousity, encourage their progression and meet their different learning needs?

My professional context

What opportunities and constraints currently operate in my classroom in relation to my teaching of science? What expectations of my teaching are held by the head teacher and other significant people in my school? What opportunities and constraints are there in relation to my responsibility and freedom to develop myself professionally?

Science teaching, learning and assessment

My pupils

How can I develop my ability to obtain and use creatively, an accurate knowledge and understanding of what they are interested in, what they already know and have experienced, what their learning needs and their present abilities to be scientific are? What do I understand about how they learn science and what more do I need to learn?

My values and beliefs about teaching in general

What are my core values as a teacher? What is my overall teaching style? How do my usual patterns of teaching (organization, grouping, task setting, assessment, recording and reporting, use of resources, including time) relate to my science teaching?

My reflective professionalism

How do I use my freedoms and responsibilities to develop myself professionally? How do I use policy, published resources, educational theory and research? How do I use methods of pupil monitoring and self monitoring to understand classroom action? How do I discuss my teaching with my colleagues? How do I reflect on all these aspects in order to understand and improve my teaching?

3   Other tutor inputs[*] (such as mini-lectures, focused practical workshops, seminars and recommended reading) to be determined in response to whole group or sub-group needs, substantive and methodological, as they arise, drawing upon actual problems from the inquiry work going on and in negotiation with the teachers.

4   Support provided for individual and group reflection on (and assessment of):

   •   the developments in thought and practice, and
   •   the personal professional inquiry qualities of course members.

Assessment

The assessment of inquiry for professional development should be:

1   Of substance and process interdependently, but with priority on the practical ethic of the inquiry purpose.
2   Person-centred and practice-centred; that is, it takes an account of personal progress in practical insight and practice taken together.
3   Professionally based; that is, thought is disciplined by the knowledge of the professional community.
4   Applicable through the involvement of a critical community of people.
5   Grounded in an understanding of the conduct of professional inquiry free from the distortions of covert rationalism.

Conclusion

The meaning of *personal professional development* as manifest in the context of extended professional inquiry can be summarized as follows.

Professional development is *personal* in that it involves several aspects of a teacher as a professional person that are interrelated. The practical,

---

*   This is the most clear-cut way in which a 'teaching objectives' (as described in the context of teaching primary science on p. 90) would play its part in an approach otherwise dominated by the notion of 'teaching people'. In this situation, the purpose of the tutor input is determined either by the course members setting their own learning objectives, which they need the tutor to assist them to achieve, or by the tutor, having formatively evaluated teachers' development to be showing a highly specific need for some particular information, knowledge or skill. The tutor then temporarily assumes the full mantle of an instructor or authority, and directs the learning. When course members consider that the objectives have been achieved, they take back from the tutor the control over their further development. In this sense, transmission episodes of teaching and learning can take their rightful place in continuing professional development – as punctuations within an overall approach of social constructivism. This view of teaching and learning is essentially similar to that of Stephen Rowland's (1984) 'interpretive' model.

reflective and theoretical aspects are not involved in isolation from one another, but together. The same is true for the emotional and intellectual aspects. It is an involvement of the teacher as a person, as well as profession-ally, since inquiry can be passionate, (Dadds, 1993; 1995) invoking feelings of humiliation and frustration as well as elation. It is personal in that it is unique, to some degree, to each person as an expression of (among other things) the individuality of each teacher's professional biography and current professional context. Paradoxically, it enables the teacher to step outside the self and see her/himself as others see her/him. Also, it is personal in that it is one's own possession.

> It is the quality of teachers themselves and the nature of their commit-ment to change that determines the quality of teaching and the quality of school improvement. Teachers are, on the whole, poor implementers of other people's ideas. Teacher development therefore ... is a precondi-tion of curriculum development, and teachers must play a generative role in the development of better curricula. Their understanding, their sense of responsibility, their commitment to the effective delivery of educational experience for their pupils is significantly enhanced when they own the ideas and author the means by which ideas are translated into classroom practice.
>
> (Macdonald, 1991: 3)

Being *professional* is an approach which could be defined as a responsi-bility for the search for improvement within one's own teaching, and a commitment to the collaborative search for improvement within the school (Ovens, 1986). It involves qualities such as self-criticism and self-evaluation; self-disclosure; openness to the perspectives of pupils, of colleagues and of policy; courage; capacities for close observation of, and accurate empathy with, others; cognitive initiative and reflective autonomy. It involves harnessing appropriate resources from academia, both conceptual and methodological, as well as standards of quality, without allowing any of them to usurp the kind of professional autonomy described here, which is about contextual-ized professional self-development.

Development means learning that is holistic because it involves many aspects of the teacher's practice and reflection on practice: not only tech-nical and subject knowledge and practical skill, but also values, beliefs, attitudes and awareness. A significant and meaningful change in one part of the interconnected whole framework of a teacher's teaching does not remain in isolation, but is assimilated when other parts of the framework are adjusted to accommodate it. This is a slow and gradual process which can be perverted but not accelerated by coercion. The framework has connections, which need to be undone or rebuilt, and which are different for each person, so development is not likely to take a linear or single path that is visible to others as smooth and rational. Gains are initially highly contextualized and tacit. Therefore, it takes an accumulation of inquiry-oriented experience in different contexts and activities in order to make tacit knowledge explicit, and for the gains to lead to broader development. However, development can lead to wide-ranging and enduring changes in professional practice which are not likely to be predictable with certainty and are not likely to be fully recognized or appreciated until later. Development integrates gains in understanding with improvement in practice. Most importantly, it is aided enormously by taking place within a context of the lively, empathic, affirming and critical friendship of a group of colleagues.

Sadly, for the rationalistic dream, development is not something which can be given to, or possibly done to people, because:

> People cannot be developed. They can only develop themselves. For while it is possible for an outsider to build a man's [*sic*] house, an outsider cannot give a man pride and self-confidence in himself as a human being. Those things a man has to create in himself by his own actions. He develops himself by what he does; he develops himself by making his own decision, by increasing his understanding of what he is doing and why; by increasing his own knowledge and ability, and by his own full participation – as an equal – in the life of the community he lives in.
>
> (Julius Nyerere, 1973: 27)

A commitment to these principles of life in the developing country of Tanzania bears comparison with the view of personal professional development of teachers advocated here because both are founded upon democratic values. The advocacy of any alternative view of personal professional development of teachers should be as explicit about its underpinning values, in comparison with these.

> The methods that I favour as a facilitator of action research are based on the following principles of democratic education which enable professionals to become persons who:
>
> • are able to take self-initiated action and to be responsible for those actions,
> • are capable of intelligent choice and self-direction,
> • are critical learners, able to evaluate the contributions made by others,
> • have acquired knowledge relevant to the solution of problems and the creation of better teaching and learning,
> • are able to adapt flexibly and intelligently to new and changing situations,

- have internalised a means of coping with complex situations by utilising all pertinent experience freely and creatively,
- are able to collaborate effectively with others in these activities, and work, not for the approval of others, but in terms of their own values and ideals.

(O'Hanlon, 1996: 185)

A vision for a 'world-class education system' for this country, which would be consistent with the meaning of personal professional development advanced by this book, would embody a more democratic (and more intelligent) balance of power between the stakeholders in schooling than currently prevails. The aims of the education of our children would be related to wider aspirations than the country's economic success, and would include the kinds of principles already indicated on pp. 212–13. In seeking such achievements for our children we would expect teachers to be reflectively professional rather than merely to be technically competent at following changes that the state dictates. Using the kinds of professional inquiry and autonomy depicted by the teachers studied here, our teachers would have the capacities to anticipate and lead change in constructively critical ways. Reflective teacher development would be the main basis for changes such as curriculum development, for a significant component of educational research, as opposed to research on education, and also for the processes of teacher appraisal and the evaluation of educational quality. All of these activities relate to the pivotal role of the teacher as a reflective professional person who has the virtues and qualities illustrated here to transcend the complexity of classroom life in inquiry for professional development.

References

Adelman, C. (1989) 'The practical ethic takes priority over methodology' in W. Carr (ed.) *Quality in Teaching: Arguments for a Reflective Profession*, Lewes: Falmer Press.
—— (1981) 'On first hearing' in C. Adelman (ed.) *Uttering Muttering*, London: Grant McIntyre.
Altrichter, H. and Posch, P. (1989) 'Does the grounded theory approach offer a guiding paradigm for teacher research?' in *Cambridge Journal of Education* 19(1).
Altrichter, H., Posch, P. and Somekh, B, (1993) *Teachers Investigate their Work: An Introduction to the Methods of Action Research*, London: Routledge.
Argyris, C. and Schön, D. (1974) *Theory in Practice: Increasing Professional Effectiveness*, San Francisco: Jossey-Bass.
Atkinson, P. and Delamont, S. (1977) 'Mock-ups and cock-ups: the stage-management of guided discovery instruction' in P. Woods and M. Hammersley (eds) *Explorations in the Sociology of Education*, London: Croom Helm.
Ball, S. and Goodson, I. (1985a) *Teachers' Lives and Careers*, London: Falmer Press.
—— (1985b) 'Understanding teachers: concepts and contexts' in S. Ball and I. Goodson (eds), *Teachers' Lives and Careers*, pp. 1–26, London: Falmer Press.
Bassey, M. (1985) 'Staff seminar on action research', Manchester Polytechnic, 6 November 1985.
Berlak, A. and Berlak, H. (1981) *Dilemmas of Schooling*, London: Methuen.
Bernstein, R. (1983) *Beyond Objectivism and Relativism*, Blackwell: Oxford.
—— (1972) *Praxis and Action*, Part 1, London: Duckworth.
Blenkin, G. and Kelly, A.V. (1987) *The Primary Curriculum: A Process Approach to Curriculum Planning*, London: Harper & Row.
Boxer, P. (1985) 'Judging the quality of development' in D. Boud, R. Keogh and D. Walker (eds) *Reflection: Turning Experience into Learning*, London: Kogan Page.
Carr, W. (ed.) (1989) *Quality in Teaching: Arguments for a Reflective Profession*, Lewes: Falmer Press.
Carr, W. and Kemmis, S. (1986) *Becoming Critical*, London: Falmer Press.
Claxton, G. (1991) *Educating the Inquiring Mind: The Challenge for School Science*, London: Harvester Wheatsheaf.
Cole, M. and Cole, S. (1989) *The Development of Children*, San Francisco: Freeman.
Dadds, M. (1997) 'Continuing professional development: nurturing the expert within' in *British Journal of In-Service Education* 23(1): 31–8.

—— (1995) *Passionate Enquiry and School Development: A Story about Teacher Action Research*, London: Falmer Press.

—— (1993) 'The thinking of feeling in professional self-study' in *Educational Action Research* 1(2): 287–303.

Dearden, R.F. (1975) 'Autonomy as an educational ideal' in S.C. Brown (ed) *Philosophers Discuss Education*, London: Macmillan.

Department for Education and Employment (1998) 'Initial teacher training national curriculum for primary science', circular 4/98, annexe E.

Department of Education and Science (1978) 'Primary education in England – a survey by Her Majesty's Inspectorate', London: HMSO.

Department of Education and Science (1988) 'Initial teacher education conference briefing paper', Blackpool.

Donaldson, M. (1978) *Children's Minds*, London: Fontana.

Doyle, W. and Ponder, G. (1976) *The Practicality Ethic in Teacher Decision Making*, Texas: North Texas State University.

Driver, R. (1988) 'Theory into practice II: A constructivist approach to curriculum development' in P. Fensham (ed.) *Development and Dilemmas in Science Education*, London: Falmer Press.

Ebbutt, D. and Elliott, J. (eds) (1985) *Issues in Teaching for Understanding*, London: Longmans.

Eisner, E. (1985) *The Art of Educational Evaluation*, London: Falmer Press.

Elliott, J. (1996) 'School effectiveness research and its critics: alternative visions of schooling' in *Cambridge Journal of Education* 26(2): 199–224.

—— (1991a) 'A model of professionalism and its implications for teacher education' in *British Educational Research Journal* 17(4): 309–18.

—— (1991b) *Action Research for Educational Change*, Buckingham: Open University Press.

—— (1990) 'Teachers as researchers: implications for supervision and for teacher education' in *Teaching and Teacher Education* 6(1): 1–26.

—— (1990) 'Validating case studies' in *Westminster Studies in Education* 13: 47–60.

—— (1989a) 'Academics and action research', paper presented to the American Educational Research Association, San Francisco, 27 March 1989.

—— (1989b) 'Why put case study at the heart of police training curriculum?' New directions in police training.

—— (1987) 'Educational theory, practical philosophy and action research' in *British Journal of Educational Studies* 35(2): 149–69.

—— (1983) 'A curriculum for the study of human affairs: the contribution of Lawrence Stenhouse' in *Journal of Curriculum Studies* 15(2): 105–23.

—— (1981) 'The teacher as researcher within award bearing courses' in R. Alexander and J. Ellis (eds) *Advanced Study for Teachers*, Driffield: Nafferton Books.

—— (1975) *Developing Hypotheses about Classrooms from Teachers' Practical Constructs*, Cambridge: Cambridge Institute of Education, Ford Teaching Project.

Elstgeest, J., Harlen, W. and Symington, D. (1985) 'Children communicate' in W. Harlen (ed.) *Primary Science: Taking the Plunge*, London: Heinemann Educational.

English, H.B. and English, A.C. (1958) *A Comprehensive Dictionary of Psychological and Psychoanalytic Terms*, New York: Longmans.

References

Fromm, E. (1976) *To Have or to Be?*, London: Jonathan Cape.

—— (1957) *The Art of Loving*, London: Jonathan Cape.

Geertz, C. (1976) 'From the native's point of view: on the nature of anthropological understanding' in Rabinow and Sullivan (eds) *Interpretive Social Science: A Reader*, Berkeley: University of California Press.

Glaser, B. and Strauss, A. (1967) *The Discovery of Grounded Theory*, Chicago: Aldine.

Golby, M., Martin, A. and Porter, M. (1995) 'Some researchers' understanding of primary teaching' in *Research Papers in Education* 10(3): 297–302.

Gott, R. and Duggan, S. (1995) *Investigative Work in the Science Curriculum*, Buckingham: Open University Press.

Graham, J. (1998) 'From new right to new deal: nationalism, globalization and the regulation of teacher professionalism' in *Journal of In-service Education* 24(1): 9–29.

Grossman, P., Wilson, S. and Shulman, L. (1989) 'Teachers of substance: subject matter knowledge for teaching' in M. Reynolds (ed.) *Knowledge Base for the Beginning Teacher*, Oxford: Pergamon Press.

Handy, C. (1988) *The Age of Unreason*, London: Hutchinson.

Harlen, W. (1997) 'Teachers' subject knowledge and understanding and the teaching of science at the primary level' in *Science Teacher Education*, Hatfield: Association for Science Education, 19: 6–7.

—— (1996) *The Teaching of Science in Primary Schools*, 2nd edn, London: David Fulton.

—— (ed.) (1985) *Primary Science: Taking the Plunge*, London: Heinemann Educational.

Hewitt, B. (1986) 'Trivial pursuit' in *Primary Science Review* 2: 13, Hatfield: Association for Science Education.

Hirst, P. (1993) 'Education, knowledge and practices' in R. Barrow and P. White (eds) *Beyond Liberal Education: Essays in Honour of Paul H. Hirst*, pp. 184–99, London: Routledge.

Hodson, D. and Hodson, J. (1998a) 'From constructivism to social constructivism: a Vygotskian perspective on teaching and learning science' in *School Science Review* 79(289): 33–41.

—— (1998b) 'Science education as enculturation: some implications for practice' in *School Science Review* 80(290): 17–24.

Holly, M. (1989) 'Reflective writing and the spirit of inquiry' in *Cambridge Journal of Education*, 19(1): 71–80.

Klemp, G.O. (1977) *Three Factors of Success in the World of Work: Implications for Curriculum in Higher Education*, Boston: McBer & Co.

Koestler, A. and Smythies, J. (eds) (1969) *The Alpbach Symposium: Beyond Reductionism*, London: Hutchinson.

Laing, R. (1967) *The Politics of Experience*, London: Penguin.

Lave, J. (1988) *Cognition in Practice: Mind, Mathematics and Culture in Everyday Life*, Cambridge: Cambridge University Press.

MacDonald, B. (1991) 'From innovation to reform – a framework for analysing change' in J. Rudduck *Innovation and Change*, Buckingham: Open University Press.

—— (1987) 'Keynote address to the Ides of March Conference' in *The State of Education Today*, Norwich: Centre for Applied Research in Education, University of East Anglia.

—— (1985) 'The portrayal of persons as evaluation evidence' in N. Norris (ed.) *Safari Two: Theory in Practice*, CARE occasional publications no. 4, Norwich: University of East Anglia.

MacDonald, B. and Ruddock, J. (1971) 'Curriculum research and development projects: barriers to success' in *British Journal of Educational Psychology*, 41(2): 148–54.

McKee, A. (1990) *How Do Teachers Learn through Experience?*, Norwich: Unit for Educational Development, University of East Anglia.

McNiff, J., Lomax, P. and Whitehead, J. (1996) *You and Your Action Research Project*, London: Routledge.

Match and Mismatch (1977) *Raising Questions; Finding Answers*, Edinburgh: Oliver & Boyd.

Millar, R. and Driver, R. (1987) 'Beyond processes' in *Studies in Science Education* 14: 33–62.

Moscovici, H. and Nelson, T. (1998) 'Shifting from activity mania to inquiry' in *Science and Children*, January 1998.

Murphy, P. (1996) 'Teachers' and students' approaches to problem solving in design and technology', paper to the European Conference on Educational Research (ECER), Seville.

Nuffield Junior Science (1967) *Teacher's Guides 1 and 2*, London: Collins.

Nyerere, J. (1973) *Freedom and Development*, Dar es Salaam: Oxford University Press.

O'Hanlon, C. (1996) 'Why is action research a valid basis for professional development?' in R. McBride (ed.) *Teacher Education Policy*, London: Falmer Press.

Organization for Economic Co-operation and Development (OECD) (1996) 'An overview of OECD work on teachers, their pay and conditions, teaching quality and the continuing professional development of teachers', paper to the 45th International Conference on Education, UNESCO, Geneva, 30 September – 5 October 1996.

Osborne, J. and Simon, S. (1996) 'Teacher subject knowledge: implications for teaching and policy', paper to the British Educational Research Association Conference, Lancaster.

Ovens, P. (1992) 'When is a journal not a journal? When it is a magazine! – the style of PSR' in *Primary Science Review* 22: 2–3, Hatfield: Association for Science Education.

—— (1989) 'The national curriculum – pot filling or fire lighting?' in *Primary Science Review* 9: 3–4, Hatfield: Association for Science Education.

—— (1987) 'Ice balloons' in *Primary Science Review* 3: 5–6, Hatfield: Association for Science Education.

—— (1986) 'Professing to be professional' in *Primary Science Review* 2: 2, Hatfield: Association for Science Education.

Ovens, P. and Ryan, J. (1986) 'Towards investigative science in a primary classroom' in *Classroom Action Research Network Bulletin No. 8*, Cambridge: Cambridge Institute of Education.

Oxford Illustrated Dictionary (1962), Oxford: Oxford University Press.

References

Peters, R.S. (1968) 'Must an educator have an aim?' in C. Macmillan and T. Nelson (eds) *Concepts of Teaching: Philosophical Essays*, Chicago: Rand McNally.
—— (1966) *Ethics and Education*, London: Allen & Unwin.
—— (1959) *Authority, Responsibility and Education*, London: Allen & Unwin.
Polanyi, M. (1962) *Personal Knowledge*, London: Routledge & Kegan Paul.
Popper, K. (1983) *Realism and the Aim of Science*, London: Hutchinson.
Power, M. (1994) *The Audit Explosion*, London: Demos.
Rogers, C. (1951) *Client Centred Therapy: Its Current Practice, Implications and Theory*, London: Constable.
Rowland, S. (1993) *The Enquiring Tutor: Exploring the Process of Professional Development*, London: Falmer Press.
—— (1984) *The Enquiring Classroom*, London: Falmer Press.
Schools Council (1980) *Learning though Science*, London: Macdonald Educational.
Schön, D. (1987) *Educating the Reflective Practitioner*, London: Jossey-Bass.
—— (1983) *The Reflective Practitioner*, London: Temple Smith.
—— (1971) *Beyond the Stable State*, London: Jossey-Bass.
Schwab, J. (1978) 'Testing and the Curriculum' in *Journal of Curriculum Studies* (1989) 21(1): 1–10 (reprinted version), originally published by University of Chicago Press in *Science, Curriculum and Liberal Education*.
—— (1969) 'The practical: a language for curriculum' in *School Review*, 78: 1–24.
Science 5–13 Series (1972–1975) *Teachers Guides* (26 titles), London: Macdonald Educational.
Sockett, H. (1989) 'Practical professionalism' in W. Carr (ed.) *Quality in Teaching: Arguments for a Reflective Profession*, pp. 115–44, Lewes: Falmer Press.
Stake, R. (1980) 'The case study method in social inquiry' in H. Simons (ed.) *Towards a Science of the Singular*, Norwich: Centre for Applied Research in Education.
Stenhouse, L. (1978) 'Case study and case records: towards a contemporary history of education' in *British Educational Research Journal* 4(2): 21–39.
—— (1972) 'Teaching through small group discussion: formality, rules and authority' in *Cambridge Journal of Education* 2(1): 18–24.
—— (1975) *An Introduction to Curriculum Research and Development*, London: Heinemann Education.
Summers, M. (1994) 'Science and the primary school: the problem of teachers' curriculum expertise' in *The Curriculum Journal* 5(2): 179–93.
Summers, M., Kruger, C. and Mant, J. (1997) *Teaching Electricity Effectively: a Research Based Guide for Primary Science*, Hatfield: Association for Science Education.
Wastnedge, E. (1968) 'Nuffield junior science in primary schools' in *School Science Review* 61(217): 639–47, Hatfield: Association for Science Education.
Whittaker, M. (1980) 'They're only playing – the problem of primary science' in *School Science Review* (61)216: 556–60, Hatfield: Association for Science Education.
Winter, R. (1989) *The Practice of Action Research: Learning From Experience*, Lewes: Falmer Press.

Index

action research: into an aspect of the tutor's role 46, 174–86; within continuing professional development 7, 157; and educational reform 170–2; epistemology 150–7, 207–8; and professional autonomy 166–9; for professional development 208–13; second order action research 8; by the tutor 1, 2, 8, 18–22, 206–7; use of audio recordings 73–8; use of a reflective journal 37, 73, 126–7; zigzagging 77, 121–5; *see also* action steps; method of this study

action steps: in Lesley's action research 114–21; and progression in action research 114–25; in Steve's action research 121–5

'activitymania' 96–9, 133

Adelman, Clem 160

Altrichter, Herbert 210, 211

Angela: Angela's story 23–31; aspects of Angela's professional development 85–95

Argyris, Chris 54

Atkinson, Paul 15

auditing professional practice 195–7

autonomy: in Angela's development 168–9; in Brenda's development 39; in professional development 142, 166–72; in Steve's development 77, 123, 170

Bassey, Michael 193

Berlak and Berlak 142

Bernstein, Richard 8, 151–4, 207

Blenkin, Geva 11

Boxer, Philip 187, 189–90

Brenda 192; aspects of Brenda's professional development 137–8; Brenda's story 31–43

Bruner, Jerome 3

Carr, Wilf 17

Chris: aspects of Chris's professional development 95–103; Chris's story 43–52

'circus' organisation of teaching 96–9

classroom visits by the tutor: Angela 24–5; Brenda 33–6; Chris 45–6; impact on teachers' development 138–40; Kay 53–4; Lesley 62–3; pedagogical development 172–86; Steve 71–4

Claxton, Guy 15–16

Cole, Ardra 144

Collaborative Action Research Network (CARN) 10

constructivist approaches 88, 98, 133, 138, 140, 143–8, 216

Continuing Professional Development (CPD): course design 5–7, 187–90, 213–16; principles 12; rationalist vs process models 188

counselling model of tutoring 174, 176–9

curriculum development 137–8

Dadds, Marion 107, 132, 209, 217

Dearden, R. F. 167–9

Delamont, Sara 15

Department for Education and Employment (DfEE) 143, 144

Department of Education and Science (DES) 147–8

dialectical tacking 153, 208, 212

Donaldson, Margaret 155